WATER IN PLAIN SIGHT

HOPE FOR A THIRSTY WORLD

JUDITH D. SCHWARTZ

St. Martin's Press
New York

www.stmartins.com

Design by Letra Libre, Inc.

An excerpt appears from Tony Hoagland's "The Social Life of Water" from
Application for Release from the Dream. Originally published in *The Sun.* Copyright
© 2015 by Tony Hoagland. Reprinted with the permission of Graywolf Press,
Minneapolis, Minnesota, www.graywolfpress.org.

Cataloging-in-Publication Data is available from the Library of Congress.

ISBN 978-1-250-06991-7 (hardcover)
ISBN 978-1-4668-7900-3 (e-book)

Our books may be purchased in bulk for promotional, educational, or business
use. Please contact your local bookseller or the Macmillan Corporate and
Premium Sales Department at 1-800-221-7945, extension 5442, or by e-mail at
MacmillanSpecialMarkets@macmillan.com.

First Edition: July 2016

10   9   8   7   6   5   4   3   2   1

To my parents,
Pauline and Alvin Schwartz

CONTENTS

INTRODUCTION

Water in Plain Sight

IT'S UNSEASONABLY WARM FOR DECEMBER IN PARIS, and the ice is melting. The ice, harvested as icebergs from a fjord in Greenland, is an art installation set up at the historic Place du Panthéon. The twelve blocks, each weighing more than 20,000 pounds, are arranged in a circle to form a clock. In winter, dusk in Paris is a leisurely affair, sprawling across the hours like lunch in a side-street brasserie. It's nearly dark when I reach the square, but the ice chunks, some taller than the people wandering among them, have their own glow, a kind of glinting charisma. People pose by the blocks, snapping photos. Children, holding onto their parents' hands, touch the ice and giggle at its smooth coldness. Some young children, in snowsuits and wool hats, are in strollers. I wonder what their parents are saying when they bend down to explain—that each drop of dissolving water ticks off another moment toward the potential destruction of earth's climate as we know it?

Water was a presence at COP21, the international conference on climate change in which 195 countries agreed to place limits on greenhouse gas emissions in an effort to curb global warming.

Water was central to the emergence of the "high ambition coalition," as island and other low-lying nations pressed for more stringent emissions limits. Leaders from states such as the Marshall Islands in the Pacific and St. Lucia in the Caribbean noted that if expected warming trends continue, their very existence was under threat.

Water was a theme at the International Rights of Nature Tribunal, held at the Maison des Métallos, formerly a steelworkers' union hall and now a cultural venue in the 11th arrondissement. Among the "cases" brought before the judges in the packed hall was the Commercialization of Nature, in which the provisions of nature, such as clean water, become products to be bought and sold. Other hearings condemned the building of megadams that would displace indigenous communities, and oil and mineral extraction that damages rivers and other water sources.

Water was on the agenda at the People's Climate Summit in Montreuil, a suburb with a picturesque old-world square at Paris's eastern edge, where more than a hundred citizen-driven workshops and discussions took place. Along with two friends, from Spain and Mexico, respectively, I headed up a steep hill to a vast, fortress-like school for a panel on water and climate. We were joined by an orderly stream of students and activists, including members of the Grandparents Climate Campaign from Norway—some very tall men and women in red hats and pinnies—en route to various events. Jean-Claude Oliva, director of the organization Coordination Eau Île-de-France, opened the water and climate forum by saying, "Water tends to be seen as related to the consequences of climate, but not as an inherent part of climate change. And yet, human activities have been affecting the water cycle in a way that is affecting climate change. This shows we can actually act on climate change through our water practices."

And water was part of numerous random conversations. I was in Paris in December 2015 during COP21 with a group called Regeneration International, a global network of activists, scientists and communicators. I was bunking in an eight-bed room in a backpackers' hostel that housed a lively nightclub downstairs. One morning I ran into Hayu Patria, who had joined our room sometime during the night, having just arrived from Indonesia. She told me that in the village where she works in East Java, the spring water is among the finest in the world. Now that the water is being privately bottled by Aqua, a subsidiary of Danone, the local people are struggling to get clean water. "They have to walk several kilometers to get water," she said. "It's hard work. It's a mountainous area so they're climbing up and down."

Water connects us all. It connects highlands and lowlands, and communities upstream to cities at the coast. Bodies of water transcend national boundaries, and so create incentives for groups to cooperate and trade. Waterways offered a means of travel long before anyone dreamed of riding on wheels. And, of course, water connects us socially: the universal gesture of peace and hospitality is to offer another person something to drink.

Water is a point of connection for many of our global challenges—as well as for solutions. Protecting water resources, such as maintaining moisture in soil, can help mitigate against climate change. The water cycle interacts with all basic biophysical cycles: the carbon cycle, the energy cycle and the nutrient cycle. The better we understand this, and the better we appreciate how water processes relate to alleviating poverty and hunger, reversing desertification, and rebuilding biodiversity, the more equipped we will be to take on the difficulties of our time.

In this book, I hope to put water in context: to explore how water works and highlight water's role in other timely concerns. To do so, I'll share stories of water innovators from around the world who are finding new routes to water security—strategies and insights with important implications for food justice, economic resilience and climate change. These stories will take us from Mexico to Africa to Australia, from deserts to mountains to rainforests.

We begin in Zimbabwe, a country in southern Africa that falls at the end of the alphabet—and which ranks near last on just about every other social and economic indicator. Here, among the wild elephants and antelope and dusty, degraded landscapes, we'll find revived rivers and pastures—and hope for a thirsty world.

ONE

THE ELEPHANT POOLS

Making Rainfall Effective

The scene which met my eyes the next morning is beyond my power to describe. Game, game everywhere, as far as the eye could see—all on the move, grazing. The game did not appear to be moving; the impression I received was that the earth was doing so, carrying the game with it—they were in such vast numbers . . . hundreds of thousands of blesbok, springbok, wildebeest, and many others were all around us.

—George Mossop, southern Africa, 1860s

WATER HAS REAPPEARED IN A REMOTE CORNER OF rural Zimbabwe, some ten minutes of scarcely drivable dirt road off the Victoria Falls–Bulawayo road and into the bush.

This new water has replenished the Dimbangombe River, which now extends a full kilometer farther upstream than anyone, including the chiefs and elders of the five local tribes, can remember. Even now, in September, the parched heart of the dry season with the hope of rain still a good two months away, there's a steady flow where the Dimbangombe now meets the slightly larger Tsitsingombe River. This revived juncture is marked by a large winterthorn tree, a tree treasured in these parts because, unlike most trees, it holds on to its green leaves through the dry months, only to drop them once it rains.

Upriver from this spot a small, marshy meadow—*vlei* in the Afrikaans language—has a clear film of water coursing over the mud. Allan Savory, who founded the organization that presides over this land, the Africa Centre for Holistic Management, says this is thanks to the new water. At nearly eighty, Savory is trim and spindle-legged in timeless bush garb: khaki shorts; a loose, buttoned cotton shirt; a felt hat with a shady brim. If it's in the heat of the day—from about noon to three, a stretch I come to think of as "the stupid hours" since the heat leaves me barely able to think—he'll be wearing shoes, perhaps a thin-soled kudu-skin pair with holes at the toe, or a tawny-shaded pair of Crocs; otherwise, not. He prefers to go barefoot. This way every step he takes is telling him something about the state of the land: the temperature of the soil, its cover, whether or not it's compacted.

"This is the giraffes' favorite area," he says. It's quiet with no animals in sight, but I imagine a herd of giraffes ambling by this very spot: their long, lanky necks pitched at an angle; shoulder muscles rippling as, suddenly and in a single unit, they break into a run.

Savory scans the vista with the intentness of someone attuned to the slightest variation in plant type or the recent presence of antelope, no matter how fleet-footed. "Ten years ago we would not have seen water here into September," he tells me and my husband, Tony Eprile.

We get back in the 4 × 4 and ramble along the dusty road to a clearing. We walk to where the river is running clean and silvery over the rocks. A red dragonfly skims by. "This part of the river goes dry after the rainy season, around April, then in July, after the coldest time of year, it starts to flow again," Savory says. "A few years back, after July the water began returning more strongly and staying longer into the eight-month-long dry season. This year, for the first time, it didn't go dry at all."

This area is home to numerous water-loving species, he says, including African fish eagle, catfish, turtles and otters, "though we haven't seen them in a while. We do have a croc in here, but he may not be here now. It's an eleven-foot croc with a slightly damaged jaw. One year he spent the dry season in an abandoned porcupine den."

Savory points out the track of a warthog, with its distinct two toes, in the dirt along the bank. Above us, weaverbird nests dangle from the trees. The air is still but for the chattering of birds and the soft rustle of grasses as we brush against them. A wave of well-being sweeps over me: this is the sound of Africa, a layering of quiet and song that fills up the space in a way that somehow makes the sky feel that much more immense. Tony spent his childhood in South Africa, so my nostalgia for this environment comes naturally—that is, by marriage. The first time he brought me to South Africa's famed Kruger National Park, he insisted we get up early so we could sit in the stillness and simply listen to the sounds.

A bird darts past too quickly for me to note its shape and color. "That's a striped kingfisher," Savory says. "I caught one in the car on the way to fetch you."

We move quietly and in single file a few yards away from the river in search of more signs of new water: Savory, then me, then Tony with his camera, striding into the grasses as if we're on a kind of water safari. We pause, and where we stand the ground is moist and all the plants are green. These are sedges, which favor moisture; they look like grass but grow in bunches, sprays of slender leaves spreading outward from the base. Savory shows us that reeds, whose existence virtually defines wetlands, are now established as well. "I never dreamt of having water here," he says. "We have Egyptian geese all year. Look, you can see water lilies—this is two months until the rain begins and there's still water. If this had been a wet year we could have explained it. But we've had seven years of average or below-average rainfall."

Finally Savory takes us to the elephant pool, where the new water has made the biggest change in the landscape. It doesn't look like much. In fact, the spot looks trashed—like, well, a gang of wild elephants had been through and ransacked the place. And that, says Savory, is the point. For the elephants don't need that particular watering hole anymore.

This had long been the site of the river's permanent pool, where elephants could water any time of year. You see, elephants like to wallow. They bathe to cool down and wet themselves in preparation for lolling around in the mud. A good coating of mud protects their skin from the harsh sun—elephants, with their delicate skin and sparse hair are susceptible to sunburn—as well as from parasites and biting insects. For elephants, baths are also an important social activity and a time in which to play and squirt each other with their trunks.

On the plus side for us humans, the lack of water everywhere else meant that you always knew where to find elephants (there are several wild herds in and around the Africa Centre's land). Savory used to bring guests to the nearby observation hide for game viewing. Often, he recalls, "I couldn't get guests out of the hide and safely cover the short walk to the car because of the damned elephants. As it got darker, one herd after another kept coming to get water." Savory and his friends would have no choice but to wait, assuming their place in the pachyderm caravan until the animals, sometimes hundreds of them, had their drink. Then the people could return to camp.

Now that the wild elephants in the area have several watering spots to choose from, they no longer have to walk several kilometers from all directions to the sole reliable pool. The pathways—centuries-old trails carved out by generations of elephants over time—are grown over with sedges and brush; without elephants digging and trampling and mucking about, the site of the pool has silted up.

The hide, a stone structure that was once prime real estate for sighting and photographing game, is deserted, its sides crumbling. Savory tells a story about the hide in its heyday. One time a guide left a group of visitors alone for several moments so they could enjoy looking at animals at their leisure. "The guide returned and there were three lions sitting on top of the hide," he says, chuckling over the memory. "The people were inside, terrified."

When I refer to "new water" at Dimbangombe, I don't mean that water has suddenly materialized out of nowhere (the amount of water on the planet remains fairly constant), or been "taken" from somewhere else. Nor do I mean reclaimed water in the sense of treated wastewater (as in, say, the "toilet to tap" NEWater program in Singapore[1]).Rather, this water is "new" in that it hadn't previously been available.

It's not that the Dimbangombe Ranch at the Africa Centre hadn't been receiving any rain. Though, admittedly, the previous rainy seasons had been lackluster, it was still near the average of 650 millimeters (a little over 25 inches), which is typical for dryland savanna landscapes. For the longest time, the land was languishing, kiln-dry and withered despite the rain, but now the ranch and the animals that dwell there are flourishing.

Through the pages of this book we'll travel around the world: to California, Mexico, Brazil, West Texas, Australia and back to Africa. At each stop we'll find new water—water held in the soil, cycled through plants, captured as dew—and gain new insights on how water flows across the land, insights that can help us replenish water sources and make the best use of what we have.

For the moment we're in Zimbabwe, a landlocked state with a wealth of big game and a deeply troubled past, where Allan Savory and his colleagues at the Africa Centre have launched and guided a mini-miracle in land and water restoration—one that offers critical lessons on how to address water problems, whether stemming from too much or too little, around the globe.

Once touted as the "breadbasket of Africa," Zimbabwe has in the last decade or so been plagued by food insecurity. Much of the population depends on international food aid; due to chronic malnutrition, one in three children has stunted growth.[2] The country's economy is so dire and improvisational that there is no national currency, the Zimbabwe dollar having inflated itself beyond relevance. Rather than carrying around Z$100 trillion banknotes, as was the case in 2009, people dig into their pockets for U.S. dollars, British pounds or South African rands. The price charged may or may not make any sense, and vendors invariably try to barter their stock in lieu of change, which they likely do not have.

There are a number of reasons for this predicament, among them Robert Mugabe's failed regime and the government-enforced land reforms. As an explanation for rampant and recurring food shortages, however, the Zimbabwe government and the global aid community generally look to drought. Indeed, the landscape across much of the country looks parched, and crops regularly wilt from moisture stress so that a season's yield may be simply written off. "Even the goats are suffering," a seventy-six-year-old subsistence farmer named Simon Sibaya told *Bloomberg News* in late 2013. "This is a dry place always, but last season what few crops we had failed."[3]

If drought is defined as a lack of precipitation, the rain records cast doubt on this as the culprit for Zimbabwe's ills. For the country's crops have also been decimated by *floods*. When the rainy season hits, it can hit hard. As I write, three months after visiting a Zimbabwe so dry and dusty it reddened the eyes, I've been reading reports of flooded bridges, homes washed away, an air force rescue of people who were stranded for two days. Not to mention the wholesale destruction of crops, the extent of which augurs plenty of hunger ahead. "Brace for More Floods," Harare-based *NewsDay* warned in January 2015.[4]

Perhaps the trouble is not quite as simple as a scarcity of water descending from the sky, though that is generally the story that gets told. In any event, Matabeleland North, the Africa Centre's home province and the nation's poorest, has been beset by the same deluges and dry spells as the rest of the country. And yet, the 8,000-acre Dimbangombe Ranch has newly formed watering holes that are luring wild elephants and other game from nearby areas. Instead of losing crops, the rural communities that work with the center are seeing improved growing seasons and getting *off* food aid. In Sianyanga Village, a young mother named Busie Nyachari says that whereas in the past they would rush to be in line to receive assistance, now "we are able to feed our families, and neighboring communities come to us for food."

Which raises the question: Is the condition we call "drought" something other than the absence of rain? And can the advent of new water at Dimbangombe teach us how to ensure that there's sufficient water to support people, the land and wildlife in regions prone to dry periods? In other words, do people in water-challenged areas have options more promising than praying for rain or piling up sandbags?

Savory wants us to have a good view of the place where the two rivers meet, so we hop back into the 4 × 4 bush vehicle and rattle our way along the improvised road. It's late morning and the air has warmed yet another notch. Still, there's a hint of breeze strumming through the grasses. Savory glances around without speaking, and I catch myself wondering if he's expecting me to read the landscape as he does. Beyond the basic visual units of river, grass and tree, I don't know what I should be looking for.

I'm humbled by the awareness that the signs and signals of this terrain—of any terrain, in fact, were I to be totally honest—constitute a language I don't speak. Savory, by contrast, is an accomplished, even legendary tracker, savvy to the subtle details that suggest an animal's recent presence or a change in conditions. He honed this ability as a wildlife ranger in Northern Rhodesia (now Zambia) in the 1950s, when his responsibilities included hunting rogue elephants and man-eating lions. He later drew on this knowledge during the long civil war that yielded Zimbabwe's independence. As a military officer he developed tactics suited to bush guerrilla warfare and established the Tracker Combat Unit that became the

elite "Selous Scout" regiment. Since then his teachings on military tracking have been used widely, including for the U.S. Special Forces.

More than a skill or even a set of skills, tracking is a way of knowing,
a kind of metaperception that involves all the senses and is grounded in
a particular place and time. It is the ultimate "now" continually referring
back in time to "then": you're fully attuned to what's happening around you
even as you're deciphering cues about what occurred beforehand. You're
thinking about today's weather and yesterday's weather and if the murky
hoofprints indicate that there'd been a strong wind. And what all of this
might mean to predator or prey and how it might inform that animal's behavior. For example, whether the lion, bushbuck or kudu is likely seeking
water or looking for shelter. Standing there with Savory on a grassy bank
within sight of that familiar beacon, the winterthorn tree, his keenness to
his surroundings is palpable.

Tony indicates a black, smallish, red-eyed bird and wonders aloud if
it's a fork-tailed drongo. Savory nods. As a child, Tony devoted much time
to poring over nature books. He hasn't lost his discerning eye. Now Savory
walks slowly toward the water, still barefoot, wooden walking stick in hand.
He waves the stick to draw our attention to the bank's left side. "That land
belongs to the national park service," he says. He grips the stick with two
hands and holds it horizontally, at chest level. "During the rainy season, the
flooding from the parkland reached three meters high. Our vehicle would
have been underwater." He moves toward some trees that line the bank and
points to where driftwood and other debris had caught on the limbs. This
tells us just how high the water was flowing during the flood.

"Right here we have two catchments, the parkland and the Africa Centre," he says. "The water coming off the Africa Centre's land only came up
to here." He lowers the stick to just above his knees. We then follow him to
where we can see the twigs and whatnot left stranded along the tree line by
the streaming current. "This one is up a meter. The other comes up three
meters." The Africa Centre's land absorbed most of the water, so that flooding was kept to a minimum. On the parkland hardly any water soaked into

the soil. Instead it streamed away, destabilizing the bank and causing erosion. As a result, the fast-running water carried off valuable topsoil along with the flotsam. Savory gestures toward the embankment on the Africa Centre side, noting the higher grass with deeper roots, and how the slope has remained intact.

"This junction of rivers—here's the whole story," he says. He invites us to consider the flooding and other problems that confront properties like the parkland, which, he says, is far from the most degraded land in the area.

The flip side of the floods—the damage caused by coursing water—is that with the water simply sluicing off the parkland, the soil there remains dry. It's a cruel irony: during the dry season everyone's waiting for rain, and when it finally arrives the greater part of it rushes away. By contrast, the center's Dimbangombe Ranch holds on to more of the rain. This is why the grasses grow high and lush, and why the wild elephants that roam the area have more choice as to where to wallow and play.

Savory looks at the parkland's riverbank that had been submerged three meters deep in floodwaters. Come the rainy months, they would likely be flooded again. He shakes his head at what waste this represents in a dry country and says, "How many trillions of gallons of water will have been lost?"

We take one more brief walk before returning to the Africa Centre for lunch, at which point Savory will return to his hut and Tony and I will be served with almost embarrassing formality by the waitstaff in the large, airy *rondavel* that serves as the main meeting area. Savory tells us about two of his early mentors, Blake Goldsmith, a botanist, and Frank Ansell, a mammalogist: "I learned more of the discipline of science from them than I did at university. Both had similar experiences in that they left school as young men and went straight into the army during World War II, Blake into North Africa and Frank into Burma. They never got a chance to go to university, but were passionate about animals and plants and became self-taught after the war. And both were later recognized for their achievements. So while I did go to university I became disillusioned with academia and began all over when I graduated, teaching myself and learning from other successful people."

Savory has long been ambivalent about the academic world, as, granted, much of the academic world has been about him. Among the most intelligent people he's ever met, he says, are some who are illiterate: local trackers and others who learn through careful observation. It bothers him that the knowledge such people command tends to get brushed aside since they don't speak the jargon and don't have degrees. He's especially troubled by the way academic institutions create divisions of knowledge, and believes this is a root cause of so many of our ongoing political and environmental problems. This is one reason he continually stresses the importance of holistic thinking and holistic decision making. He believes that the route to solving most problems transcends intellectual boundaries; zoology doesn't begin where botany ends, and vice versa. And in his experience, an African villager is at least as apt to cross disciplines as someone with a PhD.

"I remember my very first lecture when I went to university," he says. (He earned a Bachelor of Science at the University of Natal in South Africa.) "Our professor said, 'You've arrived here as useless little buggers and you'll leave the same way. But while you are here we will teach you how to learn how to learn.' That was my greatest benefit from a university education. I studied plant ecology and animal ecology. In plant science class I'd ask, 'What about the animals?' They'd say, 'If you want to be a bloody zoologist, go to the zoology department.' In zoology I'd ask about plants, and they'd tell me, "Go to the bloody botany department!'

"After university, I saw that what I'd learned didn't make sense. I could only envision ecology with soils, plants and animals as one. Plant ecology and animal ecology made little sense. I was desperate for answers to the environmental degradation I was witnessing trying to save wildlife. Where we were taught that rain falls, runs to rivers and oceans, evaporates and returns as rain, this did not for me answer what I saw on the land. When others during a rainstorm would shelter inside I took to walking in the rain to actually observe how rain, plants, litter and soil interacted—and wandering days later over the same ground to observe water evaporating out of soil surfaces."

In Savory's view, what's important is not the quantity of rain a given location receives, but rather how much *usable* or *effective* rainfall there is. It doesn't really matter how much rain falls on a stretch of land, he says, if 90 percent of the water either evaporates or streams away by the next day.

He describes a 1981 visit to Yemen, a country that struggles to keep up with its water needs and could even achieve the dubious distinction of becoming the first nation in the world to run out of water. Savory was with a team from the World Bank in the Tihama Plains, an arid region in the north of the country, when the skies opened in a heavy downpour. A full inch came down in a brief amount of time, leading to localized flooding. On the way out of town the next morning, the group stopped at a site that had flooded. The land was bone dry—so much that "I had to borrow the car keys in order to break that soil surface," he recalls. All that rain did nothing to nourish the land, thirsty though it must have been.

This is desertification—the loss of land's capacity to sustain plant and animal life. It is a story that's being written across arid and semi-arid landscapes throughout the globe, from the savanna in Africa and the steppes in central Asia to once-fertile Mediterranean farm regions and large swaths of the western United States. According to the United Nations Convention to Combat Desertification, a quarter of the world's land is either moderately or highly degraded.[5] About one and a half billion people today depend for their livelihoods on land threatened by desertification.[6] Desertification is neither inevitable nor wrought by nature's whim; rather, it is the result of human impacts that include deforestation, fire, poor grazing management, tillage and inappropriate use of irrigation—most basically, Savory says, "management that leads to a high level of bare soil between grass plants and thus less effective rainfall."

Degraded and desertified land is the backdrop for much rural poverty, which ultimately means urban poverty as well, because when land won't produce people see no option but to flock to the cities. Desertification drives the inexorable cycle of poverty, crop failure, social breakdown, unrest and repression that afflicts a nation like Zimbabwe.

It is also why we have rainfall boom and bust scenarios that have communities reeling between floods and droughts: long, sun-beaten dry stretches broken only by too much rain all at once, the notion of enough rain at the right time relegated to a far-off memory from some Edenic past. This pattern has become relentless, as flood and drought disaster news now appear as predictably as bad celebrity behavior.

And it's happening all over the world. Just to note a few countries and regions that of late have made news with this brand of back-and-forth weather extremes: Spain, Australia, Kenya, South Africa, the United Kingdom, Russia and the Amazon River Basin, not to mention the entire United States Midwest, our once vaunted breadbasket. Places like Pakistan, Thailand, Malaysia and even now Yemen have swerved from drought to floods and back, though it's the dramatic floods that usually get the photo ops: men and women pushing through chest-high water, grimly holding aloft their children. An example from my Twitter feed reports that floods in Malawi are such that half the country has been declared a disaster zone, and in nearby Mozambique the torrential rains carried away twenty-five schoolchildren.[7]

What would it take to make rainfall more effective?

To Savory, rain is effective "when the bulk of the rain (or snowmelt) soaks into the soil and only leaves the soil through plant growth, or through perennial flow to streams, springs or underground water storage, including aquifers."

This sounds awfully simple: that it's just a matter of keeping the water in the landscape. Is it possible that much of the destruction and despair caused by floods and droughts comes down to the failure to keep water in the ground? And if so, how could we change that?

Allan Savory is best known in the United States and around the world for having developed Holistic Management, a decision-making framework for land stewardship and restoration. In this approach, domestic animals—livestock—often serve as proxies for the large herds of wild herbivores that formed and maintained the world's grassland ecosystems. This use of animals is referred to as holistic planned grazing. The practice is based on two core insights. The first is that grasslands and grazing animals co-evolved, so the land needs the animals in the same way that animals need the land. This is significant, since grasslands constitute about 40 percent of the world's landmass (not counting Antarctica and Greenland) and much of this land is desertifying.

The other insight is that while plants in a landscape may be grazed too much, they can also be *under*grazed. This is the part that troubles many people, including, for a long time, Savory: it is the crux of what didn't make sense to him in those years after he left university and worked for the Colonial Service in the game reserves. At that time, there was concern because the land was deteriorating and as a consequence the animals were suffering. The administration concluded that the cause was too many animals, so they kept game out of certain areas. However, whenever they set aside land to preserve it, the condition of the land got worse. If too many animals were in fact the problem, this should not have been the case. To Savory, this was a conundrum.

Over time and through reading works by people such as French agronomist André Voisin, Savory recognized that ruminant behavior—nibbling, dunging, trampling, bunching up and moving as a group to escape predators—stimulates biological processes that promote soil fertility and plant growth and diversity. And he recognized that absent the vast, wild herds that historically crisscrossed the world's savannas, steppes and prairies, ordinary livestock, appropriately managed, could fill the niche.

This is the paradox of holistic planned grazing: ruminants acting upon the land can have a regenerative effect, when all logic and much experience suggests that cows grazing and stomping would cause it to deteriorate, as is often the case when animals graze at will. In Holistic Management circles, this laissez-faire grazing is known as continuous grazing: when a small number of animals occupies a large land area and can eat whatever plants appeal to them. Around the world, wherever there's livestock, continuous grazing is the default strategy. This tends to be the case for large cattle ranchers to nomadic pastoralists to subsistence farmers in poor rural communities for whom a cow or two represent a family's collective wealth. In many landscapes—such as those like Zimbabwe, with seasonal rains—continuous grazing causes the land to deteriorate. The animals themselves get hit with all the blame, but it's really a matter of management.

It's important to recognize that whenever people keep animals on the land, those animals are having an impact on the land—which can be a positive or negative impact, depending on how they are managed. The potential for animals that are raised for meat, fiber or labor to benefit the land they inhabit is powerful. As shown by the extension of the Dimbangombe River and its new pools for elephant frolic, this has significant implications for managing water.

One useful way to understand Holistic Management is that it addresses a basic challenge in seasonably dry environments like Zimbabwe: how to maintain moisture in the soil from the end of one rainy season to the beginning of the next. Without animals eating the grass and pressing dying vegetation into the ground, plant matter accumulates without breaking down. This blocks fresh growth and inhibits biological decay. The result: the plant material oxidizes and the soil loses carbon and water as well as the capacity to support plant and animal life. In other words, the synergy between the land and the vegetation and the ruminant's digestive process can forestall, and even reverse, desertification in grassland ecosystems.

The particulars of management depend on the conditions of the land in conjunction with the herder or rancher's goals, economic constraints and the like, and would be adapted as these evolve. The emphasis is on planning and decision making within the context of complexity (e.g., people's lives, the animals' needs, crops, wildlife, soil life, rainfall). Holistic planned grazing is not a specific formula, for such factors are not predictable. This causes great confusion, and even hostility, in part because there's a human need to codify, to say something along the lines of "cattle should be moved to new paddocks every third day," and condemn the program if it doesn't work out. Holistic Management is a system for planning for the unknown and amending as realities unfold.

I first learned of Savory and Holistic Management a few years back when I began exploring the connection between soil and climate, specifically how approximately one-third of our excess atmospheric carbon dioxide can be attributed to huge losses of carbon in soil, primarily from agriculture. The more I researched this, the more I saw a great opportunity to lower concentrations of CO_2 gas, since one can unwind the process and return carbon to the soil. As Larry Kopald, cofounder of the nonprofit The Carbon Underground, expressed it in a column on *Huffington Post*, "Nature wants her carbon back."[8] (In chapter 2 I take a closer look at soil carbon as it relates to water. Hint: carbon enables soil to effectively store water.)

I posed a question: What can you do to pull down carbon? The answer that kept coming up was holistic planned grazing. In my book about soil as a hub for our many environmental, economic and social crises—and for solutions—I wrote about Holistic Management. I found the thinking behind it compelling, and liked both its reasonableness and the improbability of cattle remaking landscapes for the good. The practice inspired my book title: *Cows Save the Planet.*

I traveled to Zimbabwe because I felt the need to see holistic planned grazing in action. I'd written about it and spoken about it, and while I'd done my homework and interviewed numerous people and visited ranches that practiced it, I couldn't get around the fact that I had not yet observed the best example of the approach, the demonstration site where Holistic Management had been implemented and documented over time. I'd heard stories and seen pictures, but that's not the same. Essentially, I hauled myself down to a remote area of southern Africa so that I could be honest with myself.

Once there, I absolutely had to meet the cows that started it all.

On our third day at the Africa Centre Tony and I wake early so we can watch the herders move the cattle. Andy Walton, the ranch manager, has planned to pick us up at six thirty. Walton is a tall, well-built fellow with a white beard and the evenly tanned skin of a man who has always worked in the outdoors. He's genial, but it's good humor with a tinge of weary cynicism. Like many whites that stayed through the transition from Rhodesia to Zimbabwe, he's bounced around. He's lost jobs and had his land apprehended and been forced to rebuild his life several times over. We'd met Walton the night before when he'd invited us to his house for sundowners, the cocktail ritual as the evening descends and mercifully cools and which has given me a whole new level of appreciation for a glass of chilled white wine. Savory was with us, as was his wife, Jody Butterfield, who co-founded the Africa Centre and continues as its Programs Director.

Walton's veranda was said to be a prime spot for game viewing. Savory had tempted us by saying that with an increase in wildlife coming to the property, it wasn't unheard of to see several hundred Cape buffalo from Walton's house. Our chatter must have kept the game away. There was at one point a troupe of baboons gathered around a pond below, somewhat mirroring our own circular seating around the low fire. But we did get to visit with Bugsy, Walton's Jack Russell terrier, who was bandaged up and miserable after an unfortunate run-in with some baboons—perhaps the same ones I'd glimpsed as the day's light was fading away.

As we wait for Walton the next morning we enjoy the sun illuminating the thatched roofs of the small chalets. It's not so much cool as not-yet-warm. Flitting about the grassy area are the ubiquitous hornbills, with their curved red beaks, shrewd yet somehow bumbling, and the gray lourie, known as the "go-away bird" for its call that sounds uncannily like someone nagging. Weaverbird nests dangle like rough, straw pompoms in the limbs of bare trees.

We arrive at the lion-proof kraal, where the herd of 500 cattle has spent the night. In western Zimbabwe, predators, particularly lions, are an ongoing problem. The woven-stick panels that had been used to keep large felines out were developed by Savory's son Rodger, who had seen similar mats used by villagers seeking protection from man-eating lions. While effective, they were also labor-intensive, so Savory and the Africa Centre staff developed portable enclosures made of boma sheeting, a lightweight but durable canvas, and this has worked well. There are four full-time and two part-time herders, all from the local villages. Every night two remain near the kraal to guard the cattle. Here in the Hwange District in Matabeleland North province, unemployment is about 90 percent. Among the tribes that live in the region, the vocation of herding cattle commands respect. These are highly desirable jobs.

Two herders are with the cattle in the enclosure. One man wrestles a young, spirited animal, a yearling, the pair kicking up a haze of dust as they turn and tussle. This is to remove its weaning ring, Walton explains when I ask about it. The ring, which interferes with nursing so that the animal will graze, is kept in place for about a month, he says. "In this country they normally wean at seven months. That's when a cow's reproductive system can regenerate to take the bull again. I like to wean in the summer, but it depends on when the calf was born. A cow will only conceive when it's in rising condition."

Rising condition. I'm no expert on animal husbandry, but the cattle appear rather thin. As a New Englander, I'm accustomed to lazy-looking, thick-middled cows, picture-postcard bovines like the ones lolling about the farms that line our country roads. Walton concedes that the cattle are less than robust, noting that this reflects the season. "It's because of the dry grass," he says. "We can control that with supplemental feeding, but we keep that to a minimum. What we're trying to breed is for cattle to be totally adaptable to the environment in all aspects. When the rains are within thirty days, they will start to improve condition."

Herding supervisor Dickson Ncube tells me that this time of year the nutritional level of the grass is down to 30 to 40 percent. From the perspective of the cows, the rainy season can't come soon enough.

The animals aren't unhealthily skinny, just leaner than I'm used to. It's also worth noting that the herd is being managed for land improvement, not to yield prime cuts of richly marbled rib-eye steak. The relative priorities are factors that would be part of the initial plan, and would therefore inform such management decisions as if or when to supplement and where to move the cattle. These cattle will eventually be processed, and in preparation those due to be sold will receive a small amount of additional feed each day at the overnight kraal.

The main task of the cattle is to make the rainfall more effective, thereby creating a more vibrant ecosystem and improved habitat for wildlife. But the income they generate is also important—it helps keep the ranch operating. As profitability is part of the goal, Walton's management strives to provide the best grazing possible at any given time while simultaneously adhering to a cattle production plan that improves the herd. This means selection and culling so that the herd consists of cows that produce a healthy calf every year. The aim is to breed cattle that get all the nutrition they need from this land without costly feeding.

Two herders start to lead the animals out of the kraal in a single line. The cattle traipse toward a sparsely wooded area some hundred yards away, steady and obedient, accompanied by a small group of goats and ushered along by a herder and the fox terrier–mix cattle dogs. The sun, heavy and shrouded in haze, is slowly lifting on the horizon. "We've got the community cattle in here to boost their numbers," Walton tells me.

It's a challenge to maintain a large enough herd to sufficiently impact the land, he says, so local owners "lend" them their cattle. The Africa Centre needs more animals to keep up the impact on the land—in essence, to keep up with the land's productivity. It costs $400 to $500 to purchase a new animal, and the center is lean on funds. While this is the fate of many nonprofit organizations, the Africa Centre has an added handicap: it's based in Zimbabwe, a nation few have had the desire to invest in.

As the cattle stream through I chat with Ncube, who's presiding over the process of moving and counting animals. He says he's worked on the ranch since 2002. He wears a torn, blue Puma cap and when I ask his age says he's "turning fifty-two." He's clearly proud of this work and his position, yet more so now that his son Duncan ("turning twenty") has joined the herding staff. He offers ongoing commentary on the various animals that have remained in the kraal. "That calf lost its cow," he says. He points to a cow that he says hasn't been producing, and so will be taken out of the herd and butchered come January. "It could die giving birth or the calf could die," he says. "We want to keep them healthy."

I'm introduced to another supervisor, Mdawini, who has bright eyes and is missing two front teeth. I remember that this is the man Savory refers to as "the Professor." Savory likes to tell the story of when Zimbabwe's minister of water development visited the ranch, and he brought Mdawini and the minister to the winterthorn tree. The three sat together and shared a thermos of tea as Mdawini, who cannot read or write, gave the official a thorough, articulate lecture in his own Ndebele language, explaining that the water has returned to the river because of the cattle hooves.

"I have seen the land change," Ncube tells me. "There was plenty of bare land. There were gullies and sinkholes. Then we started bringing in the cattle. The gully is still there, but now there is grass so there is no erosion."

By now the majority of cattle have moved into the brush and out of sight. Two herders, sticks in hand, shoo along the stragglers. It's all rather unremarkable, this slow, orderly saunter of cattle and the grazing they'll do when they arrive at their spot. And yet this is the catalyst for the improvements Ncube has seen.

Of all the ecological changes at the Dimbangombe Ranch, perhaps the one Savory is most proud of is the lack of bare ground. In his view, whether soil is covered or exposed is a key barometer of the health of the land. Soil that's covered with growing plants represents a biologically active system: the plants are taking in sunlight and carbon dioxide and creating sugars that sustain a remarkable menagerie of life forms underground.

Water, too, is cycling through the vegetation. Transpiration, the upward movement of water through plants, is a cooling mechanism; as the plant emits moisture, solar energy is released as latent heat embodied in water vapor. The vapor is then carried to cooler areas, where it condenses and falls as dew or precipitation. Water, as it moves from liquid to gas and back again in an ongoing exchange with vegetation and the sun, is continually modulating and moderating temperature. Depending on the variety of vegetation and the conditions, a plant may seal or open its valves—the stomata on the underside of the leaves—so as to retain or emit moisture.

Without ground cover, a patch of soil gets a direct hit of radiation. With no trees or grass to provide shade or to dissipate solar energy through transpiration, solar rays fall as sensible heat. In contrast to latent heat, in which the heat is dispersed, this is the sort of heat that leads Savory, albeit reluctantly, to put on a pair of shoes in the middle of the day. That bare spot becomes a microcosm of a desert, nurturing nothing and all moisture evaporated away.

There is, however, a midpoint between living plants and naked, exposed soil, which is variably called mulch, litter or soil armor. This is basic plant residue—dropped leaves, dying grasses stomped down by cattle— that serves as a protective mat. It guards against direct solar heat (you can still go barefoot if, like Savory, your feet are hardy enough not to be bothered by rough or uneven surfaces) as well as wind and the pounding of heavy rain. It also keeps moisture from evaporating and therefore the soil can support microbial life and, ultimately, plants. At which point the vegetation starts to fill in. Animals trampling on the landscape squash the plant residues into the ground, whereby it provides fodder for the billions of creatures that live in the soil. This plant matter gets broken down into nutrients like minerals, which can feed newly growing plants. Within short order, the land is on its way to becoming a thriving ecosystem.

This is what occurred over fifteen years at Dimbangombe. It is the process that yielded new sources of available water. This progression reflects the antithesis of desertification: it is the return of land function through the restoration of the water, carbon and mineral cycles. The plant litter keeps water in the soil, which allows for more plant growth and thus more carbon moving from atmosphere to soil and more water that can be held. The seasons pass, carbon and water following each other as the land rises to greater complexity and an enhanced capacity to make use of the water that rains or flows its way.

Unfortunately, what we usually get is the vicious cycle as opposed to the virtuous one I just described. When soil is left bare, water evaporates, carbon oxidizes and microorganisms die. The ground becomes a hot plate and can no longer sustain life. Water runs off the land instead of sinking into it.

It's astounding how rapidly this downward slide into desertification takes place. Two charts from the Burleigh County Soil Conservation District (BCSCD) in North Dakota illustrate this. One chart shows the extent to which bare soil heats up. On a day when the outside temperature was 105 degrees Fahrenheit, soil with living plant armor (BCSCD favors the term *armor* for soil cover) was at 87.6 degrees while nearby soil with just bits of stubble on top logged in at 107.4.

The second chart shows why this matters. When soil temperature is 70 degrees, all moisture is used for plant growth. When soil temperature climbs to 100 degrees, only 15 percent is available for plant growth. At 130 degrees all moisture is lost, and when the soil surface reaches 140 degrees the soil microorganisms die out.

Here we have the story of desertification in two handy visuals.

Appreciating what happens when soil heats up is significant because the land surface can be much hotter than the air temperature. There's a term to describe this phenomenon: *land skin temperature*. According to NASA's Earth Observatory, scientists recognized the discrepancy in 1915 in the desert near Tucson, Arizona, where at midday the temperature at 0.4 centimeters below the soil surface registered 160.7 degrees while the air temperature remained a relatively balmy 108.5.

When Holistic Management was first implemented at the Dimbangombe Ranch twenty years ago, the space between plants was 90 percent dry, capped soil, says Savory. Now, "it's hard to train people here because there are so few bare patches. We're actually preserving places with bare soil for training purposes." Similarly, at the outset 95 percent of the water would run off when it rained, whereas today 95 percent of the water soaks in. Now, he says, "I don't know how to make water flow off this land."

Many people, upward of 3 million to be precise, are aware of Savory primarily through his 2013 TED Talk, "How to Green the Deserts and Reverse Climate Change." The twenty-two minute presentation sparked a lot of attention and immediately entered that dubious media category of "controversial." To some viewers, the idea that grassland ecosystems required animal impact made complete sense. Others were bothered by an argument in such flagrant opposition to what they'd been taught. Those among the cows-are-bad contingent, which has become a highly vocal and opinionated force within the environmental movement, were particularly quick to refute it.[9]

A small minority of naysayers sought to discredit Savory on the basis of his public admission that while a Colonial Service officer in the 1960s his recommendation led to the culling of 40,000 elephants. To say that this is something he regrets is a tremendous understatement. Savory loves elephants, and has rescued many an injured and/or orphaned elephant in his day. If asked, he'll gladly provide step-by-step instructions on how to bring to safety a young elephant without causing it stress—crucial, since they are extremely sensitive animals and the level of stress can determine whether or not an elephant survives a capture. (Hint: Savory's technique involves running and pulling its tail.) At the time, he truly believed that reducing elephant numbers would allow the land to rebound and ultimately to support more wildlife, a conviction then supported by science. That reducing the elephant population had the opposite effect spurred his quest to find approaches to decision making that neither exacerbate nor merely divert the problem one is attempting to solve. What drives him as much as anything is his determination to redeem this tragedy.

There is one special elephant in Savory's life: Dojiwe, who was found as an orphan at about three years of age and adopted by the Africa Centre. The name means "she was found." Now about fourteen, she is very charming and gregarious and likes to say good morning—an affectionate guttural purr—to the guests. Since she cannot be on her own in the wild, she has two handlers so that she's watched at all times. This is a big expense, but everybody loves her and couldn't imagine not having her around. Dojiwe has tried to join wild herds, but older females chase her off. One day when we were there she got into a tiff with an elder and broke a tusk. Elephants are matriarchal, and the hope is that she will have a calf and begin her own herd. Occasionally a young bull has come courting. Sweet as she is, Dojiwe is still an elephant and disconcertingly large. At one point she was caressing Tony's face with her trunk and he jumped back. Savory said, "She's just trying to kiss you, Tony. I'm sure you've had worse."

While we tour the land, Savory points out places that were featured in the TED Talk, including what are known as the Two-Tree site and the Elbow site. He also has with him a binder with photos encased in plastic folders so we can compare the setting before us with how it appeared thirty years back. This creates an odd sensation of collapsed time, of looking at the pictures of prior desolation—of land that had been given up on—and projecting onto them the knowledge of their redemption, of seeing within the bare earth the literal seeds of imminent fecundity.

Since I've hit the dry season I don't get to see the lavish grass as in the dramatic "after" photos, but rather the before-the-rains version. Had we been here two months ago, Savory tells me, the grass would have been six feet high.

However, the dry-season grass allows me to look into the sheaves and see the consistent coverage, how little blank space remains between plants. Savory also alerts us to signs of animals, such as the hoofmarks on pathways (giraffe, kudu, "maybe a serval, one of our little nocturnal predators") as well as the cracked-off branches that tell you elephants have been this way. And, of course, dung: "That could be old hyena spoor, or baboon. Some dung you can recognize and never mistake—that's porcupine."

Animal numbers have rebounded along with water sources and land condition, I learn. "We have a higher density of lion than the park, I'm told by their lion researchers," Savory says, referring to the Hwange National Park about one hundred kilometers south.

Of the wildlife I see, mostly on late afternoon bush walks led by Africa Centre staff, what strikes me most is the sable: large, healthy herds of sable antelopes with young. Sable are gorgeous, stately antelope, with a rich, brown coat and long curved horns like scimitars. They have not been faring well in many southern African game parks, including South Africa's Kruger National Park. The wildlife authorities there have not been able to explain the sables' plight, though the antelope are known to require tall, high-quality grasses for forage.

A key change along the improvement continuum is the shift from mostly annual to mostly perennial grasses. Perennial grasses have deeper roots, and can pull up nutrients and moisture from greater depths. They store carbon and help to build soil. When degraded land improves so that it's able to support plants, annual varieties will be the first to get established. As conditions become more favorable the perennials will start to move in. Savory shows us where annual grasses are giving way to perennials. He points out that the annual grasses tend to be whitish in hue, whereas the perennials tend toward yellow. He kneels down so that we can see the green flush at the bottom of the perennial plant. It's late September, high dry season, and here's new growth, verdant as if after a spring shower. This attests to the way that perennial plants garner their reserves, and how they are primed to keep energy, nutrients and water cycling through much of the year.

Savory notes that the annual to perennial trend isn't a one-way trajectory, and that all plants have their part to play in the system. Land is never static, he says. Rather, it's "always shifting from bush to grass and grass to bush." This continuing conversion and reversion of the landscape is in part determined by animal movement, by the processes they provoke and what fills the void in their absence.

There are differences even among perennial grasses, Savory explains, as the composition reflects the particular conditions the plants have adapted to. He plucks the seed head from a blade of grass and draws our attention to the spiral stem that holds the seed. "By looking at the seed you can see that it's fire dependent," he says. He squats down and makes a corkscrew motion with his fingers to indicate how the seed twists itself into the soil. "You need sharp seeds to get into bare ground. Some seeds have awns that drill into the ground." These are the plants that would colonize land that's bare, such as a field that's been recently razed by fire.

What Savory and his Africa Centre colleagues are striving for is grassland dominated by animal-dependent plant species, which are generally more resilient and contribute to a more complex ecology than fire-dependent varieties. These plants tend to have round seeds that may reside in plant litter, residue that protects the soil from sun, wind and rain and that helps maintain moisture. The seeds would be trampled into the soil by animals in order to germinate. The animals do more than help the plants propagate; they also keep the grasses alive. Herbivores graze the vegetation before the plants oxidize, and the nutrients are recycled back into the soil through their waste.

The conditions that favor one or another type of plant are self-perpetuating; land that supports fire-dependent plants would be inimical to animal-dependent vegetation. Fire-dependent grasses can't flourish when animals are knocking down litter and dunging and pressing seeds in the ground with their hooves. Similarly, animal-dependent grasses won't grow or even germinate on bare soil. The landscape would tilt either one way or the other: in the direction of plants that sprout on dry, bare soil or toward grasses that coexist with wildlife and ground cover. Animals and plant litter would inhibit one type of grass; exposed ground would inhibit the other.

Savory has a somewhat conflicted relationship with fire. The sweet, acrid scent of bush fire was a constant in his early years, and so the smell of smoke does evoke a kind of nostalgia. Yet he sees grassland fires, including fires set intentionally as a component of management, as an ecological disaster that leaves vast areas of exposed soil and pollutes the air. "Fire is partly why water is evaporating and running off," he says. Evaporation and runoff leave the land dry, which then creates the conditions for wildfires to get out of control.

Grass burning does clear away decaying plant matter and return minerals to the soil. Postfire the land greens up nicely, Savory says, so people conclude that fire is essential to grassland health. But these two functions—clearing debris and nourishing the soil—could be performed by animals without creating pollution or bare soil. In the fire scenario, plant material undergoes *chemical* breakdown in place of the needed biological decay, and carbon is lost to the atmosphere; in the animal version, dry-season dead grass, leaves and litter decompose *biologically* and carbon is stored in the soil. The makeup of the plant community follows suit.

A light wind moves through the grasses, making a soft, brushy sound and leavening the heat. "The herded livestock were here for three days," Savory says. "They won't be here again for another two months. This will be a mass of grass in two months, if we get the rains." The two-month gap is the planner's estimate of the time required for the land to recover. Not enough recovery time and the plants and forage quality suffer; excessive rest (this would be over seasons and not, say, an additional month) leads to oxidation, bare ground, moisture loss and fire risk.

Putting in fire breaks and bringing in cattle minimize bare soil, which, says Savory, was the crux of the problems they'd faced. "I brought the five local chiefs here when we began. They said, 'We've got to put in gully control.' I said, 'We've got to remove the cause of the gullies.'" The bare soil and runoff have been drastically reduced, and now, he says, "the gully problem is gone."

Curtailing fires was a challenge in the early years, he says. This is because of the railway line that runs through the property. "Sparks from the train kept the fires going," he recalls. The rail bed is one area kept free of plants, where the vitality of the soil is sacrificed to create a stopping point for fire.

The National Railway of Zimbabwe's Northern Line bisects the ranch; the Dimbangombe stop, marked by a hand-painted wooden sign, has the steepest slope along the entire route from Cape to Congo. (Hence those fire-igniting sparks—during the civil war, when fuel was scarce, the railroad went back to steam engines to propel the train up the hill.) We'd cross the tracks whenever we took a bush walk or went to Savory and Jody's hut for sundowners or morning tea. The bare ground around the tracks acts like a canvas for stray bird feathers and animal spoor, leading to conjecture about which species had been around. Sometimes we'd hear the long hoot and then the rumble of a train going by, an oddly soothing reminder of the presence of an outside world.

The name *Dimbangombe* roughly translates to "the place where cattle can hide in the grass." The term likely dates from the nineteenth century, when the local Nambya tribe hid their cattle from the more numerous Ndebele, who were reputed to seize cattle at will. In the twenty-first century it has become an apt name, as the grass grows cow-high once again.

TWO

PIPES, PUMPS AND BEAVER PONDS

Moving Water across

the Landscape

Don't pray for rain, if you can't take care of what you get.

—R. E. Dickson, superintendent,
Texas Agricultural Experiment
Station, 1937

1. CITY WATER

The morning after I arrive in sunny Orange County, California, an hour south of Los Angeles, I am euphoric. I'd come to Corona del Mar from Duluth, Minnesota, where I'd woken up to a temperature of 16 below zero Fahrenheit and word that back in Vermont the snow had piled up to an extent verging on the ridiculous. (Later that day I'd learn one of my son's college classes in Ohio was canceled due to extreme cold.) Light and unencumbered in a T-shirt and sneakers, I head down to the beach at Little Corona. I stride along and the colors leap out at me: fuchsia (bougainvillea), purple-edged blue (morning glory), vermillion (some brushy kin to monkey flower); plants in hues I'd not dared dream of over the chilly last few months.

It's a gregarious time of day, the dog-walking hour. High-spirited dogs of varied shapes and sizes run in circles and kick up sand: alert, exquisitely groomed hounds who've only known sunshine, adored by their buff, possibly surgically enhanced owners.

Just before the beach I hear the bounding trill of a red-winged blackbird and notice a small canyon area of reeds and cattails. A sky-blue eye-level display tells me this is the Lower Buck Gully wetland area, which has been replanted and restored and, as a result, "now beckons wildlife." A second sign explains this transformation is thanks to a large restoration project to control Buck Creek's flow. As part of this project, homeowners are working to minimize "nuisance flow": the fertilizers, pesticides, detergents and pet wastes that would stream to the ocean, disturbing and possibly poisoning the habitat of tidal species.

Grasses rustle in the salty breeze as the sun rises above a bank of cloud. Still giddy from the unaccustomed warmth and sunshine, I think how wonderful it is that people are working toward improvements so that egrets, eagles and hummingbirds—species whose bright pictures decorate the signage—are returning to this tiny natural enclave in one of the nation's most densely populated areas.

Then I walk a few more steps.

Just past a row of bright blue trash cans a different sort of message catches my attention. One sign reads: KEEP OUT. SEWAGE CONTAMINATED WATER. The other begins: WARNING! RUNOFF/STORM DRAIN WATER MAY CAUSE ILLNESS.

I lift my gaze above the horizon line. Residential neighborhoods snake and curve through every visible space. From walks in the neighborhood I knew these were large, often new homes, many with three-car garages. I glance upward and in the distance see workmen carefully hosing down the steps of a three-story stucco home. That seemed a frivolous use of water, given ongoing shortages throughout the state. I wondered what that spray of water would pick up as it trickled down the canyon toward the coast. The idyllic vision of residents banding together to keep the water clean for sea hares and hermit crabs fades away in the sun-bleached light.

I pick up the pace as I hit the beach. Time to get back to the house, the tiny old-style bungalow where my friend Barbara is recovering from hip surgery—I should see if there's anything she needs. It's high tide and the waves surge and recede, leaving behind rusted bottle caps, plastic wrappers, wedges of Frisbees and Styrofoam, the rubbishy underbelly of Californian extravagance.

California's water system is hard to fathom. The sheer quantity of water that is moved in, moved around and moved out to the sea is staggering—not to mention what's treated, reclaimed and, with programs like the new $1 billion Carlsbad Desalination Project north of San Diego, relieved of its salt content. The story of California water is a tale of economic booms and busts, interests served and thwarted, and the contested fortunes of the Colorado River. Between multistate agreements, a "use it or lose it" ethic and, until recently, a total lack of legal restrictions on groundwater removal, the water situation in the Golden State is an awkward combination of highly regulated and a Wild West free-for-all. Even experts get dizzy trying to get a handle on it.

When I brushed my teeth that morning, I might have—unthinkingly, like most of us—used a quart of water. According to David Carle's *Introduction to Water in California,* the water that comes out of a faucet in Southern California may have started as snowmelt in the Eastern Sierra Nevada Mountains some 350 miles away. As it moved downstate that water would likely have mixed with other former snow and, somewhere around the San Francisco Bay area, been diverted into the California Aqueduct, a system of reservoirs, tanks, concrete conveyers, pumping stations and hydroelectric power plants built in the 1960s to bring water from the north, where it rains and snows, to southern population centers. Upon arrival in Southern California this water would combine with the more saline water from the Colorado River Watershed (point of origin: the Rocky Mountains) and water from a local aquifer that might have been tainted by industry but with dilution has been brought to safe levels.[1]

The U.S. Geological Survey reports that California uses more water than any state, though the quantity used has been declining since 1980.[2] A huge amount of energy is deployed to gather, stow and deliver water throughout the state. (At the same time, a huge amount of water is required to procure, store and distribute energy—with some of that water becoming polluted as a result.) Addressing water needs consumes about 20 percent of the state's electricity. Says Andy Lipkis, founder and president of Tree-People, "The largest single use of electricity in the entire state of California is to pump water over [the] mountains into Los Angeles."

The bulk of all this water flows toward farming. Fully 80 percent of California's developed water supply is used for agriculture.[3] About half of all produce sold in the United States comes from California (primarily the megafarms in the Central Valley), productivity that is highly dependent on irrigation. In 2014 and again in 2015, farmers who rely on water derived from the U.S. Bureau of Reclamation's sources learned that due to low water reserves and a disappointing snowpack their allocation would be zero.[4] In 2014, nearly half a million acres—5 percent of the state's farmland— was left fallow.[5] A friend who grew up in the area returned to visit family in 2014 and said she'd never seen anything like it. She described road after road lined with fruit and nut trees that were knocked over so that they would die and not draw up water.

Some have raised the question of whether growing thirsty crops like rice, cotton and alfalfa in a mostly dry, often hot landscape is the best idea. Certain agricultural endeavors basically amount to exporting water— which the region can ill afford to spare. For example, farmers in the arid Imperial Valley are shipping alfalfa to China to help feed that country's growing dairy herd. In an interview with NPR, author and University of Arizona law professor Robert Glennon said that in 2013 the United States exported more than 100 billion gallons of water in the form of irrigation-grown alfalfa, most of which was from drought-stricken California.[6]

For similar reasons, the almond has become a nut of contention. Ten percent of California's water goes toward almond farming: that's 1.1 trillion gallons annually, or one gallon per single nut. The state accounts for more than 80 percent of the world's almonds, a high-value crop that's seeing increased demand, in part because of the popularity of almond milk. The water wary say this is an abuse of water resources or even, as expressed in a *Good Magazine* headline, "Almonds Are Sucking California Dry."[7]

Much about California's water-agriculture setup doesn't make much sense. To some extent these apparent climate/crop mismatches are artifacts of arcane rules governing water rights, contracts and subsidies. It's as if the state's water-intensive agriculture were a huge, unruly machine that has become too large and entrenched to turn around. Though recently some have sought to put the system in reverse: specifically, in 2014, water districts in the San Joaquin Valley made the unprecedented request to run a forty-seven-mile stretch of the California Aqueduct *backward*— that is, south to north—to provide water to farms that might not otherwise survive the season.[8] The first-ever mandatory water restrictions Governor Jerry Brown announced in spring of 2015 emphasized domestic use, not agriculture.[9]

When we hear the term *water infrastructure* this is what comes to mind: dams, pipes and pumps; tunnels and funnels; systems engineered by human ingenuity. From copper plumbing found in the Egyptian pyramids to California's complex water matrix to China's $62 billion South-North Water Transfer Project (the latter a plan originally envisioned by Mao Zedong that has already displaced 300,000 people[10]), technological fixes have addressed the ongoing challenge of how to bring in water from the source, treat and clean water for use and consumption, and dispense with the foul stuff. By ensuring ongoing supplies of usable, drinkable, nonfetid water, basic waterworks like aqueducts, drains and latrines are a hallmark of civilization—and hygiene. Without this, a city could flourish only until some virulent, disease-causing agent hit the wells.

My elementary school class once took a field trip to a local water treatment plant. I remember reacting with awe to the deafening factory-scale machinery and concrete vats of turbid water that we looked way down into, like some sort of roiling underworld. This was the late 1960s, arguably the heyday of techno-optimism, or at least of a certain kind of big-works mechanical can-do.

For the longest time I went along assuming that the fate of the water that we needed to quench our thirst and wash our clothes and sprinkle our lawns was by necessity determined by big, mechanistic systems. The natural world played an incidental role. It wasn't until my research led me to think in terms of ecosystems that I gave much thought to how water moves from place to place—and why this has important implications for climate, poverty, politics and biodiversity.

Infrastructure is, to my ear, a cold word, and for this reason I wanted to avoid using it. But I couldn't find another way to convey the apparatus that supports water processes, the basic undergirding or hardware that enables the system to function. And the term doesn't have to refer solely to the built environment—infrastructure can describe natural systems as well.

What do we mean by infrastructure? The *structure* part suggests form, whereas *infra* comes from the Latin for "below." Which brings us once more to what lies at our feet, the soil.

2. PATCH OF EARTH

We're back again in Zimbabwe, by way of a brief video of Allan Savory on the topic of effective rainfall.[11] The clip begins with a shot of Savory, unshod and in shorts. The setting is one of the few bare patches at the Dimbangombe Ranch, maintained for teaching purposes. It must be early on a clear, dry day as the shadows are sharp, narrow and elongated.

Savory uses the wooden stick with the rubber tip that he always has on hand to mark out three rectangles, representing three separate plots on the same land. The patch on the right side is left bare. In the middle and left patches, he approximates the presence of animals, as if "a herd of buffalo or cattle or whatever" has been through. This he does by chipping up the soil with a bamboo pole, leaving hoof-like indentations. On the left side he lays down some grassy mulch to mimic the way animals would have trampled litter over the soil.

Now each of the three plots is going to get some rain—a liter of pretend rain from a plastic water bottle, the equivalent of a fairly heavy, four-millimeter shower.

A few hours later (must now be close to midday since Savory's shadow has shortened) we get a look. The plot on the right, the bare one with hard, capped soil, is dry and, says Savory, hot to the touch. He digs in with his fingers and finds little moisture. By the end of the day, he says, it will be completely dry.

On to the middle, hoof-ridden plot. This spot has retained more moisture, as the dents formed small hollows where water could pool. Still, he says, this will also dry out by day's end.

Finally we get to the ground that's been swathed in litter. Savory brushes aside the debris to find that the soil has remained damp. He can scrape into it with his fingernails and there's still moisture. He can clump up the soil in his hands and it holds its shape. Under the shelter of a layer of mulch, the soil will retain water and therefore be able to support microbial life and plants.

The plant debris helped keep moisture in the system and therefore proved to be an important, if low-tech, component of the water infrastructure of that tiny parcel of land at Dimbangombe. It served to protect the soil from (1) the sun, which would evaporate the water from uncovered ground, and (2) the erosive effects of wind and falling water.

The evaporation part likely makes some sense, since in the previous chapter we saw how soil cover keeps the ground from drying out in hot, arid climates like dry-season Zimbabwe.

But falling water?

We think of falling rain as gentle, softly gracing the land with nourishment. And for soil that's sheltered by trees or covered with mulch or living plants, and is not already saturated, this is so. But an up-close look at what takes place when those water drops strike bare earth belies the poetic notion of rainfall's mildness. In her book *Water: A Natural History,* Alice Outwater even describes it as a kind of violence: "Individual raindrops are like little bombs, gouging, beating, and battering the soil, lifting and splashing it back and forth, churning it into a pasty mud."[12]

A 2007 research collaboration between Arizona State University and Vanderbilt University used high-speed photography to document what happens when raindrops of different sizes and velocities meet bare soil. Magnified images from these experiments show water drops detonating, torpedo-like, upon contact with the soil surface. The particles fly upward like shards of glass, scattering as far as five feet away, leaving empty craters.[13]

Such drama on a microscopic scale is called splash erosion. This can then lead to sheet erosion, in which the soil is carried off by water runoff. The next phase, rill erosion, occurs as flowing water carves out small channels in the soil, and gully erosion is when those small channels turn into big channels. At which point you'll start getting big problems, since the sediment will be streaming into bodies of water, affecting water flow and quality.[14]

Bare soil has another reason to fear rain, and that's compaction. In compacted soil, water and air cannot move around. This impedes plant growth, as roots are unable to go deeper and the lack of aeration interferes with the uptake of nutrients. According to soil microbiologist Elaine Ingham, "The most compacting factor we deal with in most soil is rainfall. When that drop of water hits bare soil, rainfall is more compacting than tillage."

For more on how compaction batters water infrastructure, let's turn to Ray Archuleta, a soil health specialist with the Natural Resource Conservation Service based in North Carolina. Many know him as "Ray the Soil Guy" for his tireless championing of soil.

In a minute-or-so video, Archuleta shows viewers two glass cylinders containing soil. Sample A, on the left, has been tilled—prepared for planting by plowing and turning the soil to disrupt weeds and bury plant residues. Sample B's soil has not been tilled in forty years. The canisters get their allotment of simulated rain (this time jazzed up with red and blue food coloring.)

The results are immediate: in the container with untilled soil, the water slowly filters through, spreading moisture throughout and percolating down so as to replenish groundwater stores below. The disturbed soil, however, lets no water through. The water just sits on top. If this sample were what you were dealing with in real life, Archuleta says, "most of the water's going to run off, place your soil into drought mode and put your nutrients into the nearest lake."[15]

Bruce Ward, a much beloved Holistic Management educator and practitioner from Australia who passed away in 2012, focused on the importance of covering the soil surface, which he referred to as "the interface between earth and the air." He said that soil cover—preferably living plants or a good bit of litter—was a kind of skin. Without this skin, he warned, water runs off the land rather than soaking in, productivity goes down and whatever problems you're contending with get worse.

It's not for nothing they talk about "land skin temperature."

Ward said, "If we were to lose our skin it would hurt, it would hurt like hell. If we create bare soil, exposed soil, then that's exactly the same thing for the land. It's hurting like hell."[16]

The quality of soil on a piece of land may seem unrelated to water infrastructure. However, Malin Falkenmark of the Stockholm International Water Institute has emphasized that two-thirds of all rain that falls over the continents goes into the soil. This is in contrast to the lakes, rivers and reservoirs—those blue-colored places on the map—where we assume water will end up. In the 1990s she coined the term *green water* to represent soil moisture that cycles through plants. *Blue water* is the water in rivers, lakes and aquifers that may be drawn on for domestic and agricultural use.

Falkenmark and her colleagues point out that our engineered infrastructure projects, such as dams, irrigation, and water diversion programs, focus on blue water. Despite representing two-thirds of the world's freshwater resources, green water has been ignored and subsequently mismanaged. Changes that impede the presence of ground cover, notably desertification and deforestation, have a negative impact on green water. This is significant because water held in soil is what most directly and efficiently affects a community's ability to grow food. Indeed, while water planning and policy tend to focus on irrigation, most of the world's agriculture is rain-fed.

Water as liquid or vapor is always moving into and out of soil and plants, the atmosphere, and natural pools and byways, and so the two systems—green and blue—are interdependent. The work on green and blue water demonstrates how crucial that thin ground layer is to our global water infrastructure, the system underlying the movement of water and the fulfillment of our water needs.

Australian soil scientist Christine Jones describes how a whole-landscape approach to water management has to, paradoxically, work on the level of entire catchment areas as well as the tiny raindrop. Any time a raindrop meets the earth, she writes, one of four things can happen. That droplet of water can:

1. go *up,* as evaporation (or transpiration through plants);
2. go *sideways,* as surface runoff;
3. go *down,* as deep drainage to be stored in aquifers; or
4. be *held* in the soil before moving in one of the other three directions.

The length of time water remains in the soil where it has fallen is an important factor in the viability of a given watershed, she says. The trouble today—she's speaking of Australia but this applies worldwide—is that too much water moves *sideways,* dragging along topsoil, organic matter and soluble nutrients and depositing it in lakes and rivers. Because there's so much bare soil, thanks in part to desertification and fires and other means of undermining soil health, there's also too much water moving *up* as evaporation.[17]

This is another way to appreciate what our two videos show us. Ray the Soil Guy gave us the water-going-sideways scenario: disturbed soil becomes compacted and loses the pore spaces that would allow water and air to flow. Unable to infiltrate the soil, the water has no choice but to move horizontally—sideways—and thus we have runoff, and all the problems that entails. Savory's two uncovered plots saw their water go up: in the course of a hot day in Zimbabwe the four-millimeter rain equivalent evaporated away.

As in the African bush and on and around North America's industrial farms, all around the world we have problems with water: water shortages and runoff and floods. But maybe we can reframe our challenge as having a *keeping-water-in-the-ground* problem. For this is certainly a problem we can do something about. What we need to do is promote land management practices that enhance a part of our water infrastructure that we've been treating like dirt: the ground. The surface of the soil shouldn't have to "hurt like hell."

3. BEAVERWORKS

Where I live in southern Vermont, we have a good bit of beaver infrastructure. Friends with homes near East Road, for example, say they see plenty of beaver activity and know where there's a lodge. In early February, Jim Laurie, an ecologist and a big fan of beavers, braved an impending snowstorm (which inevitably caught up with him) and drove up from Boston to scout out beaver habitat with me. We took our snowshoes to the Greenberg Reserve, a nicely walkable nature area just south of downtown, and trekked over lofty white stuff to the wetland lookout over Jewett Brook. We saw neither a den nor newly gnawed logs, but Laurie said he believed beavers have been here in the not-too-distant past. (Beaver watchers at the One World

Conservation Center, which runs the reserve, confirm that beavers were active around that spot in 2012, but there have been fewer signs since. Beaver families move around, so they could return any time.)

The creek flowed clean and slate gray under the ice. "There also would have been freshwater clams in this water," Laurie said. When I expressed surprise, he pointed out that we get used to what's here now—or rather what's not here—and "forget all that was present in the past." Who knew what creatures had made this place their home over time? Hearing this, I regarded the brook with renewed appreciation. We followed the old trolley tracks awhile, noting a red-tailed hawk, the black specks that are tiny snow fleas, and other signs of winter life.

Also among my regular winter haunts is the beaver pond that skirts the trail system at the Prospect Mountain Nordic Ski Center in Woodford. Here's how to find it: Once you're in your boots and skis, and preferably after a quick chat in the lodge about snow conditions and the meaning of life with Steve and Kent, who know everybody's business for about four months of the year, you go up the hill into the woodland and onto Troll Road—a long, cozy corridor of pine trees. Then bear right on X-Mas Tree, curve around, and just past the junction with Loose Moose angle right again onto the Beaver Loop Trail. This will immediately reward you with a softly swerving roller-coaster-ish descent to the pond.

Got that?

A few times a season, after a solid stretch of freezing temperatures without the kind of freeze-thaw pattern that leads to ice, you can ski out onto the dam the beavers built. It's a good-sized pond, quite impressive beaver-wise, surrounded by pine. If it's a windless day the air will be still and utterly silent. There's a kind of magic in the sense of suspended time the scene creates, in the way light sketches purple stripes across the snow, in the hush. I like to ski the periphery rather than break a trail over the chaste white of the surface. At the far side, near where you traipse back through the woods to reconnect with the trail, a friend once showed me a break in the ice that marks an underwater spring. Within the dark, glossy water we saw live newts swimming around—drawn to the spot by the oxygen churned up amid the running water.

Some people call beavers "nature's engineers" for their penchant for rearranging their surroundings by whittling down trees, carving out underwater channels and using tree limbs, sticks and mud to build their dwellings and stop flowing water. Others, for the same reasons, consider them pests. Ecologists have come to understand the degree to which the two species of beaver, North American and Eurasian, have maintained and even created the hydrology on several continents.

"Scientists used to think where there was water there could be beaver," says Laurie. With greater appreciation for beavers' role in managing water, he says, "Now they see beaver and know there will be water."

What brought me to Southern California was the Urban Soil Carbon Water Summit in Los Angeles. Our sessions were held in the North American Mammals Hall at the Natural History Museum of Los Angeles County, so our backdrop included the dioramas of pronghorn, Canadian lynx and, of course, an industrious group of beaver. I got to feel particularly close to the walrus family lolling about their glass-fronted habitat. At the summit I met Brock Dolman, who codirects the WATER Institute at the Occidental Arts & Ecology Center, a research and advocacy nonprofit in Sonoma County, California. One of his projects is helping launch the WATER Institute's Bring Back the Beaver Campaign.

Dolman calls beavers "keystone ecosystem engineers" that support the water infrastructure. Beavers are often referred to as a "keystone species," meaning their "behavioral presence in the ecosystem disproportionately affects the system's carrying capacity." It's useful, says Dolman, to consider the word "keystone" in its original, architectural sense: the stone at the top of an arch that enables the structure to bear weight, without which the whole thing would collapse. Because, he says, collapse is what can happen to a watershed without beavers around to manage it.

Through their dam-building behaviors, beavers are "disproportionately affecting the flow of water, in terms of quality as well as quantity" beyond what their numbers in a given area would suggest, he says. "In essence, they are forest and water farmers. They harvest water by managing woody forests for food and use the material from the trees to build effective water harvesting things calls dams."

Beavers operate at the juncture of the water and carbon cycles, says Dolman. "They're interacting with the hydrological cycle in that they alter fluvial geomorphology: the flows and slope and meanders in a waterway. Plus, they're growing the bio-filter of forest and wetland that enhances water quality." They're also interacting with the carbon cycle: the beaver-directed water flow helps to direct the movement of sediment. And the ponds the beavers create "eventually flood onto the flood plains and expand the wetted width to build soil." Specifically, beavers build nutrient-rich, peaty soils—one reason people used to kill beavers was in order to gain access to such soil for agriculture.

Dolman and his colleagues have found historical and physical evidence indicating there were once far higher numbers of beaver in California than previously thought—and that they were native to a greater extent of the Sierra Nevada and coastal region than once believed. However, *Castor canadensis,* our North American beaver, were largely wiped out of the state by the 1830s. As of 1911, when it was estimated that fewer than 1,000 beavers were left in the state, they were protected by the California legislature.[18]

People talk about California's gold rush. But the "fur rush" is what radically screwed up the hydrological cycle, says Dolman: "I call it California's 'beaver blind spot': the legacy of the problem that beaver were so heavily trapped out and their easily observable presence so far gone that people didn't even know they'd once been there. There are huge implications for the derangement of hydrology on the West Coast: dehydration, pollution, loss of water quality and biodiversity—it's a classic hydro-trophic cascade collapse."

Dolman is riffing—his chief mode of explication—on the concept of "trophic cascade": indirect ecological dynamics that, if altered, have an outsized impact, domino-like, with the consequences amplified as we move down the food chain.

The goal of the Bring Back the Beaver Campaign is to encourage Californians to "partner with beaver as water engineers," says Dolman. "This will yield us more water, cleaner water and enhance both water and carbon storage." In an era of climate unknowns, this will bring a degree of resilience to the water infrastructure.

The story of American water largely turns on the beavers' fortunes, argues Alice Outwater in *Water: A Natural History*. Once the demand for beaver hats and hides left Europe largely de-beavered by the seventeenth century, the fur trade came to North America. By the end of the eighteenth century, beaver populations here were decimated as well. While pioneers, explorers and adventurers were moving west and forging the young country's water and transportation infrastructure—crisscrossing the Lower 48 with increasingly dense linear networks—the infrastructure largely built by beavers was systematically dismantled, one pelt at a time.

Today beavers number around 10 million, down from an estimated 200 million when Europeans arrived on our shores, a decline that's changed the nation's hydrology. Outwater writes: "If each of those pre-Columbian beavers had built only a single acre of wetlands, then an area of more than 300,000 square miles—a tenth of the total land area of the country—was once a beaver-built wetland. Now these wetlands are gone. The river of life receded when the water receded, and the primeval splendor of the land disappeared with the beaver's demise."[19]

In order to improve our water circumstances, it's important to recognize how instrumental animals like beavers have been for our water infrastructure—and to appreciate what has been lost.

4. THE SOIL AGGREGATE

Let us now leave the cuddly and enterprising world of beavers, with their paddle-shaped tails and eager kits, for a zoom-lens perspective of water infrastructure in the landscape. Specifically, we're going to look at where flow happens on and in the ground: the soil aggregate. This is water infrastructure in miniature, a realm invisible to most but which plays a key role in regulating the movement of water on land.

And the medium for this particular aspect of our water system is life— by which I mean carbon, the basis of all life forms on earth.

This requires us to take a pause to get grounded in the science. And so it's time now to bring in Peter Donovan, whom I typically call when trying to clarify scientific ideas. A few years ago Donovan ditched his apartment and sold most of his worldly possessions to move into an old yellow school bus in which he travels around the continent measuring levels of carbon in soil. I think of him as a philosopher of the carbon cycle.

I've had the chance to spend time with Donovan in part because his father, Robert, a Dickens scholar, lives in a retirement home in my hometown. Robert gave me the greatest compliment I've received on my first book to date. When I met father and son by the Lock 7 boat launch in Niskayuna, New York, a bit of local water infrastructure along the Mohawk River that was part of the Erie Canal system, the senior Donovan said, "Thank you for writing this. Now I finally understand what my son has been doing."

First, let's get a handle on the soil aggregate. Say you find yourself in the vicinity of a well-tended garden. If you grab a fistful of that good soil and let it run through your fingers, you'll note that it falls into small clumps. These are aggregates. If you try the same thing with low-quality soil, meaning dirt, it will feel different. The particles will slip through your fingers, like sand passing evenly through an hourglass. Instinctively, you'll probably sense that the soil with aggregates is better, that growing plants would prefer the crumbly stuff, and you'd be right. The soil with aggregates will likely be darker in color. This reflects the higher proportion of carbon.

What is soil, anyway? Stated simply, soil is made up of broken and weathered rock minerals (sand, rock, silt and clay), decayed plant and animal material (aka organic matter), and living organisms. Plus the air and water that continually flow through it. Soil aggregates form when you have active biology—the plants, fungi and microbes that animate the soil by the billions. (A teaspoon of healthy soil has as many living organisms as there are people on the planet.) All this infinitesimal biota, says Donovan, yields "sticky colloidal slimes from all the kingdoms of life"—strings and glues that hold the particles together.

Soil microorganisms, particularly fungi, "secrete a biotic glue. Roots and fungi also form biotic strings, which work with the glues to form a sticky network. They stick clay to silt and silt to sand and sand to clay, holding the particles together, like the mortar in masonry." Many of these gummy substances are not water soluble. This is important, as aggregates will remain stable when rain strikes the soil. However, disturbing the soil, as by tilling or compaction, damages the glues and tendrils and thus destroys the aggregate.

In many ways, soil is the last frontier. We can identify but a fraction of the soil organisms known to exist, let alone appreciate how they fit into the scheme of things. Our understanding of the realm of gluey emanations—the soil yuck-o-sphere—and its importance to soil function is only emerging.

One "superglue" that's lately received attention is glomalin, a carbon-rich protein produced by mycorrhizal fungi. (Mycorrhizal, or root-associated, fungi serve as a kind of underground trading center for plants and soil organisms, governing the exchange of carbon and nutrients and enhancing a plant's access to water and minerals.) Kristine Nichols was with the USDA Agricultural Research Service team that identified glomalin in 1996, and is now chief scientist at Rodale Institute. As she describes it, the hyphae (threadlike strands) of the mycorrhizal fungi form a kind of "string bag" for holding soil particles. The chewing-gum-like stickiness of glomalin helps bind the bits and pieces. The glomalin then forms a "lattice-like waxy coating" that maintains the aggregate, protecting it from those fierce raindrop bombardments we learned of earlier while ensuring that water and nutrients are available to associated plants.

The USDA's research service has called glomalin "the unsung hero of soil carbon storage" in that it comprises about 30 to 40 percent carbon;

importantly, carbon in a stable form that, if not disturbed, can last for decades.[20]

Back to that handful of good soil that falls into nice, distinct clumps. Well-aggregated soil is considered to have good structure and "tilth." Good soil structure means that there are spaces between the clumps that allow for air to circulate and for water to slowly filter through. Soil tilth is that property that makes soil suitable for supporting plant growth, particularly at the root zone. It's one of those you-know-it-when-you-see-it qualities, which for the most part circles back to the degree of aggregation. Soil function—what we depend on soil to do, beyond merely propping up a plant—reflects soil's ability to hold water and moderate its flow, supply nutrients, and support life within and above the ground. Practices like heavy mechanical tillage, leaving soil uncovered to dry out, and using pesticides that harm soil microorganisms are the death of tilth, and thus sabotage land's capacity to regulate water.

Soil aggregation facilitates the passage of water through landscapes. "Think of a dirt driveway," says Donovan. "You have lots of mineral dirt particles, with the small ones free to move between the large ones." He specifies the word *dirt* because this is not living soil; it's the rocky, sandy, silty stuff absent the soil life and organic matter. "They're not stuck together. The little particles are free to move between the large ones and can block the spaces. What happens when it rains is that you get a seal. It's like pouring a pitcher of water over a pile of flour. It will seal and the water will run off."

Soil without carbon is like that flour: some water can be absorbed, but not much. Soil with carbon is like a nice, fluffy loaf of bread. It's mostly composed of the same ingredients as the flour, but with leavening there's been a transformation—one that leads to a constellation of new properties, among these a structure that absorbs and holds water. (Interestingly, older farming texts call aggregation "crumb structure," reflecting the usefulness of this bread-baking analogy.)

Even the airiest chunk of bread could soak up only so much, say, gravy or hot chocolate. In the same way, water doesn't merely remain in the soil;

thanks to the filtering provided by the carbon-rich crumbly sponge, it slowly percolates down to replenish underground water stores.

Donovan likens the soil aggregate to "a dense city block full of multistory apartments and businesses full of plumbing, wiring, cabinets, clothes and books, which has acres of surface area, an enormous variety of spaces and habitats within it, a variety of life and behaviors, and a constant traffic of matter and energy." Water, air, nutrients and roots are able to move through the various chambers, or spaces, of which there are many. "In well-textured soil, about half the volume is made up of space," he says. "The largest pores, the macropores, they're the superhighways for air, water and nutrients in the soil."

If we zero in yet further on our soil aggregate—with a good bit of magnification this round—and scrutinize those compartments and the contents of the manifold fungal threads and gooey secretions, we will come across carbon. This is the product of photosynthesis, whereby plants pull carbon from the air to form sugars. A portion of these liquefied carbon compounds, the dissolved organic carbon, moves down and into the soil through the roots, where it fuels the below-ground economy.

Carbon is the main ingredient of soil organic matter, composing about 58 percent of its dry weight. It helps form the mineral building blocks—the aggregates—that hold and release water by way of the pore spaces. On a molecular level, one could say that soil carbon serves as the infrastructure for green water, the moisture essential to soil life and soil processes.

Here's what this means water-wise: every 1 percent increase in soil carbon represents an additional 20,000 gallons per acre (the figures cited range between 16,000 to 27,000) that the land can hold.[21] When soil does not allow water to infiltrate, we can understand this as a symptom of a soil carbon deficit. This was likely the case with Ray Archuleta's continuously tilled soil in his video, or the dried out soil in the Dimbangombe catchment prior to the implementation of managed animal impact.

This link between carbon and land's water-holding capacity is important in part because much of the carbon that once resided in our soils isn't there anymore. According to Rattan Lal, director of Ohio State University's Carbon Management and Sequestration Center and considered the "dean" of soil carbon, the world's cultivated soils have lost between 50 and 70 percent of their original carbon stock.[22] Where did that carbon go? Much of it has oxidized: upon exposure to the air, the carbon would have combined with oxygen to form carbon dioxide. To put this in perspective, approximately one-third of our excess atmospheric CO_2 can be attributed to soil carbon loss due to agricultural practices that break up soil aggregates and leave soil bare.[23]

The flip side is that we can return this carbon to the soil, and thus reduce atmospheric CO_2, through a variety of restorative agricultural practices, including holistic planned grazing. But that's another story, one I endeavored to tell in my previous book. In terms of water, it's become clear that keeping—or, better yet, *growing*—soil carbon is essential to keeping water in the ground.

We can't truly do justice to the topic of soil carbon without discussing humus, which is a complex and stable form of soil organic matter. Soil health educator David Yarrow describes humus as "the final product of decaying plant and animal residues" that is sufficiently stable to last thousands of years. More poetically, he calls it "leftovers from microbial feasts." Humus is impervious to microbes, he explains, so it is not vulnerable to decay. At the same time, it is a dynamic substance that's continually in the process of decomposing and being formed. In his 1936 work *Humus,* Selman A. Waksman suggests that humus is a "condition" of organic matter, and a reservoir of biochemical potential.[24]

Christine Jones says humus is more dynamic than the notion of "leftovers" would imply. She describes humus as "an organo-mineral complex containing carbon and nitrogen in specific ratios, plus a wide range of soil minerals." Like the aggregate, she says, humus can only be formed where there are fungal mycelia, such as the active area around the roots of plants. The making of humus, she says, is part of a positive feedback loop: humus enhances the soil environment and thus promotes higher plant productivity and resilience to stress; more photosynthesis means a more reliable supply of carbon for plant-dependent microbes; thriving microbial life translates to the creation of more humus.

Humus has great significance for water quality and accessibility on land. Humus can hold several times its weight in water. It also buffers the reactions of soil minerals and nutrients, ensuring their availability to plants (which means less fertilizer and other inputs) and promotes aggregation (which enhances water retention and flow).

Among soil aficionados, humus is spoken of with great reverence, as the distillation of soil's more emergent and enigmatic properties. Waksman, a microbiologist who was later awarded the Nobel Prize for discovering streptomycin, wrote: "Humus plays a leading part in the storage of energy of solar origin on the surface of the earth."[25] That sun-derived energy is carbon, which is continually in relation with water. The viability of bio-physical cycles that drive our planet's living systems—the solar, carbon, nutrient and water cycles—comes down to the relationship between carbon and water. As Donovan puts it, soil carbon—the main component of humus that, in its gluey iterations, helps form aggregates—has tremendous lever-age over the functioning of the water cycle: the holding, filtering and slow release of water upon its encounter with the land.[26]

In sum, the soil aggregate is a vital part of our water infrastructure for two reasons. First, the aggregate itself provides the architecture for the movement of water through soil, via the permeable areas within or between individual aggregates. Water is propelled through two processes: surface tension and capillary action—the cohesive and adhesive forces that may drive the flow of liquids in seeming defiance of other forces, such as gravity. Second, it is home to the carbon critical for water retention in soil.

Put another way, the soil aggregate is a link between photosynthesis and the viability and availability of water. And yet, ironically, so much of today's commercial and agricultural activity wreaks havoc on this founda-tional part of our water infrastructure.

"Our use of fossil fuels has enabled us to destroy soil aggregates faster," says Donovan, "not only in agriculture but in the soil exposure that we create to extract fossil fuels (well pads, roads, pipelines), and in the easy soil exposure that all types of earthmoving equipment make possible." He adds that the chemicals used in agriculture, including soluble fertilizers and the "-cides" (substances that kill things, such as fungicides, herbicides and insecticides), disrupt the synergy between plants and microbes— relationships that are fundamental to plant health and the formation and stability of soil carbon.

"The dynamics of soil aggregation have been understood since the 1930s," he says. "But we've forgotten about it. We thought we could re-place soil function with technology, like irrigation, and fertilizer and other chemicals. But technology cannot build soil aggregates. You need biology."

The humble soil aggregate is where processes vital to water quantity and quality take place. Yet it has remained invisible to those who design or maintain the water infrastructure most of us rely upon.

But there are signs this might be starting to change.

On my last day in Corona del Mar it rained, a soft, tangy rain that pinged my borrowed umbrella with steady but gentle force. People had been talk-ing about rain all day, and while there were spells on and off it wasn't till near evening that it began in earnest. I was out on an errand—okay, picking up a California red—and the pavement and parking lots glistened in the wet. I maneuvered over shallow puddles and running ditches that hugged the curb. *All that water streaming away with its burden of oil and chemical residues,* I thought. No doubt this would mean another round of "WARNING—KEEP AWAY" signs, along with the danger to marine life, which, alas, cannot read.

The next morning I took the Amtrak to Los Angeles, and as we ap-proached the station I saw more running water: a brackish stream moving through the center of a concrete trench. Back home I'd be looking out the

Amtrak window upon the verdant lower Hudson River, which accompanies my train trips to and from New York. This was the Los Angeles River: a fifty-one-mile-long concrete corridor that straightened and paved what had been a seasonal flow that occasionally flooded its banks after winter rains. The regular flooding became a point of contention as the area grew and industrialized. The 1939 flood, which knocked out bridges and killed forty-nine people, sealed the river's fate, and officials stepped up efforts to dam and "channelize" it.[27]

In Brock Dolman's words, this meant taking the Los Angeles Basin, a topographical watershed, and turning it into a "pipeshed," which has no intrinsic connection to its ecological setting. Indeed, this trapezoidal conveyance was among the first of Southern California's trademark freeways, built to fast-track water and whoosh it out to the sea—together with whatever pollutants were carried along for the ride. At forty-five miles per hour, the thoroughfare moves faster than much of LA's day-to-day traffic.

Happily a project is in the works to undo the Army Corps of Engineers' handiwork of some eighty years ago so that the area can once again function as a watershed. The mayor of Los Angeles and several federal and local agencies and nonprofits are planning to turn the concrete water highway into a linear park—a "greenway" with trails, recreational areas and restored natural habitat. Adventurous urbanites can already fish and kayak on the river. In artists' renderings the banks are as lush and picnic-able as rivers I might drive or bicycle by in New England.[28]

With California's population and its cultural and economic importance, particularly in agriculture, the state's water problems have become a regular feature of the news. It seems there's not enough water or too much all at once. In December 2014, after rain-watchers spent months scouring the skies to no avail, the heavens finally opened. The epic drought quickly gave way to "the storm of the decade," complete with Hollywood-worthy calamities sweeping southward along the coast: houses smothered by mudslides; highway closings and accidents; falling trees killing people and crushing cars; home evacuations and last-minute rescues. ("It turns to Niagara Falls here with water and mud," one sixty-six-year-old suburban homeowner, who'd hedged his bets with plywood, plastic sheeting and four hundred sandbags, told the *Los Angeles Times* as he responded to an evacuation order. "We were hoping to get through Christmas."[29])

And yet experts dryly observed that the deluge would scarcely make a dent in California's four-year rain shortfall. According to the website Climate Central, the state would need a dose of fifteen to twenty-one inches of rain in a month—the precipitation equivalent of five storms of similar magnitude—in order to emerge from water debt.[30] Scientists at NASA put a precise figure on the deficit: based on satellite data, the team calculated that 11 trillion gallons of water were required in order to make California's drought history. That's either one and a half times the volume of the country's biggest reservoir or enough water to fill 17 million Olympic-sized swimming pools.[31]

But perhaps the antidote to drought is not simply a matter of rainfall—but rather what we *do with* the rain. Maybe California's population centers—even the semiarid southern region—are not as water starved as we've come to believe.

This is the view of Andy Lipkis, founder and president of TreePeople, the Los Angeles–based nonprofit he launched as a teenager in 1973 to promote the vitality of the urban forest. Lipkis notes that 2013 was the driest year in the city's recorded history, with a measured rainfall of 3.6 inches. Still, he says, in Los Angeles "we throw away 3.8 billions of gallons of water for every inch of rain that falls." Even with this paltry rain yield, this comes to about 13.68 billion gallons of rain thrown away, or 3,420 gallons per person. "Our average local rainfall generates enough runoff that, if captured, would represent as much as 45 percent of our current needs. Rain can be captured and stored in cisterns and soil. We can radically reduce our needs with healthy soil."

Imagine if the Los Angeles River flowed not through watertight concrete, but rather across healthy soil and wetlands—a scenario the new greenway could help to bring about. How much rainfall would remain in the system? How much *less* water would need to be brought into the region—and how much energy would that save?

The Elmer Avenue Neighborhood Retrofit is another Los Angeles project that tries to do more with rainwater than sluice it away. Before 2010, this sixty-acre block of twenty-four homes in the San Fernando Valley had no storm drainage system, and the road was cracked and furrowed. A coalition of local agencies and nonprofits in conjunction with this Sun Valley neighborhood took several measures to address the water problem: they created bio-swales, swaths of green space with soil, plants and rocks to hold runoff and provide natural habitat; beneath the street, they built infiltration galleries that capture and infiltrate runoff to recharge groundwater stores; and they installed catch basins on both ends of the block to move water directly to the infiltration points to avoid introducing sediments and other pollutants.[32]

According to the Southern California–based Council for Watershed Health, which manages the project, the new "green street" infrastructure generates more water than all of the people who live on the street would typically use in a year. Whenever it rained the street used to flood, said Nancy L.C. Steele, the organization's executive director. "Streets are really good at moving people and cars. But streets are also really good at moving water. Let's reimagine the street. What if we reconnect the water that now rushes down the street and away into storm drain systems to the soil, which can filter out pollutants and deliver clean water to the drinking water aquifers beneath our feet?"

The story of Elmer Avenue perfectly encapsulates Ray "The Soil Guy" Archuleta's oft-uttered contention that "in many instances, what we have is an infiltration problem, not a runoff problem."

Our built infrastructure often doesn't give water the chance to infiltrate. "The way we think of it, it's as if water disappears when it hits the soil," says soil microbiologist Elaine Ingham. After rain, she says, "we want to hold the water and move water through the soil at a pace that's not too slow, not too fast so that it comes out clean. We forget about the connection with soil when we think of water as a resource."

This disconnect with soil is one reason California struggles with water shortages, Ingham says: "Look at the conduits. They're lined with concrete. There's no water going back into the soil." Ingham expresses concern that people will turn to technology to address water problems rather than reengaging with ecology. "The solution is not engineering, not technology," she says. "It's what we already know: it's through biology."

In terms of water retention, the standard-issue suburban lawn won't cut it. "In most cases, by law, the soil around a house had to be compacted," Ingham explains. "This is a requirement so that the foundation wouldn't start moving. Therefore, when you roll out the sod, the root systems couldn't go down more than two to four inches."

This isn't merely a California problem. One commonly used metric for compaction is bulk density, which gives a sense of the porosity in soil. A study in New Jersey found that residential areas built in the 1970s had turf with bulk densities between 1.75 and 1.9. The bulk density of sports fields created in 1980 was 1.97. For comparison, the bulk density of concrete is 2.2.[33]

Backyard soccer, anyone?

There's an awful lot of land out there that's impenetrable to roots of grasses, shrubs and trees, and virtually impervious to water. A NASA study found that lawns cover about 128,000 square kilometers (49,000 square miles) of the United States, an expanse nearly the size of Arkansas.[34] The lesson: just because it looks green, it isn't necessarily a thriving hub of nature—nor is it supporting the local hydrology.

However, even in dry regions there's often more water than we think. One pioneer in this area is Brad Lancaster, author of several books on rainwater harvesting. Lancaster, who lives in Tucson, Arizona, likes to use the term *urban drool* to describe the water flowing through urban streets and into storm drains—water that drips from leaky pipes, overwatered lawns and gardens, car washing in driveways, and the like. This waste or "nuisance" water can be harvested, filtered through the landscape and reused. Doing so reduces the pressure on water sources (most of Tucson's water for domestic use comes from the Colorado River, 300 miles away) and the energy system (bringing that water via canal to Tucson represents the largest single use of electricity in Arizona, as well as the state's largest source of carbon emissions).[35]

On his eighth-of-an-acre property, in a city that annually receives about eleven inches of rain, Lancaster harvests 100,000 gallons of rainwater a year. Through do-it-yourself efforts like capturing roof runoff; directing water flow toward plants with swales, sunken beds and raised pathways; and making creative use of native plants, he and his brother have created a mini-oasis on their small urban plot. They have ample shade and fruit-bearing trees; one valued crop is the pods from mesquite trees, the beans of which can be ground into flour. Harvesting water that falls or drains onto the public right-of-way adjacent to their property bolsters their land's productivity. Thanks to Lancaster's example—and tenacity—Tucson now allows for cutting into curbs to collect runoff in street-side basins. The city has also mandated gray-water harvesting capability in new homes.

One can be a producer of usable water rather than solely a consumer of it—even in the desert Southwest, Lancaster says, noting that "more rain falls on the surface area of Tucson than the entire community consumes in a typical year."

Our reliance on engineered water infrastructure is costly in terms of energy and carbon emissions. Similarly, the way we've built our cities, suburbs and industrial areas, with an emphasis on draining away incoming water, is also expensive. Our towns and cities are dominated by impervious surfaces—rooftops, parking lots, patios and the like. A city like New York, for example, has about 80 percent impermeable surfaces. Water that falls on these surfaces becomes runoff and a source of pollution. Particularly because many urban water systems are so old, this water becomes a burden to the community.[36]

To reflect the cost of handling this water, several cities, including Washington, D.C., Philadelphia, and Minneapolis, have instituted fees based on the square footage of impervious surfaces. Many municipalities offer incentives for making surfaces more permeable, including landscaping—such as rain gardens, green roofs and pervious pavements—that allows water to infiltrate and seep into the ground. The city of Charlottesville, Virginia, has open-source satellite data that serves as a map for impervious surfaces. From a water system perspective, those sprawling trophy homes now bear an additional price—and there's no hiding it from your neighbors.[37]

A vision for water infrastructure that works would incorporate all these aspects—from engineered waterworks down to the soil aggregate—to make use of the gift of rainwater and snowmelt without waste, loss or introducing impurities. In turning to technology to solve water problems, so often we are merely relieving the symptoms of an impaired water cycle without acknowledging or addressing the cause. Restoring the water cycle needs to be done with biology; our success will turn on how we manage the land and water of a living system.

THREE

THE BIRDS OF CHIHUAHUA

Water and Biodiversity

If you take away all the prairie dogs, there will be no one to cry for the rain.

—Terry Tempest Williams, in *Finding Beauty in a Broken World* (2008)

*I pledge allegiance to the streams
And the beaver ponds of America
And to the renewal for which they stand,
One river, underground, irreplaceable,
With habitat and wetlands for all.*

—Heidi Perryman, Ph.D., president of Worth a Dam

TO DRIVE THROUGH THE CHIHUAHUAN DESERT Grasslands with rancher Alejandro Carrillo is like taking a journey through rainfall past, present and future.

Also, rainfall absent, which many blame for the widespread failure of ranches in this part of northern Mexico over the last several years.

Rainfall present begins somewhere in the middle of our four-hour trek south from El Paso in Carrillo's hulking, shiny silver Toyota truck. We drive through the scantest sliver of New Mexico and south into Chihuahua State with its low horizon and broad, scruffy expanses. Toward late morning, the weather turns cold and wet. It is mid-March, the tail end—or what I'd foolishly thought was the tail end—of a relentless winter in New England. Before my trip Carrillo had told me it was hot, so I'd been looking forward to warmth, with the inward sigh of anticipated relief. With growing consternation, I watch the dashboard's digital temperature display drop from 52 to 46 and finally to 35 degrees. I zip up the hooded wool tunic I'd only halfheartedly thrown in my bag at the last minute. The rain thickens to icy slop and, for a few moments, proper, Vermont-worthy snow. Finally, a good thirty minutes past the dirt road turnoff that will take us to Las Damas Ranch, the clouds thin out and we see small birds darting amid the ground cover while solitary falcons sail above.

We get out of the truck. The quiet of the desert settles in. We have been off paved road for a while now. Through the mist, we can see the silhouette of mountains: the Sierras Las Damas, "Mountains of the Ladies," three nestled peaks that gave their name to the long defunct Las Damas Mine for which, in turn, Carrillo's ranch was named. Carrillo, forty-seven, has a master's degree in information technology from Johns Hopkins University and spent many years as an IT professional in the United States, most recently as an executive with Reuters. In 2004, when his father asked for help with the ranch, he left the industry to ranch full time. He began implementing holistic planned grazing in 2006.

He splits his time between Chihuahua and El Paso, where he and his wife, Miriam, are raising their three young daughters: Daniela, Alejandra and Paula, each one cuter than the next. Carrillo has the methodical, self-assured manner of someone accustomed to working hard and succeeding. There's an elegance about him, a near old-fashioned courtesy that's tempered by warmth and humor. He's the kind of person who is present, but gives others space.

"Look—you'll see those little birds are bunching up," he says. "Those black birds, those are prairie birds. They're responding to the rain." Small, shy birds hover and dip into the brush. There's a whirr as doves spring up, and as I follow their ascent in the sky I see solitary raptors. I flip through the pamphlet on Chihuahuan Desert Grasslands birds I'd tucked in the door's side pocket. We identify *Cernícalo Americano* (American kestrel) and *Aguilucho Pálido*, or northern harrier. Idly soaring birds of prey are fairly easy to pinpoint. Swift and skittish smaller birds, not so much. A lark bunting? Or blue-black grassquit? I switch back and forth between pages. One bird I'd been trying to label has left the branch. It could have been any number of breeds, including a Sprague's pipit or Baird's sparrow, two of several grassland species that spend the winter in the region but whose populations have plummeted as the land continues to deteriorate.

Once we get back on the road, rain past and future are on Carrillo's mind as he recounts the backstories of the various properties we pass. "When I was growing up this was the best land in the area, with grama grass up to that wire," he says, gesturing to an indifferent brownish weedy plot lined with waist-high fencing and dotted with random brush.

Tall and straight-backed in a crisp straw cowboy hat, Carrillo shakes his head. He laments the demise of good land, and the waste of it: the waste of the precious rain that's fallen upon it to no avail; the accumulated sunlight that's beamed down without finding plants upon which to bestow energy. What thirty years ago had been lush, tall grass has been reduced to bare ground and plant stubble. Carrillo points out that the effects of barren land go beyond the rampant sell-offs and bankruptcies. It has impact on the area's wildlife as well.

He's specifically thinking about the birds.

"These were the best grounds for birds to overwinter," he says. He notes that the grassland birds that winter here would now find little cover for evading predators, or seeds to eat. "Where are the birds going to protect themselves here? They get killed, or die of hunger."

Chihuahua, Mexico's largest state, is big ranching country. The Chihuahuan Desert region, which includes parts of Arizona, New Mexico and Texas as well as the northern Mexico states of Chihuahua and Coahuila, is where many of the cowboy traditions we associate with "the West" originated. (Carrillo likes to say that the word "buckaroo" comes from the Spanish *vaquero*, or cattle herder.) It was the ideal place to raise cattle, says Carrillo, "thanks to a sea of native grasslands and plenty of water from year-round springs."

However, this cherished ranching culture is slipping away—in part because, just like its neighbors across the border, Chihuahua has been in a drought,[1] which has meant a dearth of grass for cows to eat. Between 2010 and 2014, the state lost 40 percent of its cattle, with hundreds of thousands of animals dying from hunger or thirst, or sold to slaughter. Vast ranchlands that had thrived for generations are for sale or virtually abandoned.

Many failed ranches are sold to Mennonite farmers, who have been plowing up native grasslands and dousing the land with chemicals. The state is home to nearly 100,000 Mennonites, whose ancestors came to Mexico in the early twentieth century from Russia and elsewhere in Europe, often by way of Canada. Until fairly recently the Mennonites, with their horses and buggies and austere, often antiquated dress, have lived peacefully among Mexicans. But tight water sources have become a point of tension. Mennonite farms rely heavily on irrigation, and their predilection for digging deep wells, legally or not, has stressed groundwater reserves, which has led to deadly skirmishes.

Tom Barry, senior policy analyst at the Center for International Policy in Washington, D.C., who has long reported on the U.S.-Mexican border, wrote in 2013, "Mennonite expansionism into new areas of Chihuahua has set off what could well be described as the first water wars of the climate-change era." He said that while the region has been notorious for drug violence, "the drug-war crisis in Chihuahua seems likely to be overshadowed in the near future by the escalating water crisis and accompanying water wars."[2] The region's drug violence has been centered in Ciudad Juárez,

Carrillo's wife Miriam's hometown, which is just across the eighteen-foot high security fence and what's left of the Rio Grande from El Paso.

It's not just quantity but also the quality of water that's at issue. Carrillo's friend and colleague Jesus Almeida, whose ranch borders Mennonite farms on three sides, told me he once lost eighty cows in one day due to harmful chemicals in the livestock's drinking water. A laboratory in Mexico City tested the water from the earth pond beside which the dead cows were found and confirmed the presence of chemicals including Dieldrin, an insecticide that has been banned in most of the world and that increases its toxicity as it moves up the food chain.

A drive along Cuauhtémoc's sprawling Corredor Comercial Menonita gives a sense of the extent to which industrial agriculture has dug into the region. For this small city, some sixty-five miles from the capital of Chihuahua, is the epicenter of Mennonite agribusiness, with shop after shop selling machine parts, feed, fertilizer and refurbished, glossy-finished John Deere tractors. Many of the stores' broad, square facades bear the bright logos of purveyors of agrochemicals, including global companies like Monsanto.

Almeida has since had to completely reconfigure water sourcing for his animals. His cows have not been poisoned since.

The Mennonites "get the wells working, and get the permits afterwards," says Carrillo. He regularly does business with them, and admires the community's trademark discipline and mechanical know-how—invaluable for the kinds of ongoing fix-it tasks that are inevitable in the ranching trade. Yet he's concerned about the effects of chemical farming on the land and animals, as well as on people. "[The Mennonites] won't drink the water from their own wells because of all the fertilizer they put on," he says. "Almost every family has someone dying of cancer. And almost every day those dying of cancer get younger. The best business you can do with Mennonites is to sell water." Shortages of irrigation water are such that Mennonites are now leaving the country.

Despite water stress and the ongoing assault on the landscape, Carrillo and colleagues who ranch according to Holistic Management principles are thriving. As for Las Damas Ranch, Carrillo says, "comparing last year's results with 2006, when we started managing holistically, our sales have more than doubled, our hay expenses are half, and our profit is four times greater than what it used to be." Fellow rancher Octavio Bermudez, or "Tavo," says that while conventional ranches in the region produce six kilograms of meat per hectare of land, at his ranch, El Muchacho, it's double that. "We could go to twenty-two kilos per hectare if that was our goal," he says. "This is the same landscape and we use zero supplementation, which saves a lot of money. People often say that supplementing the animals' diet is an 'investment,' but if it's the same story every year it amounts to a loss."

"People say, 'It's only because you're lucky,'" says Tavo. "Our neighbors are waiting for us to fail so they can say, 'I told you so.' Thirty years later, they're still waiting."

Carrillo contends that ranches are failing because of what people have done to the land. "It's not the lack of water, plain and simple," he says. "It's mismanagement." Specifically, he targets continuous grazing, in which livestock are left to wander about and graze without restriction. As we saw in chapter 1, this practice results in some areas being overgrazed while others are overrested, both of which lead to deteriorating plant and soil quality. This scenario sweeps across the region, at the expense of land and livelihoods, Carrillo says. "The technologies that made ranching possible in arid parts of the state, deepwater wells and barbed-wire fencing, came at a price. Now cattle remain in one place until they run out of grass rather than following water and vegetation patterns. Our grasslands have become bare ground with just a few woody plants, like mesquite."

More than half of the area's land are *ejidos*, communal properties distributed to the poor and landless as part of the agrarian reforms that followed the Mexican Revolution. The people who live there, the *ejidatorios*, may have ten or twenty animals meandering over a huge tract of land. Yet the land bears the scars of overgrazing. On our drives we traverse much ejido land: dried-out fields empty but for the occasional *flaca vaca*—skinny cow—and shantytowns strewn with trash, like the plastic bags that catch on barbed wire, waving in the breeze like sorry flags.

"This is the sad reality of our whole state," says Carrillo. "Some places you don't know whether you are in Chihuahua or on the moon. This is all land that should be an Eden. We have water coming down from the Sierras. The ranchers are the ones to blame. But the ranchers blame the lack of rain, or they blame the Mennonites. The truth is that the Mennonites are capitalizing on the failures of the ranchers. People aren't profitable because we've lost the organic matter in the soil. Chihuahua used to be mostly grasslands. Now it's a center for the cement industry and U.S. manufacturing plants that pay minimum wage. The land for industry and the people who work there come from the ranches that failed. These ranchers raised cattle but they were also miners—miners of the soil."

He stops the truck and points through the open window toward the remains of a cement structure, the surrounding ground parched with but a few shallow pools holding what is left of the rain. A desert hare scrambles by. "This land hasn't been grazed for twenty years," he says. "Look at that mesquite. The roots are exposed down to one foot. That erosion represents tons and tons of lost topsoil. Where did all that soil go? It left with the wind and the rain." Now, he says, "you can get thirty inches of rain here and nothing is going to grow."

At a nearby family-owned ranch, he says, circumstances are so dire the siblings are no longer talking to each other. Other neighbors have 100,000 acres they fear they'll be forced to sell. The prospect of liberating multiple-acre blocks of land from desperate owners has potential buyers hovering over the area like canny raptors charting a predatory swoop. It isn't only the enterprising Mennonite farmers, tractors at the ready, but energy speculators as well. Northern Mexico has been found to house great stores of shale gas and shale oil, with the Mexican government touting the Chihuahuan Desert as "ripe for fracking." While Mexico's oil had long been nationalized under Pemex, in 2014 new legislation opened the industry to private and foreign investment, which has begun to pour in.[3]

All of which means that the health of this land—and the communities, traditions and wildlife it has long sustained—is very much in the balance.

Here is where our future rain comes in.

Despite the environmental and ecological pressures, Carrillo is optimistic about the Chihuahuan Desert region. "I believe the land can be better than before," he says. "The Spanish were here in the 1500s and it was a garden. There were grizzly bear in the area until the 1960s. Imagine the amount of food there had to be to grow such a large animal. I'm sure it was a gorgeous land and it can be again. We don't know how good it can be."

While this confidence may seem to belie the reality he and his peers face, it derives from the changes he's seen since practicing restorative grazing. "My granddaddy said, when there's water it rains more. When land is desertified there's no moisture in the air. No dew. Now I walk out in the morning and my feet are wet," he says. "Healthy grassland is all about the movement of the animals, just as herds of bison and pronghorn antelope kept moving when this land was wild. Our desert is very delicate. But if you do the right things it responds, beautifully."

Alas, this opinion has not caught on the way he's hoped. He shrugs. "My neighbor will say to me, "Of course you are doing well. You get more water at your ranch."

I came to Chihuahua to see the birds. Upon seeing my book *Cows Save the Planet* a few months prior, Carrillo had contacted me and told me that he and fellow ranchers who practice holistic planned grazing were working with bird conservation organizations to protect endangered migratory grassland bird populations. Several species of grassland birds, including certain song sparrows and the lark bunting, the state bird of Colorado, have seen tremendous drops in numbers—in some cases upward of 80 percent. For a long time conservationists concerned about these birds had concentrated on the summer breeding habitat, in the Western Great Plains. They've since come to realize that the deterioration of winter habitat, where the birds spend seven months of the year, could represent the largest threat to their survival. This habitat centers on the Chihuahuan Desert

Grasslands, specifically the central valley—Valle Centrales—where Carrillo and his colleagues Jesus Almeida, Octavio Bermudez and Elco Blanco Madrid work and ranch.

The good news, says Carrillo, is that they know how to grow grass, and therefore create bird habitat, through holistic planned grazing. At Las Damas Ranch "we used to have just two species, *tobosa* and *zacaton*," he says, referring to native perennial grasses that can survive through droughts and overgrazing. "Now we have multiple grasses, some taller than myself. People didn't think it was possible to have these grasses in the desert." The result of the renewed growth of diverse grasses is that the ranch is "a magnet for birds. You can see migratory, predator, nonpredator birds. In much of the state, in February and March there's no grass at all."

That this small group of ranches constitutes oases of bird habitat attracted the attention of conservation groups working to protect threatened bird populations. These include the Bird Conservancy of the Rockies, the American Bird Conservancy, and the Mexican environmental organization Pronatura. The conservation groups are now collaborating with five ranchers, with the possibility of more, to monitor bird numbers and expand the amount of land with favorable bird habitat. Ideally, they're seeking to create a biological corridor that will offer protection for desert grassland birds so that their populations can rebound.

Andrew Rothman, director of the Migratory Bird Program at the American Bird Conservancy, has visited Las Damas Ranch several times. "It was pretty evident right away that the amount of grasses there was superior to pretty much any land we'd seen in the Chihuahuan Desert," he told me. "That land was different, with plenty of vegetation and forage for cattle. What's good forage for cattle is good habitat for birds."

Rothman's field observations in Chihuahua challenged some of his earlier assumptions about wildlife conservation. "Our perception of conservation is often [to] set the land aside and not do anything," he said. "But many of our habitats are disturbed." In North American grasslands, for instance, there would be occasional, limited lightning-kindled fires or trampling from passing bison herds. "Cattle re-create some of those disturbances," he said. "This can help regenerate the landscape when properly managed."

Rothman said that birds thrive best when there's a diversity of grass heights and varieties, which forms "structures of habitat." Small, self-limiting brushfires, for instance, would generate this kind of chiseled to-pography. By moving livestock strategically one can create such textured landscapes so that you're virtually sculpting the site with cattle.

Rothman shares Carrillo's concern about floundering ranches turning to farmland. "Agriculture does not provide the habitat for birds," he said. This time of year the farmed areas are monochrome brown, endless furrows of tilled soil. No place for, say, a grasshopper sparrow to alight.

At every juncture, it seems, the birds face difficult odds. For example, center-pivot irrigation, the means favored by Mennonite farmers, requires more extensive clearing of land than other systems. One study—a com-bined effort of the Bird Conservancy of the Rockies; the North Dakota De-partment of Health; the University of Sonora, Mexico; and students at North Dakota State—used Landsat 5 imagery, Google Earth history tools and modeling to assess bird populations. The report estimated that due to habi-tat loss, "the winter carrying capacity for 28 species of grassland birds in this region has been reduced by approximately 355,142 individual birds."[4]

The land managed by Carrillo, Almeida, Bermudez and others collab-orating in the effort accounts for about 260,000 acres. With the water cycle restored on this amount of land, and the denser and more diverse grass cover that will result, how many birds can this support? Would this make enough of a difference to stem the decline of migratory grassland birds?

At the ranch we meet Almeida and Madrid, a Holistic Management educator. After a lunch of turkey mole we all head out for a walk. Distances are such that this first involves getting back in the truck. When we arrive at the chosen spot, Carrillo pauses and surveys the vista; at last, he's out of a vehicle and in fresh air on the land he loves. He looks every bit the hand-some cowboy, down to the sheen of his unscuffed black Lucchese boots.

He idly sweeps his hand through a tuft of grass and a spray of tiny seeds, dun-colored flecks, sails upward.

He says at Las Damas they do "tall grazing," which means waiting until the grass is tall and mature enough to produce seeds, before bringing the cattle in. "This ensures there's lots of food for birds," he says. "Did you know that one sparrow will eat 3,000 seeds in a day?

"This patch of grass used to be bare ground. Now it's all perennials," he continues. "What creates healthy grass is the synergy between the plants, moisture and the life in the soil, the earthworms and dung beetles. We have the birds here and also other wildlife: hares, rattlesnakes and quail. Horny toads. Lots of desert turtles. In time the mesquite will die because of the humidity. The grasses choke out the woody plants." People spend millions trying to eradicate mesquite by chemical means, he says. By changing the conditions, increasing ground moisture, the plant composition will naturally shift to grasses.

As the afternoon light begins its slow wane Carrillo takes us up the hillside, the section of the ranch he calls "the sierra," to see the bulls. We scramble up rocky turf to find some grand specimens of bull-kind: vast of shoulder, solid of haunch, languidly uncomprehending of eye. These are gentle, massive, docile creatures—and finely bred, too. One in particular has a soft, creamy white coat and delicate, lightly flaring nostrils. A real beauty.

Madrid wanders off, his head down, as he bends down to peer closely at the plants. He's smaller than Carrillo, bald, with a sweet smile, a quiet observer of nature. Over the next several days he and I will manage to communicate and become friends, pushing the outer limits of vocabulary in each other's respective languages. Nothing like long truck drives through the desert grasslands to inspire ambitious feats of linguistic comprehension. Here on the hill he's saying *"Mira, mira!"* ("Look, look!"), excited about what he's seeing: herbage with small, graceful flowers, perennials like euphorbia, sprangletop, grama grasses showing new green growth at the bottom. Carrillo joins his friend in admiration of the newly growing sideoats grama grass. He says, "I bet the birds brought those seeds."

Las Damas Ranch and the two other ranches I visit in the Chihuahua region are beacons of biodiversity. Conservation efforts, including scientific monitoring, now revolve around migratory birds, reflecting the vulnerability of the species that depend on this landscape for winter habitat. But these ranchers are mindful of all aspects of biodiversity as indicators of their success—as a sign that they are making good use of their water resources.

If Carrillo is able to make effective use of rainfall, the ground will retain moisture and support soil microbial life. Vibrant soil communities will support a diversity of forbs and grasses, which, in turn, will draw wide arrays of insects, including pollinators like bees and butterflies. And birds. Certain plants depend on birds to carry and deposit their seeds, or to break open or scarify the seeds. The richer the plant life, the more small mammals there will be. These animals, in turn, will attract larger predators. Biodiversity at one level of the food chain helps create biodiversity at the next.

After Las Damas we go to Tavo's ranch, El Muchacho (which translates to "the kid"), part of which is higher up and more forested. After lunch (salad, a chicken-tortilla casserole and a tray of desserts, including a pudding of *cajeta,* an unbelievably sweet and silky goat-milk caramel, surrounded by local pecans; at the Mexican ranches, the midday meal is a full-on sit-down affair), we walk up into the hills. We're at a higher altitude here and there are still patches of snow tucked, surreally, among the cacti.

Tavo says, "We have mountain lion and black bear, not grizzly." Tavo's grandfather shot one of the last of the area's grizzlies right on this land, something that at once appalls him and makes him proud. The current group of bears, he tells me, have learned a trick to get rid of pests: the bear breaks the diesel hose that goes from the tank to the engine of the pump, then rolls on the ground where the diesel has spilled. This way the fleas, lice and ticks keep their distance. This smart-bear innovation was captured on an animal-cam Tavo had rigged up. The camera allows him to see what else is wandering the hills. "We also have javelinas, lynx, skunk and bobcat, and there are plans to introduce the Mexican wolf. Since we've done holistic resource management we've had more wildlife. There's food for everyone."

The forest thickens as we ascend. We pass oak trees and see piñon pines up near the top. The rocks we clamber over are covered with moss and we can hear the soft swishing of a running spring.

That a functioning water cycle benefits biodiversity makes sense. Every living thing depends on water. Here in Chihuahua, the migratory birds depend for food and shelter upon the grasses that can only thrive when rainfall is effective. That's easy enough to understand. But what we don't often appreciate is that *biodiversity benefits the water cycle.*

This happens on multiple levels. For example, let's look at the grasses that are so pivotal to the survival of the birds that winter in Chihuahua. These diverse plants don't only feed and house the resident animals, insects and birds—they're also feeding the watershed. The plant life, particularly deep-rooted grasses, support the water cycle: they hold soil in place, build soil carbon and promote the formation of soil aggregates so the soil becomes a sponge—like last chapter's airy loaf of bread as opposed to the powdery flour that can't hold water. In addition, plants are continually transpiring moisture. When the ground is covered with plants, transpiration regulates soil temperature and maintains water in the landscape. In arid and semiarid landscapes such moisture is crucial.

"Everything is connected and works together," says Carrillo. "If we listen and are observant, Nature will teach us how to best manage our land."

Biodiversity—a mosaic of life forms, each thriving in its unique place— contributes to hydrological function in another important way: by *slowing down the movement of water.* We might not think that "slowness" is a desirable quality when it comes to water. Certainly, when we need water, we want it fast. If given the option, few would choose to walk several kilometers to fill a water bucket rather than turning on the tap. (Though the former option is the reality for nearly a billion people worldwide.) But if we glance back at the last chapter and our discussion of water infrastructure, the most effective scenarios—covered soil, dam-building beavers, soil aggregates—involve slowing water's course.

For example, let's consider a meadow with well-aggregated soil and compare that with one of those New Jersey lawns whose texture is not that far from concrete. When it rains, the meadow will usher the water along a leisurely path; water will filter and percolate through the soil, providing moisture for living things and building the water table. The suburban lawn, with its compacted soil and thwarted root systems, lets much of the water wash away.

The ultimate rapid vehicle for water is a man-made conduit like the portion of the Los Angeles River I glimpsed from the train. When Brock Dolman differentiated a watershed from a pipeshed, he was referring to the multiple processes water would undergo in a natural watershed in contrast to the brisk expediency of water flowing through a duct or channel.

Ultimately, all water that comes down as precipitation will run to the ocean. The signs I found at the beach at Little Corona illustrate the consequences of water moving fast versus slow toward the ocean. The restored Lower Buck Gully wetland project built up the soil channel banks and reintroduced indigenous plants to revive native wildlife. Another component was the use of gabions, rock- or sand-filled metal cages that protect against erosion and serve to slow the water flow. Moderating the movement of water through wetland soils, plants and other means is intended to improve water quality. However, the area's storm water is still moving too quickly for the natural and engineered infrastructure to manage the pollutants. Too much "nuisance flow" rushed swiftly and unrestrained into the sea.[5]

The fact is that our simplified ecosystems lose water quickly, a situation that has consequences for both the availability and quality of water. Complex diverse grasslands, with porous, living soil and covered in plants with extensive fungal networks, hold onto water. These are the grass-scapes that Las Damas Ranch has achieved now that the plant community is shifting from brushy plants, like mesquite and creosote bush, toward multiple perennial species. Such intricacy creates above- and below-ground meanders. These, in turn, slow movement and filter out debris and pollutants.

In *Water: A Natural History,* Alice Outwater writes about how different species contribute to hydrological function, each in its own way, so that we have layers of influence and interaction. She notes, for example, how the bison, or buffalo, that dominated much of our continent were part of the water infrastructure:

> The wallows dotted the plains wherever the buffalo roamed, providing drinking holes for animals and patches of moister ground that could support distinct plant communities.
>
> Buffalo wallows were dug in low areas, and they collected runoff as well as rainfall. . . . Every wallow was a pathway for runoff and rainfall to percolate down to the water table. . . . [A]n active buffalo wallow could be described as a perfectly designed groundwater re-charge pond.[6]

Having established how various species, like bison, contributed to the aesthetics and function of the landscape, she conveys what has been lost:

> This country's waterways have been transformed *by omission.* Without beavers, water makes its way too quickly to the sea; without prairie dogs, water runs over the surface instead of sinking into the aquifer; without bison, there are no groundwater-recharge ponds in the grasslands and the riparian zone is trampled; without alligators, the edge between the water and the land is simplified. . . . Without floodplains and meanders, the water moves more swiftly, and silt carried in the water is more likely to be swept to sea.[7]

Biodiversity aboveground reflects biodiversity belowground. The complex ecological systems that yielded the North American menagerie of bison, beaver, prairie dogs and grass-dwelling songbirds didn't evolve in a vacuum. Biodiversity starts in the soil. But it's not merely the presence of diverse microorganisms that supports such zoological splendor—it's also the relationships. The manifold interactions that occur within the soil food web circulate carbon, nutrients and water. This helps create the conditions for higher-order species to thrive.

We've recently been learning about the importance of biodiversity in our own bodies; the more we find out about the role of gut microflora in human health, the more it seems that each of us is not so much a discrete, single entity as a community of organisms (or, as some have put it, walking and talking storage facilities for microbes). The same principles apply to our bodies, the soil, and aboveground ecosystems: the more niches that are filled, the less chance for processes to go awry. Soil rich in varied organisms is more resilient to pathogens. Land with a range of plant species can withstand pests and the prospect of too much or too little rain. (Nature abhors a monoculture, which is why farming that way requires so many machines and chemical inputs.) The broader the array of beneficial microorganisms we harbor in our digestive tract, the greater our immunity to disease. And a complex water infrastructure (i.e., a functioning watershed) is more effective at retaining and clarifying water than a simplified system (like the pipeshed).

Outwater points out that our efforts to support biodiversity tend to center on individual species as opposed to processes or systems—particularly those driven by keystone species like beaver, which have an outsized impact on the environment. In terms of preserving and enhancing water function, however, this may not be the most useful approach:

> By focusing on the preservation of endangered species one after another, as if they were items in a catalogue, we are missing the larger, ecological picture. Without the ancestral complement of keystone

species—nature's engineers—the path that water takes through the land, and the shape of the land itself, have been simplified. . . . Without restoring the ancestral populations of engineers to at least some of the landscape, it seems unlikely that the supporting players will be able to survive.[8]

To some degree our water problems can be understood as a symptom of a too-fast water cycle. We'll look at fast/slow water cycling two ways: first by taking a macro perspective and then applying this to the level of the individual watershed.

The weird weather extremes of the last few years have many experts, including climate scientists and meteorologists, scratching their heads. In a pattern that seems like Murphy's Law—anything that can possibly go wrong, will go wrong—on a global scale, wet regions are getting more rain and dry areas are getting less. Here in Vermont at the end of March, now that we're finally enjoying a respite from the snow, it's already started to rain. The view outside my window is a soggy gray, white and silver: snow on the ground, fog above, and glistening drops of melting ice falling from the roof. Wet, wet and wet. There's a saying around here: "If you don't like the weather, wait five minutes." But these days that feels glib—as if we're dealing with a force stronger than the irony gods.

These trends can at least in part be attributed to a sped-up, or intensified, water cycle, a development that is part of the constellation of phenomena that, collectively, we call climate change. Here's one perspective on what's going on: Heat is being stored in the oceans, which are warming up near the surface, the juncture of the sea and the air. This accelerates evaporation from the ocean. In consequence, there is increased moisture in the atmosphere. Research from 2012 that measured ocean salinity concluded that the ocean-driven evaporation-precipitation cycle—what one can call the *large water cycle*, as opposed to the localized transpiration circuit we'll term the *small water cycle*—accelerated by 4 percent between 1950 and 2000.[9] In other words, moisture is going up and coming down at a faster rate. At the same time, warm air holds more moisture than cool air. With rising temperatures, water vapor may be more concentrated. So we've got more blocks of warmer, moister air moving through the atmosphere, occasionally colliding and leading to more powerful, mischief-making, record-breaking storms.

Water needs to be a larger part of our conversations about climate. Not just in terms of the impact that climate change can have on water—but also the effect that *water* has on *climate*. We hear a lot about carbon dioxide's role as a greenhouse gas. However, water vapor can be seen as the most significant greenhouse gas in that it has a greater capacity to absorb thermal heat than any other known substance. In the words of Walter Jehne, an Australian soil microbiologist, "For the last four billion years the climate of the blue planet has been controlled by hydrological processes. Over 90 percent of the global heat dynamics and balance is governed by a range of water-based processes." Water is active, in continual flux. It expands in volume or retrenches, retains or releases energy. As vapor, it conveys heat, alternately holding and releasing thermal energy as it circulates.

One theory relevant to a hastened water cycle is "Arctic amplification." The gist is that the jet stream that flows across the northern hemisphere, delivering continually evolving weather conditions, now has a tendency to get stuck. Which makes obsolete that old Vermont adage of "wait five minutes"; it may feel more like *wait five months* before the weather breaks. Jennifer Francis of Rutgers University, who studies the connection between Arctic and global climate conditions, explains that this in part relates to reduced ice and snow in the Arctic, which has altered surfaces so that they absorb rather than reflect sunlight. The result is more heat, more melting and less difference in temperature between the far north and more temperate regions. It's this temperature differential that helps drive the west-to-east jet stream in an undulating pattern. This eastward drift seems to be slowing down, so that weather systems hang on longer. A second factor is that the jet stream is curvier (the word *drunk* has been invoked) with more extreme, amplified waves. This has the effect of dragging waves of frigid Arctic air farther south, while warmer, moister air travels northward, thereby creating opportunities for improbable weather at all latitudes.[10]

The dynamics of altered polar regions and the feedbacks involved are extremely complex; what we know is dwarfed by what we don't yet understand. There is no way around the fact that we humans and fellow living creatures, all tethered to this planet, are riding into the unknown. In a powerful article in *Harper's* entitled "Rotten Ice," author Gretel Ehrlich writes about the group hunting trips in Greenland she's taken part in over the years, and how the ice has been in retreat, with glaciers calving, or shedding blocks of ice.

She observes these changes with great distress since "the Arctic is the earth's natural air conditioner." Sea ice, she writes, "is a Greenlander's highway and the platform on which marine mammals—including walrus, ring seals, bearded seals, and polar bears—Arctic foxes, and seabirds travel, rest, breed, and hunt." With dark irony she adds that in light of the rapid melting of the Arctic ice sheet, "to move 'glacially' no longer implies slowness."[11]

This is the backdrop of what we're confronting even as U.S. leaders continue, illogically, to quarrel over whether climate change is real. For all of us who came of age when technology was ascendant, it's difficult to grapple with such powerful forces beyond our control. We can understand climate denial as a kind of primitive railing against the inconvenience and indignity of elemental change, like a primal scream or tantrum. As impressive as our machines might be, we can't hi-tech our way out of climate disruption.

It's essential to embrace our humility, our place in the cosmos, and to accept what we cannot control. But it's also important to acknowledge what we *do* have leverage over. Allying with natural processes can help restore hydrological function. This, in turn, helps to restore land function and carbon, mineral and solar energy cycling. The impacts will mostly be felt locally, but at some level the feedback loops will kick in. We know so little about how these feedback loops operate. But we can nudge these processes toward restoration. And one way is supporting biodiversity, from large animals like the beautiful blond-coated bull I'd admired down to the tiniest microbes.

Which is why, when assessing environmental restoration strategies, Jim Laurie considers the watershed as a whole and poses the question: "What's out there trying to slow the water down?"

You may remember Laurie as my snowshoeing companion, trudging through the Greenberg Reserve on a midwinter Sunday afternoon in search of beaver signs. Laurie is a genial fellow with white hair and, usually, a baseball cap. The first time I interviewed him he said something that tickled me: "If there's a species out there that no one is speaking up for, I'll do it." In part this reflects his belief that biodiversity underlies the function of all ecosystems, from landscapes to seascapes; one of his projects is to revive the New England coastal ecosystem by bringing back the menhaden, a forage fish pivotal to the ocean food chain and that, when young, cleans and filters water. But it also reflects his kind spirit; he harbors a particular warmth for the underdog, a conviction that every creature, no matter how unassuming or unnoticed, is making an important contribution to our great circle of life. He has deep trust in the benevolence and wisdom of nature.

But he's not naive. In that same initial conversation, he made another comment that stuck with me: "The species that are going to remake the future are already working on it."

Laurie always carries around a white canvas bag with whatever books are most exciting to him at that moment. He's prone to pulling out a book midconversation to illustrate or expand upon a point. For twenty years he worked for Bayer Corporation in Houston as a laboratory trainer and environmental biologist. There he experimented with using biological processes to treat industrial wastewater. He later worked closely with ecologist John Todd on Eco-Machines: water-reclamation systems designed so that plants, snails and microorganisms (algae, bacteria, fungi) do the work. Laurie told me that in 1988 he read four books that shook his thinking and led him to leave his job in the petrochemical industry for good to become a full-time freelance ecologist:

Playing God in Yellowstone, in which the author, Alston Chase, contends that park policies have destroyed Yellowstone's ecology, targeting in particular the killing of bears, wolves and other predators, which resulted in an exploding elk population. "The author talked about how the elk were eating the park," Laurie said. "Chase kept referring to the loss of the 'keystone species' and I kept thinking wolves, but it was beaver. If the wolves didn't come back to the park the beavers wouldn't come back because the elk were ruining the beavers' habitat."

This was the year of the Yellowstone fires that burned 1.2 million acres over several months and prompted the first-ever closure of the park. "I was in Colorado, watching the smoke coming down," Laurie said.

Book number two was *The Turning Point* by Fritjof Capra, an exploration of systems-thinking in physics and ecology as well as a critique of the limits of contemporary scientific understanding. This inspired Laurie to ask, "How can you look at a system in the way you look at data? I'd thought that if I had numbers, I could convince people of what works. I realized that if I wanted to restore land that wasn't a good way to think about it."

Next he read *Microcosmos* by Lynn Margulis and Dorian Sagan, which opened his eyes to the idea that "evolution is more about bacteria than plants and animals." The book also emphasizes symbiosis and interconnectedness, as opposed to competition, as drivers of biology. This perspective validated what Laurie had been observing in his work. "With John Todd's Eco-Machines, we used twenty clear tanks to clean up a pond and the water got cleaner and cleaner," he says. "Self-organized beings were doing this work. I learned that we can clean water and restore systems without knowing everything. In fact, that's the only way we can do it. Nature starts self-organizing where it is. What if we can start being restorers rather than consumers? I learned that it's not just that John Todd can clean water. We can all clean water. It all comes from observation. From John Todd I learned to talk not about 'wastewater' but about 'nutrients.' Also, that we have to learn from the small microorganisms. I believe this much more now than I did then."

Laurie encountered the final entry in his transformation book list in a bookstore in Texas. "I picked out a book with a picture of a guy with a funny hat, and thought: this guy is talking about cows!" This was Allan Savory's first book, *Holistic Resource Management*. Laurie recalls: "There was an endorsement from Alston Chase. That's why I picked the book off the shelf. I got what Savory was saying: How do you keep soil microbial communities alive during the dry season? The process is primarily digestion, via animals, during the dry months."

Laurie says that biodiversity is what sustained water sources in areas that are now suffering from desertification and drought. He's spent a lot of time in West Texas, which used to be grassland plains. In the past, "every time there was a stream, there were beavers slowing it down. There were trees, thirsty trees like cottonwoods, near water, as the beavers were slowing it down. Up the hill you had prairie dogs. They would be digging holes on the higher ground, because they wanted to be able to see predators from a distance." He notes that prairie dogs are important to the water cycle since the holes and tunnels they dig allow for rainwater to move into and through the soil. This replenishes the water table and minimizes erosion and runoff.

Like beavers, prairie dogs are gregarious, furry rodents that live in groups—called towns, colonies or coteries—or in family-based clans. Also like beavers, their numbers have declined, with their population an estimated 5 percent of what it had historically been. The largest known prairie dog town, in Texas, once spanned 25,000 square miles. They have a complex warning system centered on sharp, barking sounds, hence the name prairie dog.[12]

One benefit of prairie dogs is that they control the spread of mesquite trees, tap-rooted plants that are considered water hogs and therefore pests. "In areas where there are prairie dogs, we don't have mesquite," Laurie says. "In Texas people spend millions to try to get rid of mesquite. But prairie dogs chew at the roots like crazy." Prairie dogs obtain most of their water from the plants they eat; they also, says Laurie, have their own reasons to keep mesquite from taking over: "They want to get rid of it so they can see the coyote and hawks" out searching for prey.

The transborder Janos Biosphere Reserve in the Chihuahuan Desert—not too far, as the falcon flies, from Las Damas Ranch—was established in 2009 to protect short-grass prairie and numerous threatened mammal species, including black-tailed prairie dogs. Black-footed ferrets, which feed on prairie dogs and were once deemed "possibly extinct," have been reintroduced in Janos.[13] Prairie dogs are critical for many predator species, Laurie says, and to the water cycle in short-grass prairies: "They are an active force in the ground if they're in enough numbers. It's thought the largest town had 400 million prairie dogs—and its size was half the size of New England. Say you had twenty-five prairie dogs per acre, there would be holes every twenty-five feet or so, sometimes several feet deep. This is how those land systems could breathe, how the land held moisture. If you're a drop of water and you want to make a flood, how are you going to do that?"

In the Southwest, people are starting to talk in terms of the water cycle, Laurie says. "In New Mexico there are people who put rocks down to slow the water. It wouldn't be a huge shift for people to see that animals are part of the picture. This should be the goal of every landowner out there: to slow the water down and let it go into the ground. I'd want beaver and prairie dogs. I'd also hire me some predators—owls and hawks and ferrets. And dung beetles, which make tiny holes and churn up the ground. This reverses the caliche process: it's nutrients *going into* the soil." Caliche is hardpan that forms in arid environments as minerals, primarily calcium carbonate, accumulate on the soil surface. It's the bane of desert gardeners since it blocks drainage and stymies root growth.

Brock Dolman of the WATER Institute says beaver are crucial to keeping water in the landscape because they "slow it, spread it, sink it." This is in contrast to the fate of storm water in urban areas, as the story there has been "pave it, pipe it, pollute it." Dolman is a lover of wordplay and puns. He asks, "Do we live in the *drain-age or a retain-age?* We need to *mitigate cerebral imperviousness in the actual headwaters of our own ego-system.* We need to start a *reciprocal reverential rehydration revolution!*" He speaks rapidly, in an animated patter that's a few long beats to the science-nerd side of rap.

Dolman also discusses sped-up water cycling. In a healthy ecosystem, "a raindrop that formed in a cloud in January might not get back to the ocean for ten years, a hundred years, or as part of an old-growth redwood forest, a thousand years. Today, evaporated salty ocean water pops up pure and distilled only to rain down on a parking lot in Los Angeles and rapidly run off into the L.A. River and out to the beach as a flood of polluted urban drool. It's like a nightmare, water-wise. The ocean-to-ocean journey is short-circuited. When water is held in the environment, in vegetation or soil aggregates, it stays around. It could also become part of an abundant life-filled beaver wetland. However, in our denuded, deforested, de-beavered landscape, that one drop of water returns to the ocean after ten minutes."

Increasing beaver habitat "will yield us more water, cleaner water, carbon storage." As looming climate change leaves weather patterns less predictable, this will enhance resilience, Dolman says. Beavers in the ecosystem are "like shock absorbers. Here in the West we're in a drying trend, and yet we get water more intensely, in shorter events with bigger volumes. The water we get is more rain and less dominated by snow in the higher elevations. As we lose the solid state of snow, we also lose the storage capacity of that volume: water that is slowly melted and metered out and gradually makes its way to the ocean or into reservoirs for agriculture or urban dwellers. The question is, How do we create conditions that are conducive to life? What can we do to move water into living soil that grows more plants and puts groundwater in the well to drink?"

Glynnis Hood, associate professor of environmental science at the University of Alberta and author of *The Beaver Manifesto,* has found that ponds with active beavers have a greater diversity of waterfowl and other species,

including endangered amphibians, and nine times the expanse of open water. Her field research coincided with an extreme drought in 2002, and the
only places with water were where beavers were present. Beaver ponds also
rebound more quickly from droughts thanks to the animals' engineering.
"All of these little crevices and channels—these really dynamic [pond]
bottoms, really complex—often slows the water. . . . The pond has to fill up
first before the water can continue across the landscapes."[14]

As with many things beaver, the events build on top of each other, like
twigs on logs on mud in a good-sized beaver dam: all that rodent digging
makes for deep water; deep water means less evaporation; less evaporation
slows the water cycle. Deeper ponds are prime habitat for fish, including
juvenile salmon, before they head out to sea. Dolman acknowledges that
salmon is a "totem species" in terms of its primacy to ecology and culture
in the Pacific Northwest. "If we can live in a system where there's beaver,
that will allow for salmon," he says. "If we can support a healthy salmon
population, that's a benchmark to show success. Salmon keeps us honest."

To make the point that we ignore the well-being of fellow species at our
peril, in 2009 Dolman addressed the Sonoma County Board of Supervisors
dressed as Sorax, "the Ghost of Coho Salmon Past." In his testimony he
invoked a time when California had tremendous coho salmon runs. "We
as salmon," he said, " . . . used to live in peace with the humans of this
land, and we co-evolved with the harbor seals and sea lions and our natal
forested creeks. The abundance of our families was so great that your early
pioneering families remarked, 'we were so numerous' they could 'walk on
our backs.'"[15]

Such profusion of salmon in our most populous state is hard for us to
imagine. We forget what we had, and the diminished reality of the environment we inhabit comes to seem normal and inevitable, how it's always
been. Alice Outwater highlights this disconnect between what is and what
was when she writes, "The beaver, the prairie dog, the bison, and the al-
ligator have been scarce for so long that we have forgotten how plentiful
they once were."[16]

This is a powerful point because in many natural settings, efforts to restore biodiversity are as much about imagination as anything else. We need imagination in order to have hope, and we need hope in order to act.

Every landscape holds secrets from the past—and these offer clues about what's possible. This was brought home to me in Chihuahua. At one point I was looking around Carrillo's ranch office, and on one of the bookshelves I noticed two snails: one a fossil, an impression embedded in stone; the other bleached white and coiled, like a shell you'd find on a beach. "Isn't that interesting?" he said. "Those were picked up on the ranch and that shell looks like it's no more than thirty or forty years old. Imagine that, on this land. This tells me that there was much more moisture here in the not-too-distant past."

Also at Las Damas, on the walk to view the bulls, Madrid drew our attention to a large expanse of rock with whitish marks. A deep fracture ran through the middle of the rock, as if marking the division of a primeval page. The surface was a veritable map of previous eras, with fossils etched so densely it looked like a message in an ancient language. And in a sense it was, with vestiges of life forms this place had once seen. We saw impressions that looked like trilobites, simple insect-like ocean creatures that predate dinosaurs, and the shells of ammonites, other early sea-dwellers that lived in shells. Madrid said something rapidly in Spanish and Carrillo translated: "He says maybe in some previous time the sea extended here. Or maybe it was an inland lake."

We tend to think of land as static. So that a desert has always been a desert, a rocky plain where nothing thrives, always rocky, always a frustration to farmers. Of course, history tells us this is not so. Numerous civilizations—think Mesopotamia, Phoenicia, Timbuktu—once flourished in regions where, to modern memory, there is nothing but forbidding, sandswept emptiness. But we're not always conscious of the extent to which land is dynamic, not merely as a historical anecdote or cautionary tale, but in the *now*. And that land is in an ongoing exchange with the people that live on and from it.

Land changes on a variety of time scales, and does so simultaneously. There's geological time, the eons and eras with names like Jurassic, Triassic and Devonian, that, working backward, harken all the way to the origin of life on earth and the big bang. When the fossils of primitive organisms that we found suggested that this desert grassland was, in an earlier incarnation, the site of a body of water, we were trading in the realm of geologic time.

There are also changes over historic time, as when my home state of Vermont lost its great old trees in order to capitalize on the—short-lived, as it turned out—rush for New England wool. (Our property was once a sheep farm, and we still see portions of old stone wall.) Or, say, the Fertile Crescent, where agriculture first began, being reduced to desert. As of ten years ago the marshlands around the Tigris and Euphrates Rivers, the heart of the area's plant and wildlife diversity, were determined to be 90 percent disappeared.[17]

Then we have changes that proceed along the human life span, in decades or years. That includes the deterioration of the properties that Carrillo pointed out to me, along with the recovery of Las Damas Ranch, which now supports perennial plants and has little uncovered soil; these are of this in-the-now category. This is the type of land transformation that interests me the most. For not only can we watch change occurring: we can actually influence the direction it takes.

When we do acknowledge that change takes place under our collective watch, we usually mean change for the worse—like the Dust Bowl, or the cutting down of forests in the Amazon. The thing is, we're jaded. We're continually bracing ourselves, having been trained by harsh experience to expect any news about the environment to be negative. The idea we get is that the best we can hope for regarding the fortunes of our air, land and water is that things stop getting worse.

Aren't we setting our sights rather low? Land, as we've seen, is always changing: moving toward greater or lesser complexity, enhanced resilience or deterioration, functioning or impeded water flow. It all depends on what we do with it. Once we can appreciate what nature is trying to do—for nature's predilection is toward increased function and complexity, though it may not appear that way to us—we can support that course. Indeed, we could say that every acre of land on the planet offers a choice, whether toward enhancement and health and complexity or toward degradation. It's up to us. And we can start by expanding our vision of what's possible.

Back in the Chihuahuan Desert Grasslands, the ranchers were blessed with two seasons of decent rains. When I asked Carrillo how the birds were faring, he said he thought they were doing well but urged me to speak to the ornithology professionals for a more precise assessment.

Arvind Panjabi, international program director at the Bird Conservancy of the Rockies, is very concerned about bird population trends. "Many young that make it to the wintering ground are not surviving," he says. He's hoping more research will pinpoint the reasons why. Some of the birds, such as short-grass prairie birds like sparrows, aren't losing habitat per se; the problem might be the widespread use of pesticides on farms.

The holistically managed ranches, he says, are one bright spot. "We're trying to implement practices that we believe will promote bird survival," he says. It's important, he adds, to "engage the landowners so that they're part of the solution. And to keep the ranches viable. Agricultural fields in the area have resulted in a tremendous loss of biodiversity. They're deserts—except for the doves you see occasionally, in a hayfield."

Andrew Rothman at the American Bird Conservancy hadn't been to the area recently so he referred me to his colleague David Pashley, vice president of U.S. Conservation Partnerships. Pashley visited Rancho Coyamito, a ranch I hadn't seen, run by Ruben Borunda, and said it was "quite inspiring." Borunda has only practiced restorative grazing for two years. He agreed to join the project and receive training in holistic planned grazing from the local Pronatura office because, he told Pashley, the land had long been in his family and he held noble views of the cattle-raising ethic and good stewardship. The way things were going, Pashley said, "Ruben was running out of grass, running out of water, and running out of money." And at all costs he wanted to avoid selling the ranch for agricultural land.

Pashley was previously unfamiliar with Holistic Management, so he learned about the process as well. Pronatura helped Borunda divide the land into forty different pastures (before it had been four) and ensured an accessible water source for each. The entire herd would stay in one pasture for three days and not return to that pasture for six months. They reduced the brush but left some, "because birds like to have some shrubs to dive into for protection." Locations deemed best for overwintering birds were not grazed over the winter.

"The grass has responded tremendously," Pashley said. "The combination of grazing and rain have been incredibly positive. It was very 'birdy.' I saw a lot of vesper sparrows, brewer sparrows and clay-colored sparrow, and loggerhead shrikes and savanna sparrows. This is important winter habitat for all of these birds. Baird's sparrows and Sprague's pipits are our targets. I didn't see them the afternoon I was there."

One reason Borunda's land is significant is that a breeding pair of the native, desert-dwelling aplomado falcons is known to live on the property. In the Chihuahuan Desert, there are only four known remaining pairs of aplomado, a slim, swift-flying raptor with steel-gray back feathers, white breast and reddish lower belly. They depend on open grassland habitat that's flat and has deep soil. They live and hunt as breeding pairs. The bird has been on the endangered species list since the 1980s.

"What's good for the birds is good for the people, too," says Panjabi. "People can make a difference. As an example, [Carrillo] has changed practices without the help of conservationists. We'd need to increase the scale and pace of restoration about twenty times in order to meet the scale of what we're losing. But this puts the example out there—that taking care of the land means taking care of yourself."

Creating good bird habitat and a good situation for ranchers. Enhancing the water cycle and supporting biodiversity, which in turn enhances the water cycle.

Everyone wins.

FOUR

MISSING THE WATER FOR THE TREES

How Plants Make Water

Rain rain go away, let's chop a forest down today?

—Joanne Nova of Western Australia, 2013

By this time the 1910 oaks were ten years old and taller than both him and me. . . . Going back down through the village I saw there was water flowing in streams that had been dry as long as anyone can remember. As chain reactions go, this was the most remarkable one I'd ever seen.

—"The Man Who Planted Trees,"
a fable by Jean Giono, 1953

ONE OF THE WORLD'S MOST BELOVED AND ROMAN-
tic cities has a restoration narrative at its core. Rio de Janeiro's story came
to me courtesy of Tom Goreau, a scientist with numerous overlapping spe-
cialties (his discipline is biogeochemistry) who has spent much time doing
research in the Amazon. This is what he shared:

When European explorers encountered the Guanabara Bay in the early 1500s, the surrounding mountains were covered with forests. Over the centuries the trees were steadily cut down for building and firewood, and then for sugar and ultimately coffee plantations, or *fazendas*. The city's iconic backdrop, those looming, high, bare mountains, is the result of this loss of cover. With the trees stripped and gone, soil from the slopes washed away, leaving hard, naked bedrock. Meanwhile, the city's population increased rapidly and many grew wealthy on the coffee trade. (Incidentally, coffee isn't native to Brazil but was introduced in the early 1700s from nearby French Guiana, where it was being cultivated.) It was only a matter of time before the land's fertility crashed.[1]

By the 1800s, rainfall decreased and the rivers dried up. Once-abundant springs were hardly a trickle beyond the rainy season. The city, now the colonial capital, ran out of water and people were desperate. Many fled to the countryside. People saw that their water troubles were linked to deforestation, because when there were forests there had been water. The king, Dom Pedro II, decided something needed to be done, and charged a military officer, Major Manuel Gomes Archer, with reforesting the entire area. Archer selected a variety of tree species, mostly native to the Atlantic Forest but a few exotics as well, and employed a group of six slaves to plant them. The slaves—whose names are lost to history—devoted several decades to this task, climbing and carrying saplings up steep, sometimes near-vertical inclines, and planting more than 75,000 trees. In time the forest did come back, along with the springs and rivers, and the water supply was stabilized. The Tijuca Forest, declared a national park in the 1960s, is considered the world's largest urban forest.

(Actually, my husband's hometown, Johannesburg, also lays claim to this title. Beginning in the late 1800s the planting of some 10 million trees in the city was apparently driven by the need to prop up mine tunnels. And real estate appeal: the pleasant neighborhoods north of downtown—nicely gardened and swimming-pooled, redolent of bird song—are not called the "leafy suburbs" for nothing.)

Antonio Donato Nobre is senior scientist at Brazil's National Institute for Amazonian Research in Manaus, smack in the center of the Amazon basin, where he has spent twenty years of his career. For the last twelve years he has also been a visiting scientist at Brazil's National Institute for Space Research in São José dos Campos, a small city outside São Paulo along the highway to Rio. He's from a family of scientists—two brothers, Carlos and Paulo, are both highly respected climatologists—and the account of the revived Tijuca Forest is part of his cultural, intellectual and even spiritual DNA. "I've used this story many times," he tells me over Skype. "It's a useful symbol of the incredible capacity of nature. Before the replanting there were problems with water quantity as well as quality, because of erosion from the farms. King Dom Pedro II was very connected to science. He used to travel all over the world to see science fairs. He had a friendship with Goethe. He brought over botanists from France."

Nobre says he's amused that the restituted Floresta da Tijuca is sometimes described as "pristine" Atlantic Forest, and that many local people assume the trees have always been there. "As you walk there, you still find old coffee plants that have been abandoned, as well as old fruit trees. That's proof that this area was recovered. Today Rio cannot rely on this water for its supply. But the creeks that come from these mountains are pure."

The water saga that occupies Antonio Nobre's mind today is less lofty and affirming: that is, the water crisis in São Paulo, the most populous city in the Americas. In early 2015, after consecutive years of heat and low rainfall, the Cantareira network of reservoirs that provides water to nearly half of the megacity's 20 million residents languished at a mere 5 percent of capacity.[2] Rumors of strict mandatory rationing spread as experts gave estimates of how many weeks the water supply was expected to hold out . . . fewer than ten. Some apartment-dwellers saw their water shut off without warning—for three, four, five days—while others were assigned hours for when they could run the tap. Locals have responded in varied ways: hoarding water; setting up water delivery services by bicycle; digging private wells (which may or may not meet code requirements); or leaving the area altogether, a historical echo of Rio's nineteenth-century water refugees prior to the Tijuca Forest's restoration.[3] Commentators have noted the irony that Brazil, which has been called "the Saudi Arabia of water," is confronting such a dire shortfall.

"São Paulo is following on California's footsteps," says Nobre. "We've had four years of drying up and then in 2014 a massive drought. People are anxious because it's different from some places like the southwest U.S. that have been dealing with aridity for a long time. This area has been green forever. There's always been abundant rainfall. But for most of 2014 people were looking to the horizon and seeing the same atmosphere as you'd see in the Sahara: the same layer of dust and blue sky and heat. There's no moisture and people are scared, shaking in their boots. At the same time the government has done almost nothing, as if the next wet season would save us."

For Antonio Nobre, like most Brazilians, the crisis has been a shock. He's spent his life in lush, green, water-rich settings: a childhood in the Atlantic Forest near São Paulo, not far from where he now lives; graduate studies at the wooded University of New Hampshire; decades of research in the Amazon jungle. These days, however, he's been inundated with the drought. His wife, Adriana Cuartas, is a hydrologist who works for a national center on disaster preparedness and response. Her current task is monitoring the status of the reservoirs. Each evening she would return home, sigh, and offer a somber update on the dwindling basins. For months it was dry news every day. Should Nobre choose to seek refuge in the shower—a favorite place to think, about water shortages among other matters—he'd face the indignity of his nine-year-old daughter, Isabella, scolding him and saying, "Dad, you're not saving water!" (Nothing like parental guilt: he's learned to put water-capturing receptacles in the shower.)

Not that a problem with water was a surprise to him. Indeed, Nobre has had the uncanny experience of seeing his own scientific predictions materialize right before his eyes. Late in 2014, just as the drought's severity was registering among politicians and the public, he published a scientific report entitled "The Future Climate of Amazonia,"[4] a work that reviewed more than 200 scientific articles including material from a multiyear international research effort called the Large-Scale Biosphere-Atmosphere Experiment in Amazonia (LBA).[5] From 1998 to 2008 this project, led by Brazil's scientific community, amassed an extraordinary amount of data on the processes and exchanges that characterize the rainforest ecosystem. Among the LBA's objectives was assessing "the interaction of humans with the landscape."

Nobre's paper emphasizes the role that the world's largest extant rainforest plays in helping to create and sustain a benign, "friendly" climate across the entire continent. In clear, accessible language it also conveys the grim warning that chain sawing, bulldozing, burning and otherwise trashing the rainforest stands to wreak havoc on the temperature and rainfall patterns that all—people, nations and natural systems alike—depend upon.

"I did not have a plan to publish this report during the drought," he says. "I was describing how powerful the Amazon rainforest is when it's intact, and its importance to climate throughout the region. Then as I was writing the report the drought imploded." The Amazonia report makes the case that the water that nourishes South America's landscapes turns on the fate of trees.

Unlike the story of the Tijuca Forest's restoration, says Nobre, in this instance it's the loss of trees that's having an impact.

The notion that there's a connection between forests and water sufficiency is not new. Plato and Aristotle wrote about how deforestation leads to the loss of water resources. The eighteenth- and nineteenth-century adventurer and naturalist Baron Alexander von Humboldt wrote: "By felling the trees which cover the tops and sides of mountains, men in all climates seem to bring upon future generations two calamities at once; want of fuel and a scarcity of water."[6] In his 1864 book *Man and Nature* (original title: *Man the Disturber of Nature's Harmonies*), George Perkins Marsh catalogs numerous examples of deforestation and its denouement from his diplomatic and literary travels. He wrote: "When the forest is gone, the great reservoir of moisture stored up in its vegetable mould [soil or humus] is evaporated, and returns only in deluges of rain to wash away the parched dust into which that mould has been converted. The well-wooded and humid hills are turned to ridges of dry rock."[7]

Popular histories like Jared Diamond's *Collapse* and David Montgomery's *Dirt: The Erosion of Civilizations* are full of cautionary tales of societies—the Mayans, Pacific Islanders, cases in the French Alps—that squandered their tree cover, resulting in catastrophic flooding and drought.

In order to find an example of how forest loss messes with water I don't even have to leave home. A recent copy of *Ripples,* the newsletter of the Vermont Agency of Natural Resources, informs us that European settlers dispensed with more than half the state's forest cover by the close of the nineteenth century. This was the result: "Cleared land froze more deeply in winter and thawed more quickly in warm months. While spring brought floods, the hot summer months left streams and rivers dry. Vermont historian Samuel Williams noted in 1794 that cleared land 'became warm and dry, while streams and brooks no longer supplied water.' Soil erosion contributed to the situation of streams, ponds and lakes, and gave rise to changes in fish and animal populations."[8]

As I read this it occurred to me that Vermont's "mud season," the postsnow March–April stretch that is every bit as dreary and messy as it sounds, is no foreordained inevitability. Rather, it stems from our predecessors' zealousness about dispatching old-growth native trees so that they could make room for sheep.

That forests are important to the water cycle makes logical sense. Trees stabilize the soil, which guards against erosion. The presence of trees therefore enhances soil's ability to hold rainfall rather than letting the water stream away, carrying off precious organic matter. A tree's canopy intercepts rain so that the water descends gently to the ground, not with the kind of pounding bombardment that leaves craters in bare soil or overwhelms the land's ability to absorb it.

At the Urban Soil Summit in Los Angeles, Andy Lipkis of TreePeople pointed to the quiet, unheralded absorption that trees perform when it rains: the root system of a mature tree can retain tens of thousands of gallons of rainwater—water that in urban areas would otherwise course away onto asphalt and into gutters and eventually merge with the waste stream.[9]

Lipkis shares this information in presentations, he says, "to create the model of how urban trees could and should perform if we properly design urban spaces to function as, and biomimic, forest watersheds. It is intended to create a context for how to think about designing or retrofitting for resilience. Urban trees perform some of these functions, but they barely reach their potential because for the most part, their connection to the watershed is nearly completely severed by urbanization . . . streets, sidewalks, gutters, which convey water off properties and into the storm drain system. Soil is compacted or covered with impermeable surfaces. If the soil around a tree is properly managed, then yes, the capacity of the tree to provide those water supply, quality, carbon storage, habitat and flood protection [attributes] would be greatly enhanced and, depending on tree size and other conditions, could grow to tens of thousands of gallons."

In addition, the shade of a tree canopy cools the ground so that moisture is less prone to evaporate, thus keeping water in the system. Trees recycle oxygen and water vapor, which improves the quality of the air and lends it a soft humidity. We all know how nice it is to be near trees. In Japan there's a healing practice called *Shinrin Yoku*, translated as "forest bathing," which research has found lowers stress and boosts immunity.[10]

Bill Mollison, the biologist and teacher considered the "father of permaculture," has a series of videos in which he speaks extemporaneously about trees and how they function in a landscape. He says that a tree is 93 to 98 percent water. "A tree stands there as a barrel of water," he says, and likens a forest to a kind of lake. To fully "wet" a tree, a rain shower may have to cover forty acres worth of leaf, he says. Most precipitation is intercepted by trees, which redirect the flow of rain. This "redistributes the water very differently from if it fell on a field." The tree steers the water so as to "fit its own needs. Each tree does something very different."[11]

The water that filters through the canopy, the throughfall, is distinct from ordinary rain, says Mollison: "It's the tree's bathwater. It's a much richer substance than rain." This arboreal elixir has a different ionic makeup, contains trace elements, and is less acidic than precipitated water, he says, noting, "The most nutritious pasture is near trees."

Trees in the landscape also slow the water cycle. Alice Outwater writes: "A single water molecule making its way through a stream-and-forest ecosystem is on a biological Ferris wheel. A raindrop may hit a leaf, trickle down to the bark of a branch, evaporate to come down again as rain. . . . Snowflakes that fall to the forest floor pile up in a blanket tucked around the trees, shaded from the sun."[12]

Trees contribute to environmental and human well-being in all sorts of ways: storing carbon, bestowing shade, sheltering species from birds to leopards to lemurs, luring leaf-peeping tourists to Vermont in October. Lipkis cites research from the city of Melbourne, Australia, that found tree canopy cover of 40 percent cooled an area by nine degrees. Not only does this make life more pleasant—it can apparently get kind of sticky in Melbourne—but it saves lives. "As extreme heat events have been occurring in Australia, temperatures in some of their major cities have risen to 115 degrees Fahrenheit, and above, causing people to die after three days of constant high heat without relief," he wrote to me. "Public health researchers determined that lowering peak temperatures by 4 degrees centigrade, roughly 7 degrees Fahrenheit, would be enough to save people, and have stated that people should live in neighborhoods with both dense tree canopy cover AND available soil moisture, to enable evaporative cooling. To adapt to various threats posed by climate change, City of Melbourne officials have set and begun implementing a target of 40 percent tree canopy cover over the city to achieve the seven-degree peak heat reduction."[13]

The ecological benefits trees impart are in bureaucratic terms known collectively as "ecosystem services." Such attributes make rain more effective, stabilize and enrich soil, and shield the ground from excess evaporation loss. These are functions we all know or intuit. In his report, however, Nobre says trees' importance to hydrological processes transcends water's earthward flows—he makes the case that forests are crucial to the *production of rain*. And that without sufficient forest cover, the rains of an entire region could fail.

"The Future Climate of Amazonia" is a formidable document. Reading it evokes at once awe for the massive force embodied in the billions of trees that compose the Amazon, and a chill upon acknowledging its vulnerability. Nobre describes how the Amazon rainforest hydrates a good chunk of our hemisphere and acts as an "environmental regulation machine." He refers to stretches of dense, extensive forest as a "green ocean" whose moisture, enormity, and ongoing exchange with air and wind mirrors that of its blue marine twin. He notes the clouds that hover over the Amazon rainforest resemble those that sail above the sea; like the atmosphere over the vast expanse of ocean, the air above Amazonia is clean and free of dust because it's continually cleansed and scrubbed by rain. The very term *green ocean* suggests the waves of humidity that move over and across the rainforest, a sea of vapor that supports stunning plant and animal diversity.

To really grapple with the forest-rain dynamics Nobre is getting at, we need to explore the concept of transpiration.

Most basically, transpiration is the upward movement of moisture through living plants. A plant emits water vapor to the atmosphere through its stomata, small openings on the underside of the leaves (in grasses, on the blades). You can think of this as the plant "breathing," or, more precisely, "sweating." As stomata are valves that open and close, this enables the plant to release or retain moisture, and to regulate its own temperature and that of the ground. Transpiration is a cooling mechanism; it is a means of dissipating solar heat. Without the presence of plants, sunlight would beam down directly on the landscape.

Jan Pokorný, a Czech botanist, has put together a short pamphlet entitled *What Can a Tree Do?* The piece enumerates the ecosystem services a tree provides, but is couched in the language of advertising. (As in: "The device should work in complete silence and produce no exhausts or waste. All the elements of the device are bio-degradable.")

Pokorný's tree "sales pitch" explains the extent to which transpiration consumes and transforms energy from the sun, which makes trees the world's most perfect air conditioners. Take an ordinary tree in full leaf whose crown spans five meters, or about sixteen and a half feet, in diameter. On a sunny day, our nice-sized tree would have at least 150 kilowatt-hours of solar energy shining on it. Given sufficient water, over the course of the day the tree would transpire upward of one hundred liters (more than twenty-six gallons) of water. (Pokorný says this represents three times the cooling power of an air-conditioning system in a five-star hotel room.)

The energy consumed by transpiration is now embodied in the vaporized water in the form of "latent heat"—heat potential. This is opposed to "sensible heat," or heat you can feel. (For sensible heat, think walking barefoot on asphalt midday in August.) Even in the heat of summer, a forest is pleasantly cool. In part this is due to shade, but also because the trees are transpiring—moving solar heat into a state of suspension. The heat held in abeyance will be released upon condensation, at which point the vapor turns to liquid.

The cycling of moisture via trees is as constant as it is invisible, a parallel universe of vapor, an ethereal realm. In *The Tree: A Natural History of What Trees Are, How They Live, and Why They Matter*, British biologist and author Colin Tudge brings this liquid vision to light: "It would be wonderful with X-ray eyes to see a forest without the timber. It would be a colony of ghosts, each tree a spectral sheath of rising water."[14]

In a verdant tropical forest like Amazonia, the carbon, nutrient and water cycles are accelerated: the soil-plant-sky circuit runs quickly. The furious expression of botanic energy provoked terror among the Spanish conquistadores, who called the jungle the Green Hell, *el Inferno Verde*. The rate of transpiration in the Amazon Basin is such that individual trees are veritable fountains, transferring large quantities of water from the ground and into the air like a natural spring. Nobre writes that on a given day, a single large tree in the rainforest "can pump from the soil and transpire over a thousand liters of water." As permaculture pioneer Bill Mollison puts it, "The tree has an intimate connection with rain. There's a constant exchange between the tree and the cloud."[15]

Given the 4 billion or so trees in the rainforest, Nobre writes, an estimated "twenty billion tons of water are transpired per day by all the trees in the Amazon basin. As a whole, these trees—those benevolent silent green structures of nature—act like geysers and spout a vertical river of vapor into the air that is even greater than the Amazon River."[16] Forests are such prodigious evaporators because of the intricate layering and overlapping of leaves; this creates abundant surface area for vapor exchange.

Whenever we do our calculus of water resources and look at the balance sheet, we often neglect to consider plants. Transpiration may be considered incidental to water fluxes, and often referred to as a loss of plant moisture. However, it plays a huge role in the movement of moisture into the atmosphere. In research published in *Nature* in 2013, Scott Jasechko and colleagues used isotope analysis to determine the sources of atmospheric moisture. According to the study, transpiration from vegetation accounts for between 80 and 90 percent of all moisture that ascends to the atmosphere from the continents; only slightly more than 10 percent derives from simple evaporation from land or bodies of water without plant intermediaries.[17]

We regard plants mainly as *recipients* of water—but in fact they're also key determinants of *where water goes* and *what it does*. In other words, vegetation—particularly trees, which evaporate more moisture than grasses and shrubby plants—helps drive weather and climate.

This unseen evaporated moisture is not simply lofting into the air and staying put; it's moving horizontally, along currents buoyed by wind. The Amazonia report presents the concept of "aerial rivers" whereby moisture, driven by evaporation, is transported from humid forested areas to other places where it falls as rain. Nobre notes a recent climatology review that identified "aerial lakes" that store water in the atmosphere as a kind of precipitation reserve.[18] Research in the Amazon region used isotope tracers to demonstrate that water from the forest was "exported" to other parts of the continent. The Amazon River ranks first among the world's rivers in how much water it carries to the sea: 200 million liters per second, or 17 billion tons daily. And yet, writes Nobre, the moisture flow that passes through the rainforest, the aerial river in the lower atmosphere that soars undetected above the mighty river we can see, actually exceeds this.

Nobre says the floating river phenomenon helps explain the "mystery" of why the plains east of the Andes mountain range receive plenty of rain. By contrast, other regions at that latitude—the Atacama Desert (the western edge of the Andes, deemed the world's driest place), the Kalahari, Namibia, the arid expanse of western and south Australia—are desert or savanna. He calls this the "lucky quadrangle," the chunk of South America that generates 70 percent of the continent's GNP. He writes: "The Amazon rainforest not only keeps the air moist for its own purposes, but also exports water vapor via aerial rivers, which carry the water that will produce the abundant rainfall that irrigates distant regions during the summer months."

Though it straddles the equator, the Amazon forest is always comfortably cool. Tom Goreau conducted research during the 1980s in which he compared the temperature in virgin Amazonian jungle with a nearby area that was clear-cut and overgrown with weeds. In the forest, the temperature from the hottest to coolest times of day remained within 1.5 degrees Celsius and was always "delightful." Where trees had been stripped bare, the temperature spanned 15 degrees Celsius and it got much hotter.[19]

The ambient cool that suffuses the rainforest is the product of count-less trees transpiring. It can only be enjoyed thanks to much botanical labor—the energy-intensive work of converting liquid water to gaseous vapor. In order to understand just how much energy this requires, Nobre invites us to envision the rainforest's daily evaporation yield poured into an impossibly large imaginary kettle. "If you put this 20 billion tons of water to boil, you would need 50 thousand Itaipus," he says, referring to the hydroelectric dam between Brazil and Paraguay whose power-generating capacity is second only to China's Three Gorges Dam. "And the Amazon does this for free."

Later in the document Nobre explores another paradox: why is the rainforest so rainy? To form rain droplets, water vapor molecules need some kind of particle to coalesce around: minute flecks of dust, pollen, salts or soot, bits of debris that would serve as condensation nuclei and promote the formation of clouds. Precipitation certainly happens: enough, he writes, to prompt the joke that the Amazon has two seasons, "wet" and "wetter." So something is clearly seeding the rain. And yet, as we've seen, the air in the lower atmosphere—the troposphere—above the forest is nearly empty of dusts and other aerosols. This also is true of the air above the ocean, which helps explain why many maritime stretches receive little rain. However, the Amazon region gets lots of rain—in some places, upward of nine feet a year.

How can this occur without cloud condensation aerosols?

Again, it has to do with trees. Nobre says tree leaves emit carbon-based gases called biogenic volatile organic compounds. He calls these "scents of the forest" (or, inspired by the animated films his two daughters watch, "pixie dust"). These tiny iotas of matter—"a magical powder produced by life"—induce rainforest rain, and therefore solve the lack-of-condensation-nuclei puzzle. A research team with the Max Planck Institute studied how these "scents" function in the humid rainforest air. The group found that when exposed to solar radiation, these aromatic specks "oxidize and precipitate to form very fine dust particles with an affinity for water. . . .

Poetically speaking, this is the *pixie dust* that magically appears in the moisture-laden air, and causes rain to bucket down from low clouds, i.e., the watering cans of the Garden of Eden."[20]

There's only one problem: some 300,000 square miles of Amazonia has been deforested, the size equivalent of two Germanys or two Japans. Nobre converts this to units Brazilian readers would understand: 184 million soccer fields, or nearly one soccer field's worth of rainforest lost for each person living in Brazil.

Today, he writes, the "wet or wetter" description of seasons no longer holds: "Now, there is a pronounced dry season, and the duration of the wet season diminishes progressively."

Can we blame the loss of trees?

I first learned of transpiration as a climate driver from a free booklet on the web called *The New Water Paradigm: Water for the Recovery of the Climate,* written by a group of Eastern European scientists, including Jan Pokorný and Michal Kravčík. A hydrologist based in Slovakia, Kravčík was awarded the 1999 Goldman Environmental Prize for providing alternatives to large dam projects that not only would have been ecologically damaging, but also would have destroyed four 700-year-old villages. Their publication completely upended my thinking about water and climate. In short, it fairly blew my mind. Much of the book focuses on the importance of keeping water on the land—the unheralded role of "green water." What truly grabbed me, however, was the extent to which the water cycle interacts with the energy cycle: how vapor conveys heat, alternately storing thermal energy (via evaporation) and releasing it (via condensation) as it circulates.

This offered a glimpse into the dynamism of air, that which we breathe and move through, a kind of mirror ocean riding ambient tides. Day and night, wafts of vapor wheel around the atmosphere, transforming conditions on the ground despite its weightlessness and invisibility. This moisture is, inevitably, an essential part of what creates and modifies our climate. Yet this humidity is not simply recycling moisture in a tidy, predictable way. Rather, it's diffuse and capricious, on the move, and determined by numerous other equally mysterious factors, including the presence and vigor of vegetation.

When we hear about links between water and climate, the connection tends to go in one direction: the impact that climate change may have on water sources. This is where we end up tying ourselves into knots when we say this drought or that storm may or may not be indicative of global warming. Because no single correlation can be proved, the conversation never gets beyond the chattering of talking heads.

What rarely gets airtime, however, is the extent to which *water influences climate*. In preceding chapters, we've explored some of the routes by which water has an impact on climate; in chapter 3, I noted Australian scientist Walter Jehne's statement that "over 90 percent of the global heat dynamics and balance is governed by a range of water-based processes." (Jehne says this creates the opportunity to employ cooling aspects of the water cycle as we strive to reduce CO_2 levels.) Also, we've seen how desertification can be regarded as both a consequence and a cause of climate change—that the inability to maintain ground moisture leads to a vicious cycle of unproductive land, biodiversity loss and soil carbon oxidizing to become CO_2. Plus the opposite: restoring the water cycle supports biodiversity, which, in turn, helps to bring the carbon cycle into balance. As our Amazonian adventure has taught us, plants, notably trees, have a huge influence on water. And yet, Jan Pokorný tells me, "Our understanding of the role of water and plants in landscape functioning is the equivalent of medicine before Pasteur."

Douglas Sheil is an ecologist who has been exploring the connection between forests and rainfall. An Irish fellow with a doctorate in tropical ecology from Oxford University, Sheil teaches at the Norwegian University of Life Sciences near Oslo. He also takes long research jaunts to forests in places like Indonesia, Borneo and Uganda. He helped establish the

Institute of Tropical Forest Conservation at the Bwindi Impenetrable National Park, part of an extensive primeval forest that's home to the critically endangered mountain gorilla, among hundreds of other indigenous species: mammal, bird, plant and butterfly.

Sheil works with local communities, people who continually move between crop fields and forests—areas that are respectively partially and fully wooded. "The impression among local people is that the forests attract the rain—that there's no question about that," he tells me. "When you talk to climate scientists, however, there's no recognition. If there's a forest it would be because there was water first and the forests came later."

In 2014 Sheil published an article entitled "How Plants Water Our Planet." The opening sentence is a zinger: "Most life on land depends on water from rain, but much of the rain on land may also depend on life." This isn't how we generally think about it. As if anticipating skepticism from a frowning reader, he continues: "Recent studies indicate that vegetation, especially tree cover, influences rain and rainfall patterns to a greater extent than is generally assumed."

Sheil notes that while the forces that govern rainfall over land remain stubbornly elusive to scientists—*unresolved processes* is the term often used—new research sheds light on the role of plants. He refers to the 2013 study by Jasechko and colleagues that found between 80 and 90 percent of continental atmospheric moisture comes from plants. This is extraordinary, he says, considering (1) previous estimates ranged from 20 to 60 percent, and (2) this includes evaporation from ground surfaces and bodies of water, such as lakes and rivers, which many would assume were key sources of moisture.[21]

In another study in *Nature,* published in 2012, Dominick Spracklen of Leeds University and colleagues used several streams of data including satellite observations to monitor the movement of air and rain over the tropics. The authors found that winds that moved across forested areas tended to generate more than twice as much rain when compared with winds that traveled over open areas, including land cleared for farming.[22]

Is word getting around that not only do plants need water, they also give us water? A 2015 news feature from the American Geophysical Union has a headline that plays on the link between plants, condensation aerosols and rain, and challenges the conventional wisdom: "April Flowers Bring May Showers?"[23]

Sheil stresses the role that trees in particular play in moving moisture around the globe. He writes: "Leafy tree canopies produce flows of water vapour that, per unit land area, are typically more than ten times greater than from herbaceous vegetation." He notes that even when the soil is dry, a tree's deep roots draw on moisture so as to also provide water to nearby shallow-rooted plants. And that for short time periods trees can transpire more water than they actually pull from the ground: they rely on moisture stored in their trunks, then replenish by taking in water as it condenses in cooler nighttime air. He adds that aerosol concentrations tend to be higher over forests than grasslands. (To paraphrase Jan Pokorný's *What Can a Tree Do?* brochure, a tree is indeed a wonderful "device.")

Sheil concludes that, according to the latest science (not to mention common sense), declining forest cover means less atmospheric moisture flow. And he expresses concern that we've been losing forests, particularly in the tropics.

"The Future Climate of Amazonia" made Antonio Nobre something of a celebrity in Brazil. He had given voice to people's fear: that the drought was not a fluke but an inevitable consequence of the deforestation that had happened under everybody's watch. The report was excerpted and cited countless times, and he gave interviews to journalists around the world. He appeared three times on the Sunday evening news show *Fantástico*. He told me that a national poll found that 40 percent of Brazilians knew about the report and accepted the link between water shortages and the ravaging of the Amazon rainforest.

"For the people in the street, the report made a big difference—that's exactly what I intended," Nobre says. "I'd started to articulate knowledge in a way scientists usually do not do because they are too specialized, packaging it in language that anyone could understand. The beast of knowledge was released. There was no putting it back. I'd see people in the elevator when I was going home, or taxi drivers, and some of them saw me on the Sunday program and they'd say, 'Of course the destruction of the forests is causing the drought.'" Nobre has had the experience of writing scientific books and papers for policy makers, which were "basically ignored. I decided this time I was going to speak directly to the people."

Nobre certainly had a receptive audience, since toward the end of 2014 people were in a constant state of angst about the drought. "I saw fear in peoples' eyes in São Paulo," he recalls. "For the first time, people had become really scared. It was unimaginable: what are we going to do? That fear was something that was deafening—soundless but deafening. There had been droughts in the past, but nothing compared to 2014. In Brazil we have a saying that God is Brazilian: we have good rain and soil and a wonderful climate. And then the joke that the only 'natural disaster' we have is called the National Congress. Now all of a sudden we have floods and we have droughts."

A theory called the "biotic pump," first described in a 2007 paper by Russian physicists Victor Gorshkov and Anastassia Makarieva, adds scientific ballast to the idea that forests are central to the production of rain.[24] Nobre and Sheil have each collaborated on papers with the Russian scientists; the concept is featured in both "The Future Climate of Amazonia" and "How Plants Water the Planet." The Russians' work, presented in the rarified language of atmospheric physics, challenges many long-held ideas about weather and climate. And speaks to the kind of questions a precocious five-year-old might ask, like, "Where do winds come from?" "If the water that falls as rain originated in the ocean, how do places far from the coast get rain?" Or, "Which came first, the forest or the rain that waters the forest?" It's a compelling hypothesis, but one branded with the dubious label "controversial." One biotic pump paper was published in *Atmospheric Chemistry and Physics*, an esteemed scientific journal, only after an unprecedented two-and-a-half-year-long discussion. The article appeared with a special editor's comment stating that its publication did not represent "an endorsement or confirmation of the theory, but rather a call for further development of the arguments presented in the paper for a final conclusion on its veracity (or not)." A declaration like that is unusual, to say the least.[25]

The theory maintains that natural forests act as a "pump" that draws moisture inland. Here's the gist: The concentration of trees in a forest means a high rate of transpiration. When this moist air ascends above the forest it cools, at which point the water vapor condenses. This produces a partial vacuum, a low-pressure zone, where the condensation has taken place. The result is an air pressure gradient, whereby the forest canopy draws in moist air from the ocean. Gorshkov and Makarieva contend that it's this *air pressure differential*—as opposed to a *temperature differential*, as has been assumed—that generates and drives the horizontal winds and flows of moisture that deliver rain.[26]

The biotic pump theory introduces the importance of transpiration to rain patterns. Precipitation isn't just a matter of condensation; it's a manifestation of the ongoing fluxes of transpiration *and* condensation. This principle "explains why in forested regions precipitation does not decrease with distance from the ocean, even thousands of kilometers, while the interiors of deforested parts of continents become dry already a few hundred kilometers away from the oceanic coast," Gorshkov and Makarieva write to me. "Condensation of water vapor over forests creates pressure gradients that have been shown to be sufficient to drive winds that bring moisture from ocean to land."

According to Gorshkov and Makarieva, forests don't merely grow in wet areas; they create and perpetuate the conditions in which they grow. As the physicists write on their website, "The chicken-or-the-egg problem of whether forests grow where it is wet, or it is wet where the forests grow, solves unambiguously in favor of the forests' priority."[27]

They describe a kind of "tug-of-war" between forest and ocean: with its abundance of trees—each busy transpiring moisture—a thriving forest evaporates more water than does the ocean. Thus the wooded area "wins" the tug-of-war and pulls moisture inland where it will fall as rain.

Now things get interesting—and alarming, given situations like Amazonia. Without sufficient forest cover, the Russian scientists say, water vapor is no longer drawn to a continent's interior to the same degree. The forest and the ocean keep on with their tugging, the eternal jousting for atmospheric moisture. But with a different result. Without its transpiration "advantage," the forest no longer pulls in moisture. The pump mechanism has gone bust. Rain becomes erratic and ultimately stalls, much now falling over the ocean rather than on land.

The Russian scientists associate the unusual heat waves and drought in their country over the last several years with the rapid deforestation in western Russia. They've suggested that the burning of coastal forests by Aboriginal settlers in prehistoric times contributed to the drying out of Australia's interior. Could the advent of drought in formerly wet forested areas like Madagascar, Indonesia and parts of Equatorial Africa reflect the waning of the biotic pump in those places?

There's much we don't know, including how the biotic pump interacts with circulation configurations like the Hadley and Walker cells and the El Niño/La Niña oscillations. There's also the question of what kinds of trees support the pump mechanism. Gorshkov and Makarieva say only established native forests have enough biomass to "prime" the moisture pump. They say since forests grow in specific environments—they're part of a living community and therefore develop in relation to other living organisms, down to bacteria and fungi in the soil—only mature, natural forests can fully serve this function. One couldn't substitute a monoculture tree plantation and expect to recreate the conditions of primary forest.

Should the biotic pump be confirmed, it brings new urgency to forest protection. "Most climate models recognize the role of 'precipitation cycling' in forests, but not moisture transport by forests," Makarieva and Gorshkov wrote to me. The difference is significant: if deforestation means simply reduced evaporation, the decline of precipitation would be relatively minor. If, however, rains depend on *imported* moisture and a key vehicle for transport—an intact forest—is impaired, that's a different story altogether. The physicists say, "In our model, imported moisture will decline if the forest is destroyed, especially in the inland portion of the continent. If there is no imported moisture there is nothing to be evaporated, so the water cycle will undergo a dramatic—not minor—reduction of intensity." In the Amazon, they say, this could mean a precipitation decrease up to 90 percent.

Douglas Sheil tells me he encountered Gorshkov and Makarieva's first biotic pump paper around 2007 when he was embarking on a book on conserving rainforest biodiversity. "I was working for CIFOR [the Center for International Forestry Research], collecting information on how we could better protect this forest or that forest," he says. "I was looking at hydrology and found this paper from the Russians. I said to a colleague, 'Do you believe this? If this theory is true, this is really important.'"

Sheil and his CIFOR colleague, Daniel Murdiyarso, decided to look more deeply at the phenomenon and wrote a scientific review, "How Forests Attract Rain: An Examination of a New Hypothesis." Since then he's been in close collaboration with Gorshkov and Makarieva. "I've never said they were right or wrong," he says. What's important is that ideas are made available for discussion: "Let's put it out there. That's how science works."

Something that troubles Sheil greatly is the rapidity with which a region can "flip" from wet to dry. He and Murdiyarso explain: "According to Makarieva and Gorshkov, if the near-continuous forest needed to convey moist air from coasts to continental interiors is severed, the flow of atmospheric moisture stops. Thus, clearing a band of forest near the coast may suffice to dry out a wet continental interior. Further, clearing enough forest within the larger forest zone may switch net moisture transport from ocean-to-land to land-to-ocean, leaving any forests remnants to be desiccated."[28]

Sheil adds, "It's not just local effects we need to think about, but the large-scale circulation systems are probably driven by forests more than we realize." Other researchers, too, have found evidence of teleconnection—climate occurrences in which cause and effect may be thousands of miles apart—associated with changes in forest cover. For instance, climatologist Roni Avissar, now dean of the Rosenstiel School of Marine and Atmospheric Science at the University of Miami, and colleagues at Duke University found that deforestation in the Amazon Basin correlates with lower rainfall not just locally but in distant regions, including the American Midwest.

In his 2014 Ph.D. thesis, R. J. van der Ent of Delft University of Technology used the term *atmospheric watershed* to explain how a rain-dependent region like the Sahel in West Africa may rely on transpired vapor from as far away as southern Europe. Understanding "sources" and "sinks" of moisture can help us assess potential impacts of land cover changes, he writes.[29] It's incredible to think that a farmer in Burkina Faso may enjoy good yields of millet and maize thanks to healthy woodlands in Portugal. However, the use of isotopes and modeling to study moisture recycling is showing us that when it comes to the water cycle, we all live in the same neighborhood.

In Brazil Antonio Nobre has been watching this devolve in real time—or rather, accelerated time. He writes, "Many of the model projections for the consequences of deforestation have already been observed, especially the expansion of the dry season." According to the simulations, however, this wouldn't happen until complete deforestation. At this point, about 18 percent of the Brazilian forest has been clear-cut, fallen to what he calls the "tree guillotine." Another 25 to 30 percent has been degraded, or "wounded." What does this mean in terms of its function? Has the "Future Climate of Amazonia" already arrived?

Research by University of Virginia scientists published in late 2014 in *Nature Climate Change* pointed to dire consequences of deforestation. The authors argue that environmental impacts of forest loss are global and go beyond the release of carbon stored in the trees—a common view of forests' chief relevance to climate.[30] Lead author Deborah Lawrence told the *Washington Post* that the Amazon and central Africa could have a "tipping point" of 30 to 50 percent deforestation, beyond which natural systems could break down.[31]

"We are headed for the abattoir," Nobre tells the Latin American Bureau (LAB), a UK news service.[32]

Nobre's recommendations for avoiding disaster? For one, an absolute halt to deforestation and forest burning. Since that won't be enough, he says, we also need to regenerate natural forests. It's not just about individual trees, he stresses, but the integrity of the forest system. This means restoration on an immense scale.

"The forest is our security, our protection system, like a piggy bank," Nobre tells LAB. He worries about the stress to the Amazon, and says the forest itself is striving to defend against what's been done to it, just like the human body seeks balance upon illness or injury. "The rainforest is working like crazy underneath," he says. "The climate models do not consider the characteristic of life to compensate for stress or abuse. We're led to believe the process of change is slow. But as with an alcoholic, when you've got cirrhosis of the liver it's too late. Earth's systems are responding as best they can. When they start caving, it will be precipitous. We thought [climate effects were] way out in the future because the logic of life is not built in."

He observes that an annual decline in the amount of deforestation in the Brazilian Amazon, which occurred in 2011 and 2012, is met with self-congratulation—as if merely chopping down fewer trees were enough. Laudable as less damage may be, he says, this ignores the ecological implications of the accumulated deforestation that's taken place over time. Given the proportion of the rainforest that has been clear-cut or degraded, Nobre fears the Amazon Basin may be approaching a point of no return. Beyond a certain threshold the biotic pump's traction could cease. Amazonia, then, could shift to a new state of equilibrium, more like dryland savanna. In a worst-case scenario, writes Nobre, the humid tropical biome, with all its biodiversity and capacity to sustain the region's agriculture and well-being, "would resemble present-day Australia: a vast desert interior fringed on one side by strips of wetter areas near the sea."

In other words, the lushest tropical rainforest on the globe could flip from hydration to desiccation, from jungle to desert.

Let's leave the Amazon for a bit and head over to western Kenya, where our friend (and marketer of the ever-popular "tree" air-conditioning unit) Jan Pokorný does fieldwork. Over the last twenty years he's watched the landscape grow drier. He attributes this in large part to deforestation: whereas forests once covered more than half the country, it's now less than 2 percent. Pokorný monitors how vegetation affects the distribution of solar energy, using satellite technology and thermal infrared sensors. It's a plum gig for machine geeks: he takes measurements while flying above the African landscape in a small Cessna. He shared with me an aerial photo of the area between Lake Naivasha and the Mau Forest. The mountain forests measured 19 degrees C; agricultural fields that used to be woodlands hovered close to 50 degrees C. The image shows the dark green of forests diminishing along the slope to the lowlands. The valley has clusters of deep green among the broad, pale, geometric shapes of cultivated land.

Two hundred thousand hectares of forest have been converted to agricultural land over the past two decades, Pokorný tells me. The Mau Forest was long called a "water tower" because it supplied water to the Rift Valley and Lake Victoria. More recently, the region has suffered from drought, especially during 2009's rainless rainy season. The area's gone so dry that a Japanese company stopped construction on a hydro power station; one already built, along the Sondu Miriu River, works only erratically. (The Japanese company behind the project asked the Kenyan government for compensation arguing that they were given poor hydrological data. The problem wasn't the data: it's that the hydrology had changed in the decade-plus since studies were done.) Kenyan authorities have imposed large-scale evictions in the area, ostensibly to stave off environmental disaster. There are frequent protests and skirmishes over logging and burning.

Detreeing the landscape has altered the way the ecosystem functions and self-regulates, says Pokorný. In Kenya, there "used to be a lot of rain forest. Water was constantly evaporating and above the forest the air stayed cool. Now we have agricultural land, often bare, and it's hotter and there's less evaporation. There are more days without clouds and fog. Because the air from the land is hotter, the clouds and fog disappear. The relatively dry air moves over bodies of water that now get more direct solar radiation." He notes that Lake Victoria, a large shallow lake tucked in among Tanzania, Uganda and Kenya, has shown temperature stratification, with warm water on the surface, a situation that threatens its ecological balance.

Pokorný put me in touch with Sarah Higgins, a conservationist who runs the Little Owl Sanctuary (now Naivasha Owl Centre) for injured birds near Lake Naivasha. Higgins says she's seen weather patterns vary with the forest's fortunes. When she started farming thirty years ago "we were almost guaranteed sufficient rainfall for our crops." Then came the destruction of the Mau forest, and the area above and on either side of the farm was "denuded of trees and overgrazed, down to bare earth. Our regular rainfall started to fail and we were seeing dry years, poor yields and more droughts."

However, in the mid-1990s, her late husband, Mike, planted many thousands of trees on areas of the farm that weren't suitable for crops. As these started to mature, says Higgins, "the rain is becoming more regular again. The clouds that have been passing along the Mau looking for somewhere to off-load seem to make a little deviation so that it's over our farm—i.e., our trees! This is a hugely unscientific statement, just a personal observation backed up by our rain records."[33]

Higgins's story is just that: anecdotal evidence based on someone's observations and experience. But there are reforestation projects happening all over the world and lots of similar reports, albeit not scientifically verified. Forested landscapes can be restored; with restoration ecological function does return. Can reforestation bring back the multiple, perhaps immeasurable, ways trees contribute to the water cycle? Is there a point at which there are enough trees to reinstate important mechanisms—a kind of reverse tipping point where things tilt in a positive direction? We don't know. There's no data on the extent to which the biotic pump can be reinstated because these questions have not been asked—yet.

Sheil believes reforestation can revive the biotic pump. "We can fix it. It can fix itself too, if allowed," he says. "Forests do recover . . . impressively." He refers to Ujong Kulong in Java, where you can see monkeys, wild deer and boar under large fig trees in coastal forests—all regrowth after Krakatoa's eruption and subsequent tidal waves in 1883. Since the volcano people have feared resettling the area, and the rainforest has become a national park and UNESCO World Heritage Centre, known for the Java one-horned rhinoceros.

"If we planted trees at a sufficiently large scale it would improve the climate. Even planting on a local scale can improve groundwater recharge," says Sheil. "It is just a matter of will. Think of the amount we spend on the military. If we used half that to fix the planet we'd be getting better very fast."

Nobre urges citizens and decision makers in Amazonia to do everything possible to save and restore the forest as a "healing war-effort." An oxymoron to be sure, but perhaps the language of combat will spark a response; ecological alarm bells like biodiversity loss and failing rains have yet to do the trick. In some circumstances a forest will regenerate on its own, he writes: "There is a wealth of pioneer plant species that have the ability to grow under extreme environmental conditions. These plants establish a dense secondary forest, creating conditions for the complex, lasting tropical forest to recompose itself gradually by medium- and long-term restoration." With large swaths of degenerated land, however, "it becomes necessary to plant native species. If rain still falls, the forest regenerates in replanted areas. A collection of planted trees is better than bare ground, but it is still a long way from rebuilding the functional part of the destroyed ecosystem in all its complexity."

Gorshkov and Makarieva always emphasize the importance of natural forest. The biotic pump, they write, "is a complex information-rich phenomenon," a place-based constellation of biophysical processes that have developed over the course of time. While their research suggests that simply replanting trees wouldn't be sufficient to reinstate the pump, with reforestation "it should be possible to facilitate the natural processes of forest self-recovery." They foresee the advent of "ecological medical science," the environmental equivalent of medical care for people as a means of promoting the healing of disturbed forest ecosystems.

One approach to reforestation is Farmer Managed Natural Regeneration (FMNR), a technique developed by Tony Rinaudo of World Vision Australia that's a rapid, inexpensive alternative to tree planting. Conventional planting is costly, labor intensive and, particularly in harsh, unforgiving environments—such as Niger, where in the 1980s Rinaudo was an aid worker—has high failure rates. While despairing over the blighted landscape, Rinaudo found that even in barren areas, upon closer look you'd find small seedlings and tree stumps that are sprouting. He developed a strategy to give these inchoate trees a chance to grow.

This is done by selection (choosing the most vigorous plants), pruning (steering the plant's energy toward upward growth) and protection (keeping livestock away in the initial months, and ensuring the selected shoots are not taken for firewood). FMNR requires no special skills, Rinaudo maintains. In a film clip he says, "Millions of hectares of land have been cleared in Africa, but the one redeeming factor is that many of the tree stumps are still alive."[34]

As for water, Rinaudo shared in an email some observations from a recent visit to Humbo, in southern Ethiopia. When he first went to Humbo in 1999, the hillsides had no trees. This meant seasonal rains led to floods, "causing deaths, loss of livestock and property, and destruction of crops." He's pleased by the change he's seen. In nearby Soddo the district's water source, which had also been cleared and is now being reforested through FMNR, "thirteen springs have begun flowing again, six of them running all year."

And rain? He continued: "Anecdotally we are hearing that in some areas rainfall does seem to have increased. . . . What is certain is that what rain does fall is more effective—because of lower temperatures, reduced wind speed and lower evaporation and because of increased soil moisture-holding capacity. . . . We are hearing the same testimony from Senegal to Ethiopia and from East Sumba to Myanmar: springs are returning, soils are more moist, water tables are being recharged."

I checked in with filmmaker Mark Dodd, who made *The Man Who Stopped the Desert*, and whose newest film, *Ethiopia Rising: Red Terror to Green Revolution*, looks at restoration efforts in the Tigray region, a mountainous region in the north. "You can virtually see the change in forest cover over ten years from space," he said. "The trees stabilize the hillside. That allows more water to be absorbed. Later on in the year, that helps downstream. We filmed in a wellhead at the end of the dry season. There was still a lot of water pouring out from it."

There's also Dutch scientist Willie Smits's reforestation work through Samboja Lestari, which roughly translates to "Everlasting Forest." He launched the project in 2001, buying up deforested land in Borneo to re-store habitat for orangutans, a threatened species he had come to love. He calls them "thinkers of the jungle."

In a 2009 TED Talk, "How to Restore the Rainforest," Smits describes his method, in which sugar palms are planted in rings to block fires. He employs fast-growing trees to provide a canopy for slow-growing rainforest trees. From 2007 to 2009 he reported significant changes. In addition to enhanced biodiversity (the number of bird species rose from 5 to 137), air temperature cooled while humidity, cloud cover and rainfall increased. Reviving the forested area "made it into a rain machine," he said.[35]

The first day of February 2015, the rains returned to São Paulo. "The state government was already planning the rationing of water," says Nobre.

"They were even thinking of leaving people five days without water and then two days with. Companies were beginning to relocate. Then when it started raining, the government canceled everything."

February and March turned out to be a little wetter than average, April less so, he says. "In May, now, it's dry again. Then we have the whole of the dry season ahead. People are scared. It's like a fire that's smoldering—not with open flames, but people know it's there. I think the message about deforestation and drought is there and it has to have time to operate its effect."

Preserving intact forest is imperative. Yet there's also the message about *re*forestation. After all, Brazil already has a model in the Tijuca Forest.

FIVE

FARMING FOR WATER

Industrial Agriculture's

Water-Guzzling Secrets

Fertility is the major means of managing soil to mitigate drought damage, and to give bigger crop returns when there is no drought.

—William A. Albrecht, "The Drought Myth:
An Absence of Water Is Not the Problem"

Farmers need to become biologists again.

—Third-generation Colorado farmer
Brendon Rockey, 2014

ONCE I REACH HIM ON THE PHONE, JOHN KEMPF asks if I mind waiting a few more minutes. He needs to find someone to take over the horse plow.

After the long car ride from Vermont to Ohio, I'm fine with a break to get my bearings. We are in Orwell, a small village on the edge of northeast Ohio's Amish country. Some ten miles after turning off the highway, Tony and I had started seeing large-wheeled buggies patiently weaving among the cars, and strong-looking black horses next to tidy homes. Here and there a house would have a pony—sturdy and small, its blond, shaggy mane swept across the eyes. (My day is made when I notice two children, in full Amish garb, driving a small open carriage pulled by a high-stepping pony.)

It is a beautiful spring day. As we travel we see people working in their yards, men in straw hats and women in black or white bonnets, diligently pushing small, manual mowers. The people look purposeful and unrushed, and unaware of or uninterested in the fact that visitors like us are looking at them, fascinated and yet vaguely discomfited by their differentness.

Back at the farm I wait for the horse-plow handover to take place, appreciating the sunshine and the clear, cool air. This is the site of Kempf's house and his newest enterprise, AEA Pure Dawn Farms, a permaculture farm run according to the principles and strategies that underlie his crop nutrition consulting firm, Advancing Eco Agriculture, which is just down the road in Middlefield. It's the farm's first season, and there is a slightly frenetic under-construction feel about the place: trays of seedlings lined up for planting; a leaning Porta-Potty; busy young farm hands in weathered jeans; and, improbably, a low, sleek sports car with New York license plates.

A tall, striking fellow with impeccable hair walks out of the house, and I guess—correctly—that the high-end car is his. He nods in greeting before excusing himself to rush off in pursuit of a toddler with bountiful copper curls. Quick and energetic, the little girl has the impish charisma of a child who knows daddy will follow her anywhere. The beleaguered dad is Advancing Eco Agriculture's chairman, Philippe van den Bossche, an impact investor based in Manhattan who, I later learn, once ran Madonna's Raising Malawi foundation and whose relationship status regularly got ink in the tabloids.

Such is the paradox of Ohio farmer John Kempf. One minute he's hitching up a team of horses, and the next he's on a private call with internationally renowned scientists and policy makers. On a given day he might meet with someone like van den Bossche, who looks as if he might have ambled coolly from a men's lifestyle magazine, and later confer with an employee dressed in a demure cotton cap, fluffy white apron and pleated dark skirt, like the worker who helped me to locate Kempf when I arrived. Kempf may travel by cart or car, or around the world virtual-style. But never by airplane: that is a long-held Amish prohibition he will not cross.

After an interval Kempf strides up, apologizing for the delay. Slim with curly red-brown hair topped by a crisp straw hat, he's wearing cloth pants and suspenders. He moves easily but pitched slightly forward. Kempf radiates a bright intensity that in part reflects his youth—he's twenty-seven—but also his passion for his mission: producing more nutritious crops while enhancing the health of the soil and the environment. He invites us inside his home, with its Century House 1880 plaque, and we settle around the table to chat. He has lots of ideas to share about farming and water.

I'd learned of John Kempf from another young farmer driven to bolster the quality of our food: Dan Kittredge, who grows and sells produce in western Massachusetts and is the founder of the Bionutrient Food Association. In a phone interview, Kempf shared the experience that set him on his unconventional path, that of maverick Amish entrepreneur and farmer.

During Kempf's childhood his father was a purveyor of agricultural chemicals for the area. Upon completing his formal education at the end of eighth grade, Kempf was given responsibility for fertilizer and other chemical inputs on the family farm. Despite following the application protocol, he saw that the crops were languishing. The fields were inundated with pest, weed, and disease pressure; soil quality and aggregation were poor, and yields below par. At one point he observed that plants on newly rented ground looked different—and more vigorous. Within two feet of each other, and divided only by the property line, their cantaloupe had succumbed to powdery mildew while those on the new, untreated field were thriving. Clearly, the pesticides and fungicides endorsed by the extension services were not benefiting these plants. He wondered: what went wrong with the melons on the old field? More importantly, he asked: what went *right* with the melons on the new field?

That question launched a foray into intensive study of plant nutrition and physiology from books, professionals and the scientific literature. This often meant forging links between research findings in different disciplines. Kempf found plenty of data with important implications for practitioners. However, those who might have benefited were unaware of it because the specialists in different fields and subfields didn't talk to each other.

If chemical agents were part of the problem, as he was starting to believe, it wasn't enough for Kempf to simply swear off chemical additives. He wanted to know why those particular crops that had been bathed in chemicals were flagging whereas similar untreated plants flourished. He sought to understand precisely which mechanisms the amendments had set in motion, or put to a stop. Through years of study and experimentation—remember, he started in his midteens—he settled on a holistic model of plant health, nutrition and development. Based on this framework, he has built a successful consulting business.

I wanted to talk to Kempf about the water needs of crops. This, it turns out, is not as straightforward as we're led to believe. Kempf has learned that the factors that contribute to plant resilience also help determine how crops take up water. Plants vary in water usage efficiency, he says, depending on their stage of development and the state of their health.

Chapter 4 highlighted the notion that rather than being passive recipients of water, plants actively influence the flow and cycling of water. I wanted to hear Kempf's insights on whether plants grown as crops also manage water—and whether healthier plants are more effective managers. Specifically, I was anxious to learn how understanding healthy plant-soil interactions can inform farming practices so we can make better use of water.

In this time of trepidation about water, driven by shortages in the Southwest and particularly in California, there's talk about the water footprint of various foods. I take issue with the one that gets the most ink, that of a hamburger, because the 450 gallons of water for a quarter-pound patty[1] is predicated on growing grain to feed the animal, which is a poor use of resources and results in meat that's less healthful than pasture-raised. Also, as we've seen, restorative grazing can enhance land function so that more water remains in the ecosystem. But plant-based foods don't get off easy either. We're told, for example, that a tomato "costs" about thirteen gallons of water,[2] eight ounces of broccoli accounts for 19.5 gallons[3] and, notoriously, that an almond requires a gallon per nut.

Could it be that healthier, more resilient tomatoes, broccoli heads or almond trees use water more frugally and therefore need less? If so, this seemed something we might want to know. And that is how I found myself on a sunny, late May Friday afternoon at John Kempf's kitchen table in Orwell, Ohio, a large wooden bowl of nuts and dried fruits set between us for periodic snacking.

Our discussion—or rather Kempf's high-voltage disquisition, which I strive to keep pace with in longhand—leaps from here to there and back, circling around the linkages between high-performing plants, healthy living soil and water efficiency. The best place to start is with Kempf's conceptualization of plant health, which he illustrates pictorially as a pyramid where four levels ascend toward a peak of optimal resilience, function and efficient water use.

Stage one is successful photosynthesis: the plant converts simple sugars to complex carbohydrates and polysaccharides. This stage imparts resistance to the basic soil-borne pathogens a plant would encounter.

At stage two, the plant synthesizes complete proteins. Since many common crop pests—aphids, whiteflies and larval insects—cannot digest complete proteins, this adds another layer of protection.

Stage three marks a higher level of nutrition in which surplus energy is stored as lipids, fats and oils, making for stronger cell membranes. At this point crops can stand up to airborne pathogens like blights and mildew and many bacterial threats.

A plant that reaches stage four produces "plant secondary metabolites," the aromatic compounds—think essential oils, i.e., that which makes, say, rosemary smell like rosemary—that embody the plant's immunity, properties that are then conferred to the animals and people that eat the plant. Crops at this pinnacle not only repel a higher order of pest and pestilence, but also have more resources with which to attract pollinators, neutralize toxins and withstand stresses.

What does this have to do with water?

A great deal, says Kempf. First, he says, consider how crops use water. Plants require water for both photosynthesis and respiration, distinct processes that use water differently. Photosynthesis employs water to create sugars and build biomass. In respiration, the plant metabolizes (breaks down) sugars in order to reap that energy. Respiration is most prevalent at night, when no photosynthesis occurs. Some liken plant respiration to "breathing," a metabolic process that takes in oxygen (O_2) and emits CO_2. Plants with a high level of nutrition need less water for both photosynthesis and respiration. Plus, they maintain a positive balance between the two processes: when the balance tilts toward photosynthesis, there's growth; more respiration means growth is curtailed. Kempf says good nutrition can significantly reduce a plant's water requirements.

Here's why: when a plant is proficient at drawing nutrients from its surroundings, photosynthesis becomes efficient. I contacted David C. Johnson, senior project specialist at New Mexico State's Institute for Energy and the Environment, who explained: "If the plant can grow more efficiently, fixing more biomass in a shorter time, then it may use less water as compared to a plant in a low fertility or low carbon soil, struggling for nutrients and marking time."[4]

Efficiency also supports the plant's ability to produce lipids, says Kempf. "When plants reach optimal levels of health they'll begin forming elevated levels of fats, oils and lipids. You can see this by the glossy waxy sheen on the leaf surface. That coating is insulating that plant, cooling it and preventing rapid water loss. Therefore, nutrition has a big impact."

Johnson adds: "Since plants thrive best within certain temperature ranges, less water is needed to control these temperatures, making the system more water efficient." Plants that produce lipids, Kempf explains, cool themselves without relying on evaporation and therefore losing water.

This is particularly relevant to respiration, as higher temperatures increase the rate of transpiration. Plants with a moisture-conserving lipid coating do not need to burn through water to maintain temperature and therefore do not experience lackluster growth.

The important thing to recognize is this: a plant cannot get there alone. To paraphrase that oft-quoted African proverb, "It takes a village to raise a child," we can say, *It takes a soil community to feed a plant.* Any farmer or gardener who successfully nurtures plants is working in partnership with microorganisms, consciously or not.

"Plants are no different from us in that they are hugely outnumbered by microbes—and depend on them for so much," says Johnson. "These plant/soil microbial community systems are much like us. We are outnumbered ten to one in cell count when we compare the number of cells in our body to the number of microbial cells we have. These microbes help digest our food, generate nutrients for us, synthesize vitamins, detoxify carcinogens, promote cell renewal and activate and support our immune system. We are finding now they even control our appetites and cravings and are able to turn on and off genes in our body that regulate brain development and emotional behavior. We, as a supraorganism, are totally dependent on the form, function and proper operation of our microbial 'symbiont' partners and disruptions can promote catastrophic consequences. I expect plant/soil microbial systems are no different."

When I'd talked to Kempf a few years back he made an enigmatic comment that left me feeling I was student to a Zen master. He'd said, "Soil is to the plant as the rumen is to the cow." This is what he meant: A cow's rumen, the first of four compartments in a ruminant's digestive tract, goes to work on the forage the cow consumes, fermenting and processing it for the animal to assimilate. In the same way, soil is the site where nutrients are broken down and provisioned for the plant to take in.

Kempf says he regards soil—meaning the entire living soil community—as the digestive system of the plant. The plant, he says, essentially "outsources" the task of digestion to the surrounding soil. In consequence, the process of nourishing a plant cannot be considered in isolation. Soil conditions and soil microbiology are integral to how well a plant crop is "fed."

This sheds light on the term *plant nutrition*, which refers to the availability and absorption of the chemical elements a plant needs to grow, develop and sustain itself. As Kempf emphasizes, this is not a formula. You can't simply provide crops with set amounts of mineral nutrients and expect them to thrive. Additives would have to be what a given plant needs, and provided in a form the plant can absorb. Nourishment is not a one-size-fits-all recipe. Rather, a plant's nutritional status is the culmination of multiple interactions between the plant, the atmosphere, the soil and the mineral substances essential to living processes.

The role of soil in plant nutrition has huge implications for the amount of water that crops need, Kempf says. A plant primarily takes up water through its roots, so moisture at the root zone, the rhizosphere, is its main reservoir. Plants growing in healthy living soil will form relationships with root, or mycorrhizal, fungi. These fungal networks can tap into water sources that a plant's own roots are unable to reach, expanding the plant's range up to several hundred times.

As a result, associations with mycorrhizal fungi keep plants hydrated during periods of water scarcity. "When you have soil at a certain level of dryness, the film of water around each soil particle becomes so tightly bonded that the plant roots can no longer extract it," he says. "But mycorrhizal fungi can, and they extract and provide that water to plants. There's an intelligent ecosystem at work. As plants dry out, mycorrhizal fungi will automatically extract water and transfer it to plants."

These beneficial fungi also solubilize minerals, meaning they break down substances so that they can be carried in water. This makes nutrients that might be present in the soil, such as phosphorus and many key micronutrients, available in a form a plant can utilize. And, in turn, it enhances a plant's nutritional level, enabling it to attain higher states of vigor and resilience. This supports the production of complex compounds. Among these are lipids that coat the leaf so that water cleaves to its surface, thereby adding another means of safeguarding moisture.

All these great things root fungi do for plants are part of the carbon-trading deal, as our plants are keeping fungi happy by feeding them sugars through the roots. It's not that mycorrhizal fungi are altruistic. Rather, these relationships are an elegant form of biological barter that benefits both plant and fungus. As well as the soil: mycorrhizal fungi are pivotal to the formation of soil aggregates and the long-term storage of carbon in the soil. And this is significant for drawing down excess carbon in the air.

In each previous chapter, we've seen that carbon and water tend to move in tandem. In healthy soil systems, they're following each other into the ground; in dysfunctional systems, they're moving into the atmosphere. Mycorrhizal fungi in agricultural settings also get into the game; mycorrhizal fungi follow carbon, and water follows mycorrhizal fungi.

Plant nutrition is critical to a crop's ability to make the best use of water. I'll explain point by point, but here's the takeaway first: *It's all about living soil.*

Perennial and annual plants interact with all manner of microbe, both fungi and bacteria. In the crop production world, attaining a favorable fungal/bacteria ratio in the soil, generally associated with higher productivity, is considered a kind of Holy Grail. "Many soils are bacteria dominated, and soil microbiologists, permaculturists and many different groups talk about the need to build soil fungal communities," Kempf says.

But how? Applying mycorrhizal products, he says, rarely works.

Kempf posits a sequence of events he calls the "Soil Regeneration Cascade," a model for how well-nourished crops and living soils feed, reinforce and enhance each other in a way that maximizes the use of water. As he describes it, the soil microbe community evolves as a kind of wave: the initial sugars sent by plants into the soil stimulate bacterial growth, and as plants grow and transmit more complex compounds—notably, lipids—the composition of organisms shifts toward fungi. In the wave's initial ripples, plants get the benefit of bacterial metabolites, byproducts of bacterial work that provide mineral nutrition in a more complete form than simple ions. When this happens, Kempf says, "a plant's energy efficiency goes up dramatically."

To clarify: Kempf distinguishes between two models of plant nutrition. In one, crops absorb nutrition dissolved in soil moisture in the form of ions, or simple charged particles. This is the model in farming today, which he says is basically "glorified hydroponics" that reduces the role of soil to "provid[ing] a base for the plant." This system is artificial, he says, because it is not how plants operate in nature. The other, less easily studied in a lab, is "real-world agriculture" in which plants procure nutrients through synergistic interactions with soil organisms. When a plant is fueled directly by microbial metabolites, Kempf says, it can access nutrients at lower moisture levels.

He explains that while ions are only transported in water, microbial metabolites can be absorbed in low-moisture conditions. Plus, converting simple ions to complex compounds—such as converting nitrate to amino acids, the building blocks of protein—consumes a significant amount of a plant's energy. With complete compounds available to them, the plants now enjoy an energy surplus. That spare energy is stored as fats, just as it is with people and animals. Robust plants nourished in a biologically active system may have three times the lipids needed to form cell membranes, he says. As it did with surplus sugars, the plant now begins sending lipids through the roots as root exudates.

This in turn begins to tip the microorganism balance toward fungi, including mycorrhizal fungi, which get to work on the lipids, breaking down the substances as far as they can be broken down. This activity, described by the less-than-appetizing term *fungal digestion,* is pivotal to the production of humus.

Humus, you may recall, is a stable material that's at once a sink for carbon and a sponge for water, the loamy earth's own hallowed elixir. What

Kempf proposes here that's new is this: the lipid content determines the cut-off point at which plant matter can no longer be digested. Plants form lipids once they reach a certain threshold of vitality and nutrition. Therefore, Kempf suggests, what governs the creation of humus is not the quantity of plant material—the biomass—but its lipid content, which rises according to the level of plant nutrition. In other words, humus formation is to a large degree contingent on healthy plants.

The connection between healthy plants, carbon and fungi in the soil, and water efficiency is starting to gain traction. Research, including the Rodale Institute Farming Systems trial that's been in operation for thirty years, has documented improved water use efficiency and water holding capacity on farms that practice organic methods compared with conventional systems.[5]

New Mexico State's David Johnson studies soil microbiology to better understand which conditions support increased carbon in the soil. While he wasn't specifically seeking data on water use, what he found on that score surprised him: soil that sustained larger fungal populations and higher carbon levels *doubled* the crop yield that land could produce with the same volume of water.[6]

"A healthy soil microbial community and plant system appears to be able to extract needed nutrients and water on the Walmart shipping model: everything just in time," he says. This activity "requires energy, and the plant-soil-microbe system elegantly shuttles this energy when and where it is needed and has many feedback mechanisms to assess when it has a sufficient amount of a nutrient and then reduce the energy flow for that process."

Even with optimal soil conditions there are limits to plant production, Johnson continues, "most likely limited by the amount of sunlight available, with the next limiting factor being water. Nature does everything in small steps. The energy release from the chemical bonds in energy molecules, such as sugar and starches, is done in small steps with a small component of energy utilized in each step. In nature, water was also done in small steps previous to the extraction of carbon out of the soils. We now do not have the capacity to slow down this flow of water. Some soils do not even let the water into its structure and it becomes runoff. In other soils it flows through too rapidly and leaches nutrients into water resources: our streams, lakes, aquifers and oceans. Carbon in all its forms—soil organic matter, aggregates, mucilages, glues, glomalin, humic substances—helps open up a soil so it can receive the water while also giving the soil the structure and capacity to store that water. In our sandy soils in the Southwest, a 1 percent increase in soil carbon promotes a quintupling of water storage ability."

When you're growing crops, it doesn't matter if the water arrives by thunderstorm, pipe, sluice or sprinkler. The moisture needs to stay in the system, and that requires living soil with a high carbon content. Says Johnson: "It is not what you get, it is what you keep that is important."

John Kempf's Soil Regeneration Cascade illustrates a notable, and even admirable, attribute of plants: their proclivity, when in a fully functional system, to create the conditions to ensure that they will thrive. In this instance, the plants' wish list consists of soil that's rich in humified carbon. Later I'll share more on the clever strategies of plants from Australian soil scientist Christine Jones. For now, I'll leave you with this assertion from Kempf's website: *We know that healthy soil will lead to healthier crops. Interestingly enough, however, the fastest way to regenerate soil is to grow extraordinarily healthy crops.*[7]

Now for the problem: none of this great stuff is going to happen if chemical inputs like fungicides, pesticides and herbicides are added to the soil. It does stand to reason that spraying to kill off fungus precludes alliances with mycorrhizal fungi, the fungi a farmer wants. And that might seem a tolerable loss, even a calculated one. But the reality is that chemical amendments inevitably kill more than the targeted species. In a biologically dynamic setting like living soil, this sort of collateral damage is rarely benign. Destroying one set of pests may provoke exponential growth in others, only to throw an entire system out of balance. Or, as we've seen in the "superweeds" scenario, species may build up immunity to the very formulae intended for their demise so that they rebound in greater force. Other practices that disrupt a functional soil community, such as heavy tillage, fallowing fields and leaving bare soil, will also interfere with the reciprocal relationships and processes that support a plant's efficient use of nutrition and water.

Understanding the biological consequences of chemical applications helped Kempf solve the mystery of the mildew-y melons. The cantaloupes' high-input regimen altered interactions between plants and their microbe neighbors in a way that stymied processes essential for the crop's viability, let alone its full, round, sweet, orange-hued cantaloupe-ness. Kempf came to the conclusion that there was no way to get a good crop while using chemicals that destroy soil organisms. And that trying to cultivate plants this way was a matter of squandering perfectly good time, money and water.

But wait: maybe we can't assume that whatever water a farmer employs on his or her crops is perfectly good. For the next thing Kempf wanted to talk about was water quality—specifically water used for irrigation on farms.

The advent of irrigation is the quiet backstory of civilization. The ability to move water from where it is abundant to where crops need it enabled people to remain in one place, to set up agricultural shop. This set the stage for the development of towns, cities and large, stable institutions.

According to Sandra Postel's book *Pillar of Sand: Can The Irrigation Miracle Last?*, the deliberate management of water to grow crops began around 4000 BC in the Fertile Crescent, areas served by water from the Tigris and Euphrates Rivers and the Nile. People "used flooding and dug a ditch and diverted some of the river's flow . . . to water their crops during the dry season," writes Postel. "By artificially applying water to their fields, farmers found they could grow an extra crop. Areas that were too dry to support crops at all could be turned into productive fields. For the first time, large food surpluses appeared, freeing a portion of society to pursue other activities," including the arts and scholarship.[8]

Agriculture's need for water has proved a fount of human ingenuity. The time line of the Irrigation Museum, a project of the Irrigation Association, based in Fairfax, Virginia, notes such early achievements as a water measurement device dubbed the Nilometer (Egypt, 3500 BC), cement piping for water (Romans, 2000 BC), and the *Sakia* or Persian water wheel, which consisted of several buckets strung along a moving belt pulled by oxen (500 BC). The exhibit presents the development of irrigation through the centuries. (A drop of irrigation trivia: during a 1976 baseball game between the Oakland A's and California Angels, the sprinklers mistakenly came on, interrupting play for several minutes.[9]) Recent innovations have brought tremendous precision to the art of delivering water to plants. We can now choose from microsprinklers, microjets, subsurface drip lines, and bubblers—and microbubblers—each of which may be directed and/or activated by lasers, soil tensiometers, remote sensors, timers and delays.

As Postel points out, the "miracle" of irrigation has come with costs: "It made agriculture dependent upon a network of hydraulic infrastructure—including dams, canals, and levees—that was a natural target of enemies. The infrastructure also needed to be maintained, which required vast amounts of organized labor, some of it provided by slaves." Then there was the inescapable hazard of degraded soil, particularly that caused by salt buildup: "In dry climates, evaporation of water from the upper layers of soil can leave behind in the root zone a layer of salt that is damaging to crops." She cites research that suggests soil salinization from irrigation played a part in the downfall of civilizations, including in Sumeria, the Indus River Valley, and Mesopotamia.

We face the same vulnerability, says Postel, even as we're increasingly reliant on irrigated agriculture. Compared with the year 1800, which she says marks the dawn of the modern irrigation age, today more than thirty times as much land is under irrigation systems of one kind or another. And yet, according to the United Nations University Institute for Water, Environment and Health, every day the world loses some 2,000 hectares of farmland to salinity. In total, about 20 percent of global land under irrigation—the square-mile equivalent of France—has been left unfarmable due to accumulated salts in soil.[10] A related problem is waterlogging, where water at the root zone impedes the flow of oxygen. Ironically, this is a consequence of irrigation; without proper drainage the water table can rise, slowing growth and diminishing yields.

Irrigation has created a groundwater crisis as well. In many places around the world, including Mexico and the western United States, we're drawing down water reserves several times faster than can be replenished by natural processes. The Ogallala Aquifer, which provides agricultural water for eight states in the Great Plains, is being depleted at an alarming rate. Postel, who is director and founder of the Global Water Policy Project, writes: "As much as 10 percent of the world's food is produced by overpumping groundwater. This creates a bubble in the food economy far more serious than the recent housing, credit, or dot-com bubbles, for we are meeting some of today's food needs with tomorrow's water."[11]

Christine Jones, who initially entered public debate when she took on conventional wisdom on Australia's dryland salinity crisis, echoes Postel's warning about irrigation. In an e-mail she wrote: "Over the history of humankind, every irrigation system, everywhere in the world (other than water diversions in the wet tropics) has failed. Taking entire communities—and sometimes civilizations—with it."

We know irrigation presents its own problems. We hear about squabbles over sources of water, such as the Colorado River, whose total allocation far exceeds the amount actually there. We read about the race to drill for water at lower and lower depths, which Tom Philpott describes as a "hydrological arms race" in *Mother Jones*.[12] And some spectacular episodes of subsidence, in which so much water is removed from below that the ground sinks, along with whatever schools, roads and bridges happen to be nearby, have made this national news.[13]

For the moment, however, let's hear the plant's perspective.

When it comes to irrigation, water is not simply water, Kempf says. He means that the sources of water used for crops—be it well, river or reservoir—vary as to the mineral salts that they carry. The degree to which salts are present in water is referred to as "hardness," generally described in terms of grains per gallon. ("Salt" in this context is not what you'd sprinkle on scrambled eggs, but the combination of elements with a positive charge [cation] and negative charge [anion].) Kempf says that poor water quality, specifically water with high levels of calcium carbonate (lime), is a problem not often acknowledged in public discussions of agriculture—but one that affects crop production and, ironically, leads to a higher use of water.

"The level of minerals affects not only plants' ability to absorb water, but also how the plant can absorb nutrition," says Kempf. "Hard water requires more energy, and therefore nutrition, to break it down. When water quality is poor, more water is required." Farms do regularly test for water quality, and he says that when a potential client's water source has more than five grains per gallon he recommends that it be treated.

"When farms irrigate with poor-quality water there are multiple effects," he says. "It ties up all the nutrients that have been applied in the form of fertilizers. It significantly suppresses soil biology. And what often happens is that sodium and calcium bicarbonates accumulate in the soil profile. This leads to salinity."

By binding nutrients and inhibiting biological processes in the soil, hard water undermines the plants' ability to reach higher stages of health. This results in less-resilient crops and precludes the water-saving efficiencies that characterize robust plants. Plus, additional water may be needed to correct the problems associated with poor-quality water. For example, soil salinity is typically addressed by flushing the area with large amounts of water. That's why salinity tends to be a problem in dryer areas like Australia and the Northern Great Plains in Canada and the United States. Here in Vermont, for example, our copious rains would easily wash out excess saltiness. However, Kempf is not talking only about places like California, where he says the situation is endemic. "Ohio, Pennsylvania and the entire Midwest have this problem," he says. "But no one talks about it."

At the close of each growing season, the Advancing Eco Agriculture team gathers for a debriefing. "We sit around as a group and go through our entire list of customers," Kempf says. "Who got the results that we would have expected? And whose results were we not satisfied with? The farmer might be ecstatic. He might have gotten a 20 or 30 percent increase in yield. But in many cases we may feel there's still a lot left on the table here, much opportunity for improvement.

"When we went through this process in the fall of 2014, we discovered that there was one common factor among all the farms that, by our standards, were doing poorly. It was that they had poor-quality water. In particular, they were putting on foliar applications [spraying directly on leaves] with poor-quality water. Whenever a farmer puts on applications with hard water, particularly water that has bicarbonates, I would say it's not going to be 100 percent effective." It's gotten to the point where the company will not work with clients unless a water quality problem is addressed, he says. "If a farmer wants to work with us and has poor-quality water, we will not sell him the product unless he changes the water because we know the program won't work and that he'll blame it on us."

The company sets a limit of five grains of hardness per gallon for foliar water and ten grains for irrigation. "Eighty-five percent of all the water used on farms in this country falls into this spectrum—in excess of five grains per gallon," Kempf says. "We don't hear about it in the Midwest because we get rain that flushes the toxins out of the soil. If we did not get rain we would have the same problems as in California to a lesser degree."

It's impossible to fully address water quality without discussing nitrogen. According to Christine Jones, farmers globally apply more than $100 billion in nitrogen fertilizers to their crop fields and pastures each year. Less than half of this is actually taken up by plants. The remainder, between 60 and 90 percent, "is leached into water, volatized into the air or immobilized in soil."[14] That excess nitrogen will inevitably cause problems. In terms of the atmosphere, increased fertilizer use is associated with the rise in emissions of nitrous oxide, a greenhouse gas with 300 times more impact than CO_2.[15] As for water, the USDA's Economic Research Service estimates that removing nitrates from municipal water supplies costs Americans more than $4.8 billion each year.[16] We can thank excessive use and poor management of nitrogen (and phosphorus) fertilizers for algae blooms and the 6,000-square-mile dead zone in the Gulf of Mexico. Because nitrogen fertilizers are relatively cheap, farmers have an incentive to apply more rather than less. The UN's Food and Agricultural Organization suggests that nitrogen fertilizer use worldwide will continue to grow, surpassing 200 million metric tons (220 million tons) in 2018.[17]

Jones says the ecological fallout of widespread nitrogen fertilizer use goes far beyond pollution. Inorganic nitrogen alters biological systems in the soil in a way that results in a greater use of water. The problem, as I heard her articulate it at the 2014 Quivira Conference in Albuquerque, is that "in pursuit of yield we've uncoupled the linkages between carbon, nitrogen and water."

If irrigation is the story of farming, nitrogen is what drives the story of the Green Revolution. All living things require nitrogen; nitrogen compounds, such as amino acids, are central to the production of proteins. As it happens, there's plenty of nitrogen around; it accounts for 78 percent of our atmosphere. However, the N_2 gas is very stable, and not available to plants. The nitrogen needs to be "fixed"—its bonds severed—via lightning or nitrogen-fixing bacteria in the soil or in the root nodules of legumes. Usable nitrogen is also present in plant and animal waste, albeit released slowly. Keeping enough nitrogen in the system has been an ongoing challenge for farmers. Most relied on manure, composting, and crop rotation or cover crops, particularly from plants in the legume family, like peas and clovers.

Everything changed in 1909 with the arrival of the Haber-Bosch process, an energy-intensive, high-heat means of synthesizing plant-ready forms of nitrogen from nitrogen gas, literally creating fertilizer out of thin air. The manufacture of nitrogen fertilizer brought about increased crop production, industrial-scale farming operations, and the advent of high-yield plant varieties—all features of the Green Revolution, which began in the 1940s and both served and propelled the dramatic growth in world population. (The Haber-Bosch technology also facilitated industrial warfare, as it's integral to the mass production of explosives, like mustard gas, nitroglycerin and TNT.)

Jones stresses the difference between organic nitrogen, which is the most prevalent form in natural systems, and *in*organic nitrogen, found in synthesized fertilizers. In her Quivira talk, Jones invited us to consider nitrogen in a natural system. You can tell that plants are nitrogen-deficient when they turn yellow, she said. As an amateur gardener I know this as I sometimes get yellowing with my tomatoes, particularly on the lower leaves. But if I look around now, in early summer, from where I sit on my back deck, I have a panorama of all kinds of trees and shrubs and unstoppable kiwi vines and nowhere do I see the slightest hint of yellow. Somehow, then, these plants around my property are getting their daily dose of nitrogen. Lightning isn't doled out that evenly, and aside from some clover among the grasses, there are few legumes. So it must be through associations with nitrogen-fixing bacteria.

"I've never seen a nitrogen-deficient plant in a natural ecosystem," says Jones. "Obviously there's something we're doing in agriculture that's interfering with the biological fixation of nitrogen." Practices that inhibit natural nitrogen fixation include keeping bare fallows, inappropriate grazing, using fungicides and pesticides, and applying high rates of nitrogen fertilizer. She calls nitrogen a "double-edged sword," as adding it offers apparent results while at the same time disrupting the systems upon which the crops depend. Farms become reliant on synthetic nitrogen to compensate for impaired soil, Jones says; they need to be weaned from it, as from a drug.

The transfer of fixed nitrogen to plants, in the form of nitrogen compounds like amino acids, takes place via the hyphae of mycorrhizal fungi.

The fungi do not themselves fix the nitrogen. Rather, the nitrogen compounds are part of the trading network for which mycorrhizal fungi often act as broker. In a thriving soil system, plants send carbon exudates out through their roots. These sugars are bartered with microbes and fungi for minerals the plant needs, including nitrogen, often through a mycorrhizal intermediary.

If we zoom in to the cellular level, we see that nitrogen and carbon are inextricably linked: chlorophyll, where photosynthesis takes place, is part of a protein complex, which means it must contain nitrogen. Therefore, photosynthesis cannot be achieved without nitrogen. At the same time, the plant cannot procure nitrogen without carbon compounds that can be exchanged for it.

In bestowing nitrogen upon plants without asking them to "pay" for it with carbon, we've disturbed the arrangement. "When crops and pastures are not performing, we tend to want to add something to the soil to fix it, and that's usually nitrogen. By using inorganic nitrogen we're short-circuiting the pathway," says Jones. "The plant doesn't need to provide carbon to microbes in exchange for nitrogen, and therefore the plant is not getting the other nutrients the microbes are also providing."

With no need to deal in carbon, plants get lazy. "Due to the use of synthetic nitrogen, there's a loss of carbon in the soil," says Jones. "Therefore the soil no longer has structure, and water-holding capacity is reduced. And because plants are not getting trace elements, plant immunity is down. This leaves them susceptible to pests and disease and now farmers need expensive pesticides. It messes up the food chain. Plus, we need more water because the soil isn't retaining it." She stresses that the plants may look just fine—certainly no yellowing since there's nitrogen galore—but the edifice that supports them is crumbling.

Jones urges us not to underestimate these invisible alliances that she calls, collectively, "the microbial bridge." "We have to remember that plants can't move, but they do signal. Minerals are not just floating around in the soil, they are bound up. They need bacterial and fungal enzymes to release them. The plant provides the biochemical energy, the fuel, for these ecosystem processes." In so doing, the plant helps to build soil.

In terms of water, Jones says, "we now know that in order to sequester carbon, we also need to sequester nitrogen. The building of soil aggregates through carbon and nitrogen co-sequestration results in greater water infiltration, less evaporation and greater water-holding capacity. Nitrogen must be obtained through a microbial intermediary in order for carbon to be channeled to the soil. What happens when we interrupt the cycle is that we start to lose function in soils. The plant is in the drivers' seat, but needs microbial partners."

Jones laments that the way agricultural research is conducted distorts our understanding of the plant-soil system in what John Kempf calls "the real world." "Experiments are undertaken in greenhouses and laboratories in ways that reduce the influences of biological processes," she says. "To reduce 'background noise,' inputs are tested in a homogenous, often sterile environment. If experiments were undertaken in biologically active soil they would often get totally different results."

Can we reconnect carbon, nitrogen and water in our agricultural systems? Think about how vibrant our crops could be. And how much water we could save.

Back in Ohio, young men and women working on the farm stop in to report to Kempf about work they've finished and when they'll start the next morning. Kempf says the Pure Dawn Farms team now consists of three full-time employees, five seasonal employees and nine interns—the latter from as far away as India and Brazil. I take a handful of nuts and cranberries and reflect on an earlier part of our conversation when I'd asked Kempf, perhaps inappropriately, what kept him in the Amish community.

He said he liked "the place Amish have for children and young people. They are granted a strong sense of belonging and community. It's the entire community structure. Young people are given responsibility to the family and for community events, and spend most of their time contributing and not receiving.

"Let's say a boy's father is a carpenter in construction. By eighteen he's working with power tools. By the time he's twenty-one he has all the knowledge he needs to start his own business if he wants to. I observe this partly on the farm. I have interns from all over the world. They are passionate about permaculture, healthy food and a healthy ecology. But I can put them side by side with an Amish boy who will exceed their workload by several times. Not that he's working harder, but that he knows how to work with less effort. It's a combination of experience and body mechanics." I don't ask about gender roles, but that ease of work, a kind of bodily oneness with a task that I could never achieve, gave me something to ponder.

Scheduling conversations concluded, Kempf turns back to me and I ask him about the large trough visible through the window. He shrugs and acknowledges that it looks messy out there. This, he says, is a pond-in-progress that was built four days prior. When completed, the pond, now eight feet deep, will collect rain from an area of nearly two square miles. Establishing the pond reflects his concerns about water quality.

"There's a very good reason why we're depending on rainwater stored in ponds as our primary source of irrigation water on this farm," he says. "I believe that's the direction that agriculture needs to go in. We need to completely ignore subsurface water, and for the most part we need to ignore rivers and streams and to allow them to flow naturally. We need to build ponds and reservoirs near the sources of that water before it flows into the rivers and streams and use that for irrigation."

For the farm water system, he says, "I could have drilled a well for this entire farm for about $4,000. Instead, I'm installing this and another pond that will cost us about $60,000. That's why most farmers don't do it—because they're looking purely at the investment cost. I know that the $60,000 pond that I invest in will help me grow a million-dollar crop. The water that the $4,000 well would get would give me an $800,000 crop. The investment will pay for itself several times over."

He explains that well water is usually hard water because it's been filtered through the soil and limestone layers, picking up minerals, particularly carbonates and bicarbonates, along the way. "It's the equivalent of overapplying limestone to soil," he says. "We have a term we coined in the company to get people to stop doing it. We call it 'constipated soil.' Because everything shuts down. Biology shuts down. Mineral nutrition shuts down. And it's like everything is plugged up and it doesn't work."

Can water stress be relieved? I took part in the 2014 Chicago Council on Global Affairs Symposium on Global Agriculture and Food Security, and on the panel on water, A. G. Kawamura, a farmer and former California secretary of agriculture, talked about water-saving strategies being used in California, including "circular systems that reuse water over and over on the farm" and reverse osmosis units wheeled in and out of greenhouses. He said, "We see that within a few decades people are going to call waste a thing of the twentieth century."

That comment stuck with me. And yet the smarter use of water can only take us so far. Certainly it's important not to be reckless with water, as we have been. But it's also important to understand the dynamics of plants, water and soil. Otherwise we're just working at the edges of the problem. For example, at the Chicago Council event there was also much discussion about developing "drought-tolerant crops" through biotechnology. It's difficult to see how this can get farmers through water shortages when the methods of growing said crops, notably the use of chemicals, interferes with the soil's ability to store water and the plant's ability to make efficient use of it.

Soil Carbon Coalition founder Peter Donovan has for long stretches parked his school bus home near agricultural land on California's Central Coast, giving him much opportunity to ponder water and farming. "The whole system involves producing plants with tillage and irrigation," he says. "There's a tremendous emphasis on the efficiency of irrigation, but it's all technology: drip irrigation with moisture sensors in the soil to time it better. But because of the tillage and the loss of biodiversity in the soil, you need more water because you're not capturing or holding water. It's farming on soils without structure or biodiversity. The real efficiency is biological, which few people are paying attention to."

By biological efficiency, Donovan means maintaining the integrity of soil aggregates, and keeping the ground covered with plants to support the soil food web and avoid surface evaporation. He notes the irony of hand-drawn protest signs in California complaining about the cuts to farm water that he's seen on bare-tilled fields that, he says, "wouldn't hold an ounce of rain." Such placards bear messages like, "Stop! the Dust Bowl" or "Water Cuts = Lost Jobs." This in no way diminishes the anguish of people dependent on the survival of these farms, but real security will come not by squeezing every last ounce from the Central Valley Aquifer or Colorado River, but by boosting carbon stores in the soil.

The failure to do so results in wasted water, as well as lost agricultural productivity. Donovan is fond of a video from the South Dakota National Resource Conservation Service that shows how various management regimes affect how quickly water soaks in—or how much runs off. On the west side of the fence, under a grazing system that yields healthy, diverse plants, all the water was absorbed in just over ten seconds.[18] On the east side, under continuous season-long grazing, it took more than seven minutes. That's the difference in the soil's capacity to absorb water. The narrator, NRCS grazing specialist Stan Boltz, says every inch of water that runs off represents a loss of up to 150 to 200 pounds of production per acre.

We're then shown a field recently converted to cropland, where the remaining grass had been treated with an herbicide and corn was drilled in without tillage. Here, the water doesn't fully soak into the sampled spot for a full 31 minutes and 13 seconds. "Every minute that goes by is another inch of rain that's going to run off the land," says Boltz. Not only is that a loss of precious moisture, he points out; flowing water whisks away sediments, including nutrients, its "wealth," from the soil. The video opens with the question, "When the rain comes . . . will your soil be ready?"

Singing Frogs Farm in Sebastopol, California, has made water retention a priority. Upon launching their eight-acre vegetable and fruit operation in 2009, farmers Paul and Elizabeth Kaiser made a commitment to building soil rich in organic matter. Their guiding strategy involves not just what they do, but what they *don't* do—namely, plow and till. On the farm's website, they explain that by breaking up aggregates and exposing particles to oxygen, tillage "works much like a bellows on a forge creating rapid and dramatic combustion of the soil's nutrients (such as carbon and nitrogen) and volatilizing them into the atmosphere where they combine with oxygen to form carbon dioxide, nitrous oxide and other potent greenhouse gasses."[19] They point out that while organic systems may avert the wholesale destruction of soil organic matter, whenever there's tillage the soil life, soil aggregation and water-holding capacity will be compromised.

I heard Paul Kaiser speak at Quivira, where he reported how organic no-till provides resilience despite Northern California's capricious rains. A neighboring farm irrigates for three to four hours every day, he said, whereas Singing Frogs Farm uses one hour of drip irrigation every five to seven days. (Part of the differential reflects the method of irrigation: with sprinklers, some water evaporates before it even meets the plant.) He described a recent weather episode that saw eleven inches of rain tumble from the sky after ten months of zero precipitation. "The neighbor's plants drowned and had 100 percent crop loss," he said, while Singing Frogs lost nothing. He said the farm's productivity is nine times the state average.

Another water-conserving strategy with multiple benefits is off-season cover crops. Between the trees at Dixon Ridge Farms, an organic walnut operation near Sacramento, California, there's a lush carpet of wintertime green, a mix of plants including legumes for added fertility. The crops' root systems create pore spaces that allow water to slowly percolate into groundwater reserves. In a video, state conservation agronomist Dennis Chessman assures people about a common concern: cover crops won't "rob" the cash crop of the water it needs. For one thing, he says, the cover is grown at a different time of year. Plus, "we've got to get water into the ground for the water to do the plants any good." The cover crops develop soil structure, enhancing water flow. After their season the plants die back, creating a mulch that traps moisture so it moves into the soil. This also protects cash crops from too much water. In the same video, orchard owner Russ Lester says after big rains, uncovered soil seals over and becomes impervious. To illustrate, the video now pans across tired-looking trees standing in mud and water. Though the trees are dormant, the roots are starting to grow, he says: "Just like us, if they are under water, they basically are going to drown."[20] Lester conservatively estimates that the use of cover crops cuts his water use by 20 percent compared with other systems.

It's important to understand the dynamics of water. The plants aren't down there in the soil divvying up the water, arguing about who gets what. Rather, it's about evolving synergies—the ongoing interactions of plants, water, soil and living organisms. Lester points out that irrigation water also benefits wildlife. "I have hawks and raptors and honey bees that wouldn't be here if we didn't irrigate," he says. As water, once used, doesn't simply disappear, it's not always useful to compare foods by how much water is required to grow them. So much depends on management and, as Allan Savory says, making "effective use of rainfall."

John Kempf hopes his 160-acre farm will "show people what the earth can be, and its potential to produce exceptionally healthy crops," and high-light "the potential of plants to be extraordinarily healthy, regenerate the local ecology, and provide food as medicine." Noting California's water crisis, he says, "We can't grow avocados and papayas in Ohio. But we can grow a lot of salad greens and other things."

This first year, he says, they're focusing on annual crops to serve their CSA (community-supported agriculture) supporters and set the stage for cover crops. "We need to build resiliency into agricultural systems so that we can handle what has been happening over the last half decade—which is six weeks of drought followed by six inches of rain in three hours," he says. "That means two things: being able to manage that water when it comes, and store it; and being able to transfer that water back to the farm in the form of irrigation. I see an agricultural ideal in which plants can regulate water on their own. That's possible, but not probable on most farms today because the soil is too unhealthy to support the level of plants that would be able to do that. This is our first year on the farm. We're not there yet."

In 2010, David C. Johnson and his wife, Hui-Chun Su, developed a composting method for the USDA. The process yields compost that's low in salinity (that was the original goal) and rich in microbial life, with a high fungal to bacteria ratio. In field trials, this shift to fungal dominance combined with increased diversity in the soil microbial community has produced twice as much plant growth as the world's most prolific terrestrial ecosystems, which are swamps and rainforests. Plus, an astounding 70 percent of the carbon the plants produce is sent back into the soil.[21]

With so much carbon returned to the soil, the implications for carbon drawdown are huge. In Johnson's latest study, soil carbon was captured at twenty to fifty times the rate shown in previous studies of no-till farming methods. And not just captured, but kept: soil respiration—which we can think of as earth's exhalation, as soil microorganisms release CO_2— decreased as much as four-fold. Our current, low-performing soils may reap similar amounts of carbon, says Johnson, "but their fertility is so low and their carbon-use efficiency is so low that [most] of the carbon captured is respired."

Food and environmental security is often presented as an either/or proposition, as if the directive to "feed the world" requires concessions in terms of ecological integrity. But as Johnson told Kristin Ohlson, author of *The Soil Will Save Us*, the synergies between plants and soil microbial communities in advanced, highly fertile soil could allow for the capture of the equivalent of a year's anthropogenic CO_2 emissions on less than 11 percent of the world's cropland.[22]

Given the urgency of drawing down carbon, this is an extraordinary statement. Particularly as we're not talking about high-tech geoengineering schemes like injecting CO_2 under the ocean or scrubbing CO_2 from the sky. It's simply allying with plant-soil-microbe dynamics to make the most of sunlight, water and nutrients. In other words, a farmer's objective—maximizing photosynthesis—is a goal that will help us grapple with water and climate challenges.

We have a choice ahead of us. We can, through our agricultural practices, create the conditions under which we will thrive—just as plants build carbon- and nutrient-rich soil. Or we can continue to do what we've been doing.

SIX

DEW AND THE DESERT

What Goes Up Must Come Down

Up there is another ocean—

—"Clouds," in *Lost Woods: The Discovered*
Writing of Rachel Carson

All water is a part of other water . . .
Cloud talks to lake . . .
dew takes elevator into cloud.

—Tony Hoagland, "The Social Life of Water"

KATHERINE AND MARKUS OTTMERS LIVE AND WORK
in the dry steppes of far west Texas. Since rains can be few and far between, they've designed the main building at Casa de Mañana—their fifty-by-fifty-foot "rain barn," the off-grid headquarters and enterprise launch pad for Ottmers Agricultural Technologies—to collect both rainwater and condensation. But they had no idea of just how much water they harvested solely from dew until one morning in winter 2012 when the valve burst on one of the water tanks.

Markus was doing ironwork outside when he noticed water gushing from the tank. "Hey, Brad!" he called to his coworker. "Go see how much water is in there. It can't be full. We haven't had any rain in four months." Not only were they rainless; they'd been providing for a herd of some fifty goats, and between six and eight people were regularly taking light showers at their place. Conscious of every bit of water used, Markus knew it was in the neighborhood of fifty to seventy gallons a day.

Brad checked, and the tank was completely full. The Ottmerses continued to monitor the tank, and rose at four thirty the next morning to check its status. Sunrise was yet hours away and stars saturated the sky. This sparsely populated area puts on a night sky as clear as you can find stateside—not just the bright starry dots, but the smudgy sweep of distant galaxies in between. And here, at the edge of the Big Bend, in the midst of Texas's multiyear drought, a bleary-eyed Markus discovered that water was streaming into the tank at a rate that amounted to about sixty gallons a day, enough to cover nearly all of their water needs.

"I was wondering who the water fairy was," Markus recalls. He walks over to the tank and shows us the gauge that told the story. A tall, restless Texan, he possesses an impatient turn of mind that flits toward puzzles and plans that most would dismiss as quixotic if not impossible. It's a quality common to many who work in the loosely defined realm of permaculture, a model for agriculture that emphasizes functional design and draws upon principles observed in natural systems. Among his other areas of expertise—precision earthworks, glass blowing, welding, straw bale and geodome home construction, mycology, and beehive removal and rescue—Markus is a certified permaculture trainer. Katherine and Markus, both from the Texas Hill Country, met in 2008 when she took his permaculture course in Kerrville, dubbed "Kerrmaculture." Katherine, too, is a master of many trades. She's long worked as a landscape designer and has since become a certified Holistic Management educator.

Markus's instinctive mode of action is improvisational, a tendency that's revealed throughout the operation. The barn and outdoor working area are strewn with electrical parts and metal and wheels and plastic piping, combinations of which might be perched on a table as if they'd been tinkered with and then abandoned. But it's an ordered chaos: at any moment, Markus can tell you exactly what he's trying to accomplish, the stage of any given project, and what he's doing that's new.

The source of the collected water—the water fairy that proved more generous than anyone had guessed—was condensation, he tells us. "That water going into the tank is from the roof, because you can see I'm not standing out here with a squeegee," he says. "This is because there's heat on the roof, and breezes coming through. The roof cools off, and then the warm air flows create the condensation."

The barn was structured for solar gain in the winter and shade in the summer, says Markus. While maximizing comfort, so precious in this harsh environment, the design also accentuates the temperature differential. The volume of water is made possible by a four-foot difference between the upper and lower roofs, he says. Because of how the building is situated, the galvanized tin upper roof is "superheating" in the afternoons. It extends over the lower roof, casting a shadow and breaking the sun. Air flows through the building thanks to two air vents: one at the top of the superheated roof and another low on the north side. "The more we can bump up the difference between hot and cold, the more we can create moisture."

An inspiration from nature, he says, is the Namib Desert beetle, which survives in its ultra-arid home on the western coast of southern Africa by harvesting condensation from ocean fog. As the Namib Desert has scant surface water and an annual rainfall around five millimeters, dense fogs become the "lifeblood" of the surprisingly varied wildlife that lives there.[1] Here's how the insects have worked it out: The beetles stand on a crest of dune and, as fog rolls in from the sea, lift their legs as if doing a handstand. Tiny droplets of water roll down their bellies and into their mouths so they can drink. This particular talent has spurred both commercial[2] and philanthropic enterprises based on mimicking beetles' penchant for gathering water.[3] Some designs emulate the patterned surfaces on the insects' back that combine both water-attracting and water-repelling surfaces, though it seems that what's called "fog-basking behavior" is at least as significant.[4]

"The beetle puts its ass to the wind," Markus says. "We built the building copying the beetle." He drops down on bent knees and wiggles his backside in a fair if inelegant approximation of an insect scoping out the mist.

The rain barn is oriented to the east, he says, the source of their desert breezes. Dry as the air might seem, the winds carry water vapor. Enough to bolster the water supply for the Ottmerses and whoever among a continually evolving circle of friends and colleagues might be staying on-site; enough so that an east-facing building with heat-absorbing metal and cooling drafts can regularly "bask" in condensation.

And yes, they drink the water, which is filtered through a Brita gravity pitcher. The water tank is aerated with air stones and an air pump, the kind of system you'd put in an aquarium. The inflow and outflow is completely screened, and the piping from the tank has an inline sediment filter.

As a result, the Ottmerses don't feel the same stress about water that troubles many of their neighbors. When Tony and I checked into the Wild Horse Station, a group of rentable cabins tucked into hills along the route to the ghost town at Terlingua—community booster bumper sticker sighted: HOTTER'N HELL AND COOLER'N SHIT—the proprietor, Louise Hammer, respectfully encouraged us to be sparing with the water.

"That's what's going to get us down here," Hammer said. She lamented that though they've had higher than usual rainfall, complete with greened-up hills and banner wildflower displays, "all that rain isn't helping us." Alas, she told us, the water table has been falling.

By contrast, up the road at the Ottmerses' place the water tanks are keeping pace with people's needs. A refreshing after-siesta rinse can be had without guilt. Katherine and Markus's dwelling, a one-time Katrina FEMA trailer, has air-conditioning, and a bucket by the three-step entrance catches the condensation drip. At any given moment, a chicken from among their mixed flock of seventy or so egg-laying or stew birds may stop by to take a drink. On one corner of the FEMA trailer roof, there's a tiny gap where the condensate gathers. In the heat of the day, many of the bees from the closest apiary dart up to that spot, nabbing sips of water before going off to forage or to rejoin the hive. It's an entire ecosystem fueled by variants of dew.

I met Katherine in Albuquerque at the 2014 Quivira Conference, an annual event devoted to enhancing Western landscapes. I was immediately intrigued by the way she talked about water, how she seemed to have a different relationship to it than anyone I'd met. She told me about "guzzlers," instances like that winter day when condensation from the roof caused the water tank to overflow. She said that in the desert, "we don't have a lot of rain, but we have 'moisture events.'" She told me about "nutrient dense fogs" with morning mists so thick "you can't see the truck in the driveway." She described how such events, which may materialize between five and eight times a year, kindle something in the vegetation: "The plants are a lot happier with that little bit of moisture. Everything shifts right after that, as if there's been some nutrient exchange."

I was charmed by Katherine's evocative use of language—I'd later learn that she'd been a student of linguistics—and unusual way of looking at things. She said she and her husband ranched at the bottom of Big Bend Valley, a place so remote it's "like living on the moon." A keen awareness of the patterns, movement and gifts of water seemed to inform everything they did. "We're so sensitive to water that we can tell the little shifts in the moisture in the air," she said. "We're like the desert plants that way."

Over the months, from our respective landscapes and very different sorts of winter, we kept in touch. In March she wrote, ecstatic about the drenching rains that seemed to wake up the earth after several dry years: "Wildflowers so crazy good that professional photographers are coming out of the woodwork to take pictures! This place is starting to look like Ireland! The desert has grown a green fur." She sent photos of moisture events: bands of fog riding the horizon, thick as smoke. She shared news of the "explosion" of Africanized bees that followed the blaze of wildflowers, which meant paid bee removal work for Markus. "One of the biggest tricks out here on the moon is to get a gig and make a living," she wrote. "You don't need much currency. There are very active bartering, trading and non-cash transactions."

Between the epic, transformative fogs, the water-making roof, and the hyperperceptive desert plants, I figured if anyone could share the nuances of condensation, and how to use it to advantage in an arid landscape—indeed, how to eke out moisture in a desert climate, a timely question given the spread of desert conditions across the globe—it was this admirably self-sufficient pair. And so, in high summer Tony and I once again fly to El Paso for a trip into the Chihuahuan Desert. This time, rather than driving south into Mexico, we hew to the U.S. side of the border heading eastward into Brewster County, where little more than 9,000 people fill an area larger than the state of Connecticut. Here, in the biggest county in a state known for bigness, multihour jaunts for groceries and supplies are a given and *neighbor* is a relative term.

The towns and exit signs quickly thin out once we leave El Paso. It's well into the 90s as we veer south from the junction at Van Horn and pass through mostly vacant scrubland. On the road there's a disconcerting mirage effect, likely caused by the heat and reflected clouds. The asphalt seems to glisten as if wet from rain, and then as we approach the shimmer dissolves. Stretch after stretch of this and I begin to understand how distance and heat in a punishing landscape can make one feel a little crazy, with water always tantalizingly one span of highway beyond, perpetually beyond your grasp.

Past Alpine the hills are green and full of flowers, variations of yellow and white among silvery grasses and shrubby stands of mesquite and scrub oak, testimony to the ample rainfall Katherine described. In this high chaparral we see cattle and horses, pretty and robust, and flowering yuccas and agaves. We rise and dip past Cathedral Mountain (6,800 feet), Elephant Mountain (6,230 feet) and a backdrop of high mesas that reminds me of the Las Damas Mountains, on the Mexican side of this same desert, that give Alejandro Carrillo's ranch its name. The sky is the powder blue of a boy's baby blanket. As we move into lower elevation, the ground has more bare patches between the brush and rock. I remark to Tony that with restorative grazing this would be beautiful grassland. With all my reporting on Holistic Management, I realize, I've developed a knack for backseat grazing.

We arrive close to 6 p.m., and as it's still awfully hot we park ourselves at a table by a large, whirling fan that keeps the air temperature within the realm of tolerable. Katherine explains that she and Markus go back and forth between their two properties: Casa de Mañana, where we are, and Rancho de Mañana, the ranch her sister purchased for her in 2010 and which we will visit tomorrow. (In Spanish the names mean "House of Tomorrow" and "Ranch of Tomorrow," respectively.) The ranch is about a square mile, just shy of a "section" in land surveying terms. It's on an old trading trail on which goods were carried by camel. Who knew there were camels in Texas? They did fine with little water but apparently their soft feet, ideal for traversing sandy terrain, fared less well on rough, rocky paths.[5]

"We chose the ranch because it has water," Katherine says. "The water flows under the land. In the desert, you're not going to see it sitting on top." A "running riparian sponge" fills with rainwater and spring water; at times the wild burros that roam the property can kick at the ground and access water. "People say if it's not permanent water, it has no value. If it's water in the soil or air, it has no value. Nothing has value unless you can get it out of your tap." This was once seen as prime agricultural land and was farmed for the area's cinnabar mines, significant sources of mercury ore. The land includes part of Alamo de Cesario Creek, and there are cottonwood trees that indicate a dependable source of water. (*Alamo* is the Spanish word for cottonwood.)

Among all the couple's other projects they've managed to put some work into the ranch, including installing a four-foot culvert and gravel-filled French drain to redirect flow, and shaped the land surface so that it retains water. "Markus put in a permanent berm and swale with really precise GPS input," says Katherine. "This has meant three million gallons of water that we're able to keep on the land. We've already gotten increases in well-level depth."

Katherine initially had a herd of Nigerian Dwarf dairy goats on the ranch, in part for the milk products but also to restore the land. This plan ended tragically. "In 2014 we'd had them with a buck, and we were within a month of kidding season," she recalls. "Markus and I were working in Kerrville and there was a family on the ranch taking care of the goats. There was a mix-up of communication and the animals were left too long in a pasture with Johnson grass." Under certain conditions, this grass produces prussic acid, which is toxic to animals and humans. In this instance, there was a hot day followed by a freeze, and all fifty-eight animals died. Katherine tells the story: "We got a call that five goats died. Then another call. Then it was clear none survived. I'm tracking it back to the lack of leadership on my part. I was doing too much." Devastated, Katherine and Markus took on some projects back in the Hill Country until their neighbors urged them to come back to the area.

"The challenge is to find enterprises to keep both properties going," says Katherine. She facilitates the Texas Chicks Working Group for producers of non-GMO, pastured poultry products and helps local women with business plans. Some of this is paid work; most is for building community. They just became a commissioned guide service with the Big Bend Ranch State Park. They're also launching a women-operated, women-run, women's guide service. These days, however, their main business is bee removal—a vocation that's not for the faint of heart.

Out here bees are no small nuisance. Around the time I visited, two people in the region died from being attacked by Africanized, aka killer, bees, in one case when a man's bulldozer disturbed a hive. As the name suggests, these bees are not native. Call them uninvited guests. Southern African bees were originally brought to Brazil in the 1950s in order to breed a more productive variety. ("Mixing stoner Brazilian bees and hyperactive bees," says Markus.) Several swarms escaped and have since been traveling up through the United States, wreaking havoc along the way.

Markus has been asked to do bee removals in houses and barns and places like the Fort Davis National Historic Site, a building in Presidio that was once Pancho Villa's armory, and Big Bend Ranch State Park, where bees established themselves in a composting toilet. "Bees that are sweet bees, we rehive them in our apiaries," says Katherine. "We harvest wild honey and make wax products."

While we're waiting for the others to return from swimming at a nearby ranch (near by South Brewster County standards) we go out for a stroll. Markus shows us how he's worked with the land's contours to steer the water where he'd like it to go. "The water comes in here, and makes a slight curve this way," he says, pointing out various plants, some of which are in flower. Behind where he's built a berm, it's ten degrees cooler—a bit of microclimate refreshment that we all take a few moments to savor. "The water here is six feet deep and the trees are taller," he points out. If similar principles were applied at the nearby O2 Ranch, says Markus, "you could change the weather," he says. The ranch he refers to is 275,000 acres, more than 400 square miles. Weather is to a large extent determined by the movement of water and water vapor, he says—and we have great influence over its flows and patterns.

Markus gestures toward the east where there's a large, dark gray cloud the shape of a cartoon alien spaceship. He says, "A thunderhead. Someone's getting rain over there." This is a cumulonimbus cloud, otherwise known as a storm cloud, the kind of cloud that makes the sky go dark. This particular specimen stays where it is so just one spot somewhere off in the distance gets the benefit of its cooling bounty. "A secret of the desert is that our most extreme weather, our strongest heat, triggers thunderstorms," Katherine says.

Katherine says their larger goal is "oasification," bringing life to their desert landscape beginning with the soil. Across the arid Southwest, she says, "the land is not in motion. And when you take things out of motion they're dead."

Animals are key to this vision. She quotes permaculture founder Bill Mollison, who once said, "'The humid environment of the desert exists in the rumen of an animal.' You can't have soil in the desert without having animals." For now they're working with chickens, quail and bees, but she hopes to incorporate more animals as well. Nor does she discount the people: "Everywhere there's a person, that person is carrying and transporting things and so we pollinate. We bring our seeds and our actions and our waste and our ideas. In that sense we play a similar role to the herds. Here we are the largest animals in the landscape. Like animals managed well, we can act upon the land in a positive way."

As a landscape designer, she says, "I was doing permaculture without telling anybody about it. People would spend $80,000 to $100,000 on landscapes, and they didn't have anything to eat from them." Her work began shifting toward native, wild plants and edible landscapes, and she recognized the social and ecological implications of land restoration. "I went from being a doomer to a prepper to a new agrarian," she says. "I'm a new grandmother, and that makes me ask, Where are we now? A lot of people are asking that question. When you move to the desert you're directly addressing an issue: degraded land."

Katherine says there's a movement of people rallying around the goal of greening the arid lands that sprawl across far west Texas. Those involved share several sources of inspiration: Geoff Lawton, an Australian permaculture educator who created a productive ten-acre oasis on dry, salty land in Jordan[6]; Masanobu Fukuoka, the late author/philosopher whose "Do-Nothing Farming" suggests strategies for revegetating desert lands[7]; and the Israeli kibbutz as a model for communal living and technical innovation. She says this part of Texas falls along an ancient migratory route known as the Rio de la Vida, or "River of Life," which runs from the Four Corners down to

Lake Titicaca in the Andes. The Rio de la Vida corresponds to an energetic ley-line, or sacred pathway, recognized by traditional people. Indigenous lore included a prophecy that the time when grains again flourish in the Four Corners area will spark a period of prosperity for all people. Those who choose to be desert dwellers are cocreating something out of nothing here, she says. "It's time to kick-start this landscape for human habitat."

It's dark now and the others now living at Casa de Mañana—Ember, in her twenties and from Nebraska; Don, also from Texas, an elder with knowledge of medicinal plants; and Stacy and Lee, a father and son related to Markus from the Hill Country—have returned, plenty hungry. Lee is newly thirteen, and his after-school curriculum at Casa de Mañana includes blacksmithing, beekeeping, mapping, and learning about the chicken business. Markus lights the shoulder-high torch lamps that border one wall and we sit down to dinner. After a day of penetrating heat, once the air passes a certain threshold of cool there's a great, physical sense of relief, a shared reprieve, however fleeting, that creates a feeling of intimacy. We all go outside to look at the night sky, remarking on its clarity; blink, and you'll miss a shooting star. A light breeze brushes my skin, air that will circulate between the roofs as we sleep, yielding tomorrow's water.

Condensation is all around us. It's when you pick up your cool drink on a summer day and water droplets have formed on the glass. It's when you step out onto grass early in the morning and your feet get wet, or when you get in a car that's been sitting in heat and your sunglasses steam up. It's when you're walking in the city and a few drops fall on your head. You look up to see if it could possibly be raining despite the immaculate blue spanning the sky, and realize it's just the drip from someone's noisy air-conditioning unit. Condensation is at work every time it rains or snows.

Most simply, condensation is the process of water in its gaseous form turning to liquid, what scientists call a phase transition. There is always water in the atmosphere, even in a dry environment like the Chihuahuan Desert and even in a drought. The condensation part happens when warm and cold collide. As when the nighttime air hovers over a pond whose surface has been warmed by the sun and a bank of fog materializes. Or when the evening breeze circulates between the sunbaked upper roof and the shaded plane below the Ottmerses' rain barn.

The dew point is the temperature at which the atmosphere is fully saturated with moisture. Once the air temperature cools beyond the dew point, the moisture will condense to create clouds, fog or dew. Arid environments have wide temperature swings—hot during the day and cold at night—so that the air consistently crosses the brink at which dew will form, a discrepancy that, as the Ottmerses' experience demonstrates, you can make use of.

Condensation is the reverse of transpiration, its meteorological mirror. Transpiration absorbs latent heat. Condensation releases this withheld heat. This doesn't necessarily mean a temperature increase. Rather, the conferred heat contributes to the amassing and ascent of clouds. When water shifts from liquid to gas, the molecules spread out; when water vapor becomes a liquid, the molecules retract and move closer together.

Condensation scarcely comes up in conversations about water. And yet many ancient cultures had a tradition of collecting dew for drinking or cultivating plants. When in synagogue, I've always noticed that the "standing prayer," the Amidah, includes a blessing for rain during the winter while in summer we thank God for "life-giving dew." In the past I've regarded this as merely poetic, but now understand that dew was important in ancient times. Israelites built low walls around plants to capture moisture, and throughout the region and elsewhere it was common to gather morning dew from carefully assembled piles of stones.[8] In many cultures, ways of maximizing condensation fall into the realm of folk wisdom. For example, Tony told me that in the Western Desert of Africa, where his uncle Robert served during World War II, South African troops used to arrange their sleeping tarps so as to collect valuable drinking water.

There are a few philanthropic efforts that rely on condensation. For example, the Canadian nonprofit FogQuest uses mesh fog nets to bolster water supplies for rural communities in several countries including Nepal, Ethiopia, Eritrea and Guatemala. FogQuest is also working in the Atacama Desert in Chile, deemed the driest place on earth, but where a brewery is now making beer from fog-harvested water.[9] An Italian project, Warka Water, builds towers that capture rain, fog and dew water in the atmosphere for people in remote areas in Ethiopia who lack access to clean water. The design is modeled on moisture-collecting examples in nature, such as cacti, spiderwebs, leaves of the lotus flower and that fog-catching icon, the Namib beetle.[10]

For using condensation to grow plants there's the Groasis Waterboxx, which employs several strategies, including the collection of dew, to nurture trees in degraded lands. This program earned Dutch inventor Pieter Hoff a *Popular Science* "Best of What's New Innovation of the Year Award" in 2010.[11] An Israeli company called Tal-Ya (Hebrew for "God's Dew") Water Technologies has devised reusable dew-collecting trays that capture condensation and direct it to the roots of plants. Inventor Avraham Tamir says the system allows growers to avoid the salinity problems that are common with irrigation since condensation distills and therefore purifies the water.[12]

For the most part, however, few in either the industrialized or the developing world are looking to condensation for answers to water problems. Dew and other forms of condensation seem ethereal as opposed to practical, serendipitous rather than dependable. One can only conclude that these distilled beads of moisture, no matter how winsomely clasped among flower petals, wouldn't make a dent in our water challenges—even in the aggregate. For those drips and droplets are only incidental, whereas the real water action must be in our rivers, lakes and reservoirs.

Not everyone agrees; in fact, many would say that we've overlooked a vital water source. Or, pulling from the headlines, condensation represents a "Mist Opportunity."[13] There's much potential condensation out there. To put this notion in context, water in the form of vapor exceeds the amount in the world's rivers by a factor of five.

Peter Andrews, an Australian farmer and horse breeder, is a condensation champion. The developer of Natural Sequence Farming, a model for ecological restoration based on reinstating the way water moves across the land surface, Andrews emphasizes dew's significance to what he calls the "daily water cycle." In an interview with the Australian Broadcasting Corporation, he argued that dew is "the most important water on the landscape, and it's the purest."[14]

Andrews drew his interviewer's attention to the types of plants that are riddled with barbs and thorns. These include nuisance plants like prickly pear, Bathurst burr, and Paterson's Curse—weeds whose very names have sharp edges. "The condensation occurs first around those furry leaves, like Paterson's Curse, and the thorns that other things have got—that's their job. Their job is to harvest that atmospheric water and cover the ground when everything else has failed, to keep it in a state that, when it does rain, the recovery will happen."[15] Andrews, whose belief that each weed has an ecological value has raised ire in his country, adds that dew softens spiky weeds so that cattle are able to graze them.

Fellow Australian Chris Henggeler says he pays as much attention to dew as to other sources of water. Henggeler manages Kachana Station, a nearly 200,000-acre tract of rugged, inaccessible rangeland in Western Australia's Kimberley region. When he leased the land in 1989, it was barren and desolate. He attributes the property's remarkable transformation to keeping water on the land, and says dew has played a key role.

When managing land, Henggeler wrote to me in an e-mail, "often we tend to overlook and undervalue the work performed by microorganisms and the importance of observing what's happening at micro-environmental levels. Similarly, we tend to ignore what could be termed the 'micro-water-cycle.'" He said that a core goal of his is to have healthy vegetation on the land— robust plant communities that "create and maintain stable microclimates," distinct pockets of favorable conditions and ambience, like the cool mini-oasis at Casa de Mañana that was a welcome refuge on a scorching day.

Such verdant enclaves, says Henggeler, enhance water on a larger scale by (1) attracting moisture in the air, and (2) retaining and recycling the moisture transpired by plants in the form of dew. The plant and microbial life keeps moisture in the local environment. This moisture allows for cooling processes like transpiration to take place. In a living system moisture generates more moisture, of which dew is one manifestation.

In a "brittle environment"—places with seasonal rains like Zimbabwe and northern Australia as well as many parts of Texas—this can mean the difference between a lush, productive landscape and a drying cycle leading inexorably to desertification. The margins on which land turns are that fine. Henggeler says, "There are all those additional microorganisms that can keep active throughout extended periods well after the rainy season—as long as they get a 'watering' each night."

On summer mornings I love the feel of dew on my feet and, in my flower garden, the way round droplets lie cradled in leaves and blooms, like pearls. To me these are sights that radiate well-being, a sense, perhaps transient like dew itself, that all is right in the world.

Ohio farmer John Kempf says he regards dew as an intrinsic part of the earth's 24-hour cycle of inhalation and exhalation, and that dew formation and volume indicate the health and vigor of growing plants. In the ultimate expression of dew, he says, "the droplets are perfectly round. They are standing straight up from the leaf as if they are balanced on the tip of a pin, though there's almost no contact. When there are threshold mornings, mornings when it's almost at the dew point but not quite, healthy plants will form a strong amount of dew and unhealthy plants will form none. I've seen it side by side in the same field. All you need to destroy that capacity—the plant's nutritional status and its rootedness in place—is to spray that plant with a fungicide or insecticide. And it's gone."

Some plants, such as coastal trees and ferns, are able to take in condensed water through their leaves. For the most part, however, condensation serves plants two ways: cooling the plant to minimize water loss, and falling onto understory plants or the ground where it can be taken up by the roots (this water is called "fog drip").

Animals also make use of condensation. Glenn Gall, who has holistically managed sheep and cows on land near Oberlin, Ohio, says, "My sheep hardly need to go to the trough once grasses are four inches high." In 2012, when his flock had grown to forty-five animals on five acres, he says, "enough moisture was provided on the surfaces and in the grass to satisfy the sheep over some periods of days. Even into early afternoon on sunny days, I would get wet ankles from the dew."

In places where water is at a premium, an understanding of dew can help one make best use of the moisture available. "Condensation is an important strategy for planting here," says Katherine Ottmers. "You plant where the morning sun can't hit the leaves until a time after the dew dries. You situate the plant so that there's something to block the eastern light for an hour or two." This allows water to soak into the root zone before that Texas sun really starts bearing down.

Peter Andrews's observations about thorny, thistly plants calls attention to another principle: certain plants "specialize" in fog, having evolved to harness the recurrent condensation in their environment. For example, Arizona rainwater harvester Brad Lancaster says that condensation—in this case fog—built the majestic forests of the Pacific west. "Coastal redwoods are phenomenal at capturing moisture," he told me. "In the summer, while they have no rain, these trees are creating their own rain. The needle structure changes from the top down. They've adapted to comb the moisture from the air. This dramatically increases the amount of precipitation available to the tree and the understory."

It is hard to fathom just how much moisture it must take to grow such a massive tree. UC Berkeley researcher Todd E. Dawson found that redwoods glean between 25 to 40 percent of their water from maritime fog. The fog drip then furnishes water to the dense, varied understory. The coastal trees will ultimately transpire this fog-borne water, moving moisture inland and supporting rain and snow in the interior. And it's not only moisture that's wafting in from the sea: the winds off the coast roil the waters so as to lift nutrients to the surface, and this becomes part of the mist.[16]

Which brings to mind the "nutrient-dense fog" Katherine had mentioned when we initially met. A few years back, Katherine's sister had purchased a home with some land on the edge of the Laguna Hills in Southern California. Markus observed that its orientation to the ocean made it a great place for a garden, and helped to create an edible landscape. The plants are flourishing in part thanks to the regular fogs, he says.

"Dew is the most consistent water source there is," Markus says. He and Katherine believe there's value to the hydrological cycle, because that predictability—embodied in dew or the summer rains referred to locally as "monsoons"—allows one to plan. Katherine says she recently took part in a drought-mitigation workshop with Richard Teague, a range scientist with Texas A&M University who, like Allan Savory, is originally from Zimbabwe and studied in South Africa. Teague stressed the value of regular sources of moisture during a period of climate change and instability. "Professor Teague said that today we should *all* consider ourselves to be in a 'brittle' environment," she recalls, in reference to the term Savory employs for places with seasonal rainfall, landscapes whose viability turns on holding on to moisture. "This is because no one's getting the regular rains anymore."

The plan for the next day is to go out to the ranch, but not till the heat of midday since Katherine wants to show us how the cottonwoods "rain." On certain hot days, she explains, cottonwoods on the ranch seem to pump out water, with a drip so steady you can watch it fall into a cup. "We've seen the ground pick up so much water that near the trees we had five pounds of mushrooms."

This puts us in the unlikely, bordering on masochistic, position of waiting until the temperature becomes utterly unbearable and then forging out into the scorching glare. To bide time we gather around the table, eating eggs and tortillas, chatting and periodically checking e-mails, as the large metal fan twirls valiantly beside us.

For many new-breed desert dwellers, Katherine says, Hurricanes Katrina and Rita were a "game changer." Don, who was living in Jasper, Texas, during the storms, says the weather systems "came and sat over us. I bought gasoline to help people who were stuck on the freeway without any. Everyone was sleeping on the upper deck of my apartment building. The whole place turned into a community."

Katherine says so many fleeing the storms came to Kerrville that people ran out of gas and water. In anticipation that such crises will continue to happen, some who saw firsthand the vulnerability of our food and energy distribution systems have chosen to prepare for resilience. "There will continue to be movements of people for a lot of reasons," she says. "We have an opportunity to create community in the desert. People want to be part of the paradigm shift. I like to think of Casa de Mañana as one big art project. Our canvas is degraded land."

She says that aside from the new metal roof, the rain barn was built from salvaged materials. The building's frame was assembled from surplus oil field piping. The sign at Casa de Mañana's entrance reads "Bloom Where You Are Planted."

A little after noon we decide the weather is sufficiently sweltering and miserable, so we stuff a cooler with snacks and water bottles and pile into one of the pickup trucks. Stacy has offered to drive. This turns out to be a very good thing as the recent rains have washed out part of the road to the ranch, requiring some heroic path shoveling on his part. Even without the messed up road it's a long drive through old mining country—gold, agate, silver and opal in addition to cinnabar—which might only be fifteen miles but it's hot and bumpy, flat and harsh.

Near the property Katherine draws our attention to a chunk of road that always has flooding problems. She notes that had the gradient been slightly different, it could have impeded water flow and therefore supported vegetation. This would have meant building soil rather than losing more to erosion with every rain.

Roads should be constructed with hydrology in mind, she says: "We can create waterworks through the roads in rural development. We're bringing in equipment and breaking up the ground anyway. It's low-hanging fruit. Here roads are infrastructure as well as means of communication. We can make them water creating instead of water draining."

Stacy stops the truck and we step into a silent, stony moonscape. There's an acacia tree growing straight out of the rock. Lee scrambles over a boulder and finds indentations that look like seashells—similar to what we'd seen across the border in Mexico. Katherine tells him that around here people have found dinosaur fossils, and this launches him on a rock-collecting spree that only abates when they become too heavy to carry in the heat.

We walk along the creek and soon Tony spots an animal that we think might be a goat—maybe Leo, perhaps the lone survivor from Katherine's herd—which we later determine is an Aoudad Barbary sheep, an animal native to Africa and brought to the desert Southwest. We pass yucca blooms, desert willows and Goldenball leadtrees—*Leucaena retusa*—which Katherine says is considered a sign of water.

We're guarding our energy and sipping water frugally but it's not so bad, perhaps because I'd expected that conditions would push me to the limits of endurance. We walk through some verdant, grassy areas—the result of holistic planned grazing with the goats. The creek widens and we reach a crescent-shaped pool where the water is several feet deep and about as clear as outdoor water gets. Slender minnows zip about in tiny groups. "This means water's been here a long time," Katherine says of the little fish.

I cool off by wading in and splashing my face while Katherine strides all the way in and lays flat on her back. After a few moments of bliss she gets up and shakes herself off. She says she wears layers because it holds the cool longer. "Sometimes I'll wear thick wool sweaters in the summer. I can get them wet and since it takes longer to dry out I get to wear my evaporative cooler!"

A few minutes later we reach the stand of cottonwoods and happily settle ourselves in the shade. Though I hadn't noticed a breeze the leaves rustle: gentle chimes. The banks of rivers and streams in the Southwest used to be dominated by cottonwoods, says Katherine. "Then they were cut down for fuel and wood, and because it was thought they used too much water—as opposed to seeing them as part of the water table. In the past there was a canopy of taller trees and beautiful grasslands, and there was open, flowing water."

We listen for drops of water, waiting to see if the tree will weep for us. Katherine pulls out a bag of nuts and sighs. "Maybe it's not hot enough," she says. I ask how hot it gets around here and Stacy says he's seen it as high as 117 degrees Fahrenheit. He says heat tends not to bother him, but when it's that hot "it's like having a hammer on your head, or your stomach."

"Looks like we have some visitors," Tony says, and we glance up to see six wild burros bunched together, alert, big-eared and idly curious. They stare at us intently and it becomes clear that they would like us to leave so that they can enjoy the shade of the cottonwoods. It's about time for us to move on anyway, so we gather our things and give up our prime desert real estate to the patiently waiting animals.

Casa de Mañana is situated at 3,200 feet elevation, "the lowest of the high steppes," says Markus, and as low as he's willing to go since even slight differences of elevation can be consequential out here. "I recently worked a job in Presidio," he says. "I could feel the temperature drop when we came back." This despite Presidio being just slightly lower in elevation.

Changes in elevation also affect condensation. Air temperature cools as it moves upward. Since cooler air holds less water, it will more quickly reach saturation (which is why dew forms at night). In Big Bend National Park, the least-visited national park whose main entrance and headquarters are just a few miles from Terlingua, the amount of rainfall varies according to terrain. The park's desert areas receive between five and ten inches a year while the Chisos Mountains get fifteen to twenty. Katherine says, "In trying to green the desert there are two things that control the game you're playing: elevation and topography."

Rain is a product of condensation, but water can't do it alone: H_2O molecules need a surface to condense upon in order to form the droplets that fall as rain. This is where "condensation nuclei" come in: the flecks of particulate matter around which moisture coalesces. As Cynthia Barnett, author of *Rain: A Cultural and Natural History,* has said, "There has to be a little tiny *something* for the drop to *cling* to. So, there's a *tiny* bit of dust or even a tiny bit of bacteria . . . You know, I hate to tell you this, but there's no such thing as clean rain."[17]

Not all that sky-dwelling stuff will actually seed the rain. Australian scientist Walter Jehne draws a sharp distinction between hygroscopic (water-attracting) particles and what he calls "haze micro-nuclei," which do not attract water. The hygroscopic particles are precipitation nuclei: they become the kernel for water droplets that fall as rain. The particles may be ice crystals, salts or bacteria produced by plants. Cumulatively, precipitation nuclei form dense, lofty clouds. Such clouds have a high albedo, or reflectivity, so that much of the solar radiation ricochets back into space as opposed to being absorbed.

Haze micronuclei, Jehne explained in an email, are much smaller than precipitation nuclei. Rather than serving as scaffolds for raindrops, these specks condense water vapor to form haze microdroplets. Such droplets never get either large or heavy enough to fall as rain, he says, and so they linger in the atmosphere, creating a kind of persistent, humid haze. While precipitation nuclei coalesce as solar-reflecting high-albedo clouds, haze micronuclei contribute to the absorption of heat radiation. Plus, he says, as the haze microdroplets remain suspended in the air "they prevent evaporated or transpired water . . . falling back to the Earth as rain."

Jehne says the makeup of atmospheric nuclei determines what happens to the water vapor up there: whether we get precipitation or a persistent rainless haze; whether we enjoy fluffy clouds and cleansing rain showers or the kind of global dimming that has cast a pall over much of the rapidly industrializing developing world (a scenario known as the "Asian Brown Cloud"). In other words, these unseeable specks have important implications for the constellation of weather-related phenomena that, in the aggregate, we call climate change.

Here's why this concerns us: the balance of particulate matter floating around the air has been tilting toward those haze micronuclei. This can largely be traced to human activity, says Jehne. While a wide range of aerosols may become micronuclei—including pollen, volatiles from trees and compounds produced by marine algae—there are "also pollutant particulates and some three to five billion tonnes (metric tons) of dust from bare, eroding soil surfaces."

According to an article in NASA's *Earth Observatory*, man-made particulates may derive from burning from land clearing, fossil fuel combustion, even indoor cooking stoves and cigarettes: "Deforestation, overgrazing, drought, and excessive irrigation can alter the land surface, increasing the rate at which dust aerosols enter the atmosphere." The darkest airborne particles, such as black carbon, at once absorb heat and shade the ground surface.[18]

All that dark, dusty stuff we've lobbed into the air has apparently been toying with the planet's solar and water cycles. The NASA report says that swirls of anthropogenic particles soar around the globe, with large swaths of airborne "micro-dirt" wafting over Asia with its busy factories. Aside from altering patterns of absorbing, reflecting and scattering solar radiation, this aerial onslaught has an impact on precipitation: "Broadly speaking, aerosols are thought to suppress precipitation because the particles decrease the size of water droplets in clouds. However, under some environmental conditions, aerosols can lead to taller clouds that are more likely to produce lightning and strong downpours. In a few places, meteorologists have detected a cycle in which the frequency of thunderstorms is connected to mid-week peaks in aerosol emissions."

The article adds that research on pollution and biomass burns indicates "the black carbon warms the surrounding atmosphere and can cause cloud droplets to evaporate," a development that "turns clouds into a smoky haze that suppresses precipitation."[19]

Jehne has dubbed this scenario the paradoxical term *humid drought*. He says the humid hazes that trap heat are "aridifying," which also sounds contradictory. Such phrases, enigmatic as they are, do convey the kinds of uncomfortable weather conditions people around the world are enduring. One example is the "heat dome" that descended over the Middle East in July 2015. In the Iranian port city of Bandar-e Mahshahr, the heat index—what the air felt like—reached an astounding 165 degrees Fahrenheit, the temperature of a fully cooked turkey. The heat index is a combination of air temperature (in this instance 115 degrees Fahrenheit) and the dew point, which, at 90 degrees, meant extremely high humidity.[20] The aforementioned Asian Brown Cloud, a layer of haze that now sits over the region around the northern Indian Ocean for several months a year, has reportedly reduced the monsoon rains by as much as 20 to 40 percent.[21]

Aerosols affect the environment in complex ways; en masse, the tiny particles can brighten or dim, warm or cool. Whether light is assimilated or beamed skyward is determined primarily by surface color: dark-hued specks absorb light while bright or iridescent particles reflect it. As for temperature, Jehne says whether warming or cooling dominates depends on the composition of nuclei: heat-trapping haze microdroplets or precipitation nuclei.

These rain-producing particles play a fundamental role in fashioning our environment, says Jehne. And he laments the damage we've inflicted on the equilibrium among nuclei—and therefore to the rhythms of natural rainfall. "The importance of the precipitation nuclei is in not only producing cooling clouds but in creating the rainfall that all life and the global hydrological cycle and thus our stable climate depend on. We have grossly impaired the production of these biological nuclei and thus their cooling and rainfall effects." One way we've altered precipitation dynamics, he says, is by destroying up to three-quarters of the earth's primary forests—a project we humans have been working on for the last 10,000 years.

Precipitation nuclei are a product of our natural environment. Therefore, says Jehne, revitalizing our landscapes—as we've seen happen in places as varied as Zimbabwe and Arizona, Mexico and Ohio—can return the aerosol regime to stability. But given feedback loops, we shouldn't delay. For example, a forest burn not only means more dimming, drying micro-ash; it also diminishes the production of the precipitation nuclei that seed our raindrops.

Jehne says, "Restoring these natural processes via the regeneration of our landscape is now critical, not just to secure adequate rainfall and water to sustain bio-systems and their cooling latent heat fluxes but to restore the former levels of high albedo clouds that naturally helped cool the planet."

The nuclei needed to coalesce these cooling, rain-making clouds, Jehne specifies, are much larger than the haze-producing variety and highly effective at attracting and coalescing haze micro-droplets into raindrops. A significant portion derives from plants. Some suggest that the rain dances common to many cultures have a scientific basis: by dislodging and hoisting into the air rain-generating "bio-aerosols" in the soil and low-lying vegetation, people may actually incite desired rains.[22] In a sense, this echoes what Jehne says we need to do—except that rather than kicking up the potential for rain, we'd be planting it.

With the summer monsoons now a week behind them, the Ottmerses brace for a dry period. And a busy one: a time to get things done as the population is at its most sparse right now, Big Bend tourism at its quietest.

Katherine and Markus make an interesting pair, as he's impatient and geared toward action while she's more reflective.

"Here's where I'm at now," she says. "I feel we're in the Anthropocene." She says this philosophically. That humans have and are changing the Earth is no longer a matter to be debated, she believes, but rather than ruing the fact, we need to embrace the responsibility it entails. "We can be the beavers on the landscape, the keystone species."

"The drought has been an opening for change," says Katherine. "People are buying degraded lands. It's affordable."

Markus says that while scarcely acknowledged in public debate, "the largest social justice issue is land access. This is the cheap stuff."

With all their challenges, Katherine resists the notion that their land has less value. "What we're doing is oasification, and this is our incubator," she says. "We can see where the water is in the landscape. Water is never lonely and always moving."

SEVEN

STORM WATERS DREAMING

Dousing the Flames in Australia

You sing the country before you burn it—in your mind you see the fire, you know where it is going, you know where it will stop.

—An elder in Arnhem Land in the Northern Territory

There's time enough for everything in the Never-Never.

—Jeannie (Mrs. Aeneas) Gunn

CHRIS HENGGELER MANAGES KACHANA STATION, A chunk of rugged terrain in the Kimberley that spans nearly 300 square miles, close to the combined area of New York City's five boroughs. As with much of Western Australia state's rural lands, it's on a long-term pastoral lease from the Crown. The Kimberley, with a long, craggy coastline running eastward along the Indian Ocean and Timor Sea, is about as remote and thinly peopled a region as you can find. Try to imagine the outback of the outback: dramatic canyons and gorges awash in hues of ochre; eighteen-foot-long crocodiles lazing on the river banks and forked-tongued goannas sunning on rocks; eye-catching birds like the red-tailed black cockatoo and the rainbow lorikeet; sparkling waterfalls, like "the Horries" (for horizontal), which flow sideways (only in Oz). It's hot year-round. It's not so much temperature that marks seasonal shifts but rather the things you need to worry about, namely fires or floods. Water, not enough or too much all at once, is a constant challenge. Kachana Station averages close to thirty inches of rainfall a year, not a paltry sum, but falls into the "brittle" category as precipitation comes all at once.

Henggeler brought his wife, Jacqueline, and their two small children to Kachana full time in 1991. The family set up a small camp on the property, portable steel structures with roofing-iron cladding. The sides are propped up by metal poles, to allow for lifting for ventilation, and shade or protection against driving rains. The Henggelers live here to this day. Aside from a tenuous Internet connection, their 1972 Cessna 206 is the family's primary link to the outside world. While conceding that most folks would by now have bought or built a proper dwelling, Henggeler says, "We decided that an aircraft was more important than a house."

Apart from fifteen kilometers of north-south tracks, there are no roads to or within Kachana Station. Given frequent washouts and the reality that wet-season storms mean four months of impassable roads, the building and maintenance costs weren't worth it. Says Henggeler, "Air kilometers are less expensive than road kilometers." It took several weeks to bring a tractor and truck to the valley, so vehicles are used sparingly. To get in or around, you've got three choices: fly, walk, or ride a horse or one of their small ponies. Henggeler downplays the notion that this level of isolation represents hardship. "We aren't that remote," he says. "As the crow flies, we're only 120 kilometers from Kununurra, forty-five minutes from starting up to touching down. That's less than some people commute to their work. I've worked in places that are more remote." Kununurra, with about 6,000 permanent residents, is the region's population center.

When Henggeler first visited the property in 1985 with his brother, Karl, and business partner, Danny Waser, he found a desolate, worn-out landscape that had not been managed for decades. Land surfaces were riven by gully erosion, waterways so full of silt they scarcely flowed. Some tired-looking shorthorn cattle moseyed about, browsing on what green they could find and further compacting the dirt. Wide areas were swept clear by recent fires, leaving brown and dusty soil.

It didn't take long for Henggeler to decide: let's invest.

Resolving to make a go of such unpromising ground may seem an unlikely choice for a young man with his future before him. Yet Henggeler's background makes this kind of foolhardiness seem oddly inevitable. He grew up in northeast Rhodesia (now Zimbabwe), the child of Swiss parents with international roots and a love of nature. His father, Bob, in particular was an avid conservationist and hunter who supported the family on a small farm. Bob experimented with high-density grazing and a focus on building biodiversity. Although the broader framework of Holistic Management was not available to him, Bob observed how the land worked and successfully reintroduced zebra and antelope species like eland and impala to the property.

Henggeler attributes his keenness to take on Kachana to what he learned from his father. "I would not trade my childhood for anything," says Henggeler. "A lot of what I'm doing now is just continuing in my father's footsteps. In the Rhodesia high veldt we had deteriorating catchments, rivers sanding up and deteriorating soil. It's the same thing you see when you're flying over the Kimberley."

One shadow over the family was the repeated loss of land. Henggeler's maternal grandparents' land in Hungary had been seized during the Second World War; his paternal grandfather and great-grandfather lost properties as well. And through the 1960s, Rhodesia was growing increasingly tense. "I was fifteen when I realized that we were probably going to lose the farm," says Henggeler. "My father said, 'You need a broader education.'" He finished high school in Switzerland and by the time he graduated, in 1978, the farm was in the middle of a war zone.

With no more than a sense of what climate suited him—warm and sunny like his home country—Henggeler went on the road in search of a place where challenge derived from the elements, not political whim. "Within three months in Australia I realized I could easily commit to living here, rather than spending the rest of my life chasing the end of the rainbow." Australia was in the midst of a cattle boom, so it was easy to immigrate as a stockman. Henggeler did stock work until he got a place to study veterinary science. After three months in Sydney he realized cities were not for him and headed back to station life up north. With Danny and Karl he became engaged in real estate, which remains a source of revenue. But properties in more settled areas, like Queensland, were beyond his financial reach. And not all areas were viable. "Australia is harsh and unforgiving," he says. "If it doesn't rain in five years you have to pack up your bags and go. It needed to be somewhere where there was water."

Henggeler sent me the 1940 short story "Far Enough," by South African author Stuart Cloete, which he says inspired his quest. The piece tells the tale of Danie de Wet, a simple Afrikaans man who asks for nothing more in life than to run his farm, smoke his pipe and tell bad jokes. When an English fellow, suspecting gold or diamonds, pressures de Wet to sell his land, the farmer tries to outwit him by naming a price so outrageous that no one could possibly pay it. But the Englishman easily comes up with the money and de Wet, stunned and horrified, is forced to leave his beloved home. As the story ends, de Wet is content with his new, larger house and farm in a distant, secluded spot—having established that no precious metals lurk anywhere on the property.

Kachana means "very, very far" in the Zimbabwe vernacular.

"I was looking for something nobody wanted," Henggeler says. "A place where we could raise children without having to sleep with loaded weapons next to our beds. I stumbled on that place in 1985. There was surface water and sunshine. True, there was a major lack of soil. But I thought that management could work that out. If it were easy, we would never have had the opportunity—someone else would have done it."

Henggeler and Jacqueline, a pediatric nurse, raised three children—a daughter joined them in 1995—at Kachana. Now young adults, the children received education via the School of the Air, a correspondence program that had used the Royal Flying Doctor Service radio and now relies on the Internet. "There would be anywhere from six to twelve students in an area four times the size of Switzerland," Henggeler says.

Though the enterprise is called Kachana Pastoral Company, Henggeler doesn't sell livestock, beef or dairy. The "product," rather, is restored land or, as Henggeler puts it, "enhanced natural capital." He regards his approach as "environmental capitalism," which entails recognizing and making use of the income opportunity inherent in twelve hours of free solar energy. "All this is beamed at us. We just need to harness it," he says. "I think of this as solar real estate. And I look at myself as a capitalist. The goal is to build your asset base so it can sustain you. I didn't want to be exporting nutrients off the property in an unsustainable manner. The basis of all economics is the environmental foundation. The social and financial gains are the result, the interest that can be sustainably generated."

It's the legacy he'll leave to his children that motivates him, he says. Had he pursued a more immediately lucrative path, what would that give them? "Do I use my own wits and educate our children to out-compete neighbors in a global competition for diminishing resources?" he asks rhetorically. "Or do we try and learn how to generate new wealth and not compete?" Central to creating wealth at Kachana, he says, is better managing the water that falls from the sky.

And the cattle? That's his "middle management," Henggeler says. "These cattle had never seen humans before we arrived. Now they're working—they're more like oxen. They're our plumbers and electricians on the landscape." He says that with proper stewardship, the livestock enhances the land by providing healthy vegetation, fertilizing the soil, stabilizing creeks, minimizing erosion and creating low-fuel fire buffers.

Given the magnitude of Kachana Station and the limited "upper management"—that would be humans—he is targeting a few specific areas. He reports that in these locations, mostly within a few kilometers of camp, they are growing grasses faster than they can expand the herd and the proportion of bare ground has drastically diminished. The cattle are healthier and there are ten times as many of them. A creek that was a desiccated channel in the early 1990s now has clean, flowing water throughout the year. More springs are surfacing and locally endangered plant and animal species are thriving. For example, he's been seeing cabbage tree palms, river reeds and corky-bark acacias; as for birds, there's the Gouldian finch and purple-crested fairy wren, both spectacularly colored. Creeks flow longer into the dry season and the land rebounds more rapidly from bushfires.

That is when, Henggeler says, they get it right. As they're still learning, the fires do occasionally beat them. In these cases the recovery does take longer.

Fire, as everyone in Australia knows well, is a cunning force.

Australia has always been a singular place. It is both island and continent, and home to one of the oldest living cultures on earth. It has the dubious distinction of having been colonized by convicts. It is at once highly urbanized and underpopulated; the rural outback, which includes the Kimberley and spans three-quarters of the continent, is home to less than 5 percent of its residents. It has strange and wondrous creatures, most famously the iconic marsupials, like the high-bounding kangaroo with baby—a "joey"— stowed in a belly pocket. And some of the world's most lethal: the predatory saltwater crocodile (the "saltie") and some supervenomous snakes (one harbors enough poison to kill 100 people).[1] Even the cuddly looking koala, another marsupial, has sharp claws and teeth and will attack if disturbed. Australia enjoys an extraordinarily rich and exclusive biodiversity; more than 80 percent of Australia's mammals, reptiles and plants are native to this continent alone.[2]

In an era of ecological instability, Australia's "specialness" is often seen in its heightened vulnerability to climate change. It is the world's driest inhabited continent and has headline-grabbing dramatic weather extremes. In 2013 Australia's Bureau of Meteorology famously added dark purple to its weather maps to denote over-the-top heat waves, the no-longer-rare days when air temperatures breach 50 degrees Celsius (122 Fahrenheit). Higher than 52 degrees Celsius and the map gets coded pink. Australia's history since European settlement has been riddled with droughts and floods so dire they're etched in the books as significant natural disasters. The millennium drought, known colloquially as the "Big Dry," persisted for fifteen years until finally doused by epic rains and floods in late 2010 into early 2011.

As for wildfires, the most devastating since 1851 have names, including Black Christmas and Black Tuesday. Most recently and most deadly were the Black Saturday bushfires of 2009 in the southeastern state of Victoria, which killed 173 people. An estimated 60,000 bushfires, many of them extensive, flame through Australia each year; between one-third and one-half of these are attributed to arson.[3] Establishing a psychological profile of would-be "firebugs" and determining ways to deter them from flinging lit matches is an ongoing social challenge.[4] (Here in the United States intentional fires are also a problem, although not discussed to the same degree.[5])

The sheer extent of Australia that goes up in smoke is mind-boggling. According to a report by Walter Jehne for the Australia-based research nonprofit Future Directions International, between 30 and 120 million hectares (74 to 296.5 million acres) are burnt by wildfires annually. A further 100–200 million hectares may be burnt each year in fuel reduction and stubble burns. That's a patch of earth somewhat bigger than the nation of Liberia and perhaps as large as Sweden.[6] The carbon emitted from these conflagrations outstrips that derived from fossil fuel use.

Many see Australia, with its huge, vivid blazes and over-the-top weather, as the poster child for climate change. There may be an element of schadenfreude to it: we do get floods, droughts and wildfires in the States but *nothing like that!* "Australia is often called the lucky country," science journalist Linda Marsa wrote in "The Continent Where Climate Went Haywire" in *Discover* in 2011. "But the floods of the past year hint at a new, less fortunate chapter in Australia's history. On many fronts, Oz is a land under siege."[7]

In referring to Australia's distinctiveness I don't just mean today. I'm speaking also of the island through *geological time.* Understanding Australia's unique ecology can provide insights about how a place's environmental conditions influence the plant and animal species that thrive there. It's a two-way path: the water cycle affects which plants and animals are suited to the environment, and the ecological impact of plants and animals helps determine the hydrology of a landscape.

Author and environmental activist Tim Flannery is devoted to exploring Australia's environmental backstory. A former director of the South Australian Museum and a mammalogist and paleontologist, he's been credited with the discovery of twenty-nine new species of kangaroo.[8] Flannery's 1994 book, *The Future Eaters: An Ecological History of the Australasian Lands and People,* examines how human migrations to Australia have altered the landscape. Controversially, he calls the Aboriginals who arrived from Southeast Asia between 45,000 and 60,000 years ago the first "future eaters," in that their predation of the continent's rich resources diminished the environment they depended on. Without question, however, the Aboriginal people lived in far greater harmony with the landscape than the Europeans who began colonizing it in the late eighteenth century—arguably the true "future eaters" who accelerated the process of depleting Australia's natural bounty and upended its fragile ecological balance.

The land down under was once part of Gondwana, the southern hemisphere's supercontinent. Around 55 million years ago Australia began to detach, at which point the landmass embarked on its slow northward drift. The timing (give or take a million years) is significant as this was during the Cenozoic period, or the Age of Mammals, so that Australian fauna developed in relative isolation.

Australia is sometimes referred to as the "oldest" continent; over the eons, the land surfaces and structures have been extremely stable and remained fairly flat. In many places, features from the Gondwana period like rock formations and riverbeds can be seen today. This is because unlike most of the globe, the continent has experienced little in the way of volcanic or seismic activity, geological processes that spark tectonic uplift and create and renew land features. During more recent ice ages Australia's latitude was to the north of where the ice sheets formed and so its land largely averted the disruption of glaciation.[9] Across most of the world, over hundreds of millions of years, volcanoes bathed landscapes in nutrient-rich volcanic ash and glaciers delivered sediments and rock particles to build and shape soils. In Australia, however, the land was steadily weathered and covered by salty inland seas that evaporated to dust. This has left a legacy of mostly nutrient-poor, highly saline soil, particularly in the north.

In response to low fertility, plants and animals evolved to be frugal with energy, writes Flannery. But rather than limiting the variety of species, he argues, the strategies used to forge a niche and survive yielded a wealth of diversity. He says a reason marsupials have been more successful than mammals that have placentas and carry their offspring longer is that the pouched animals have a lower resting metabolism and can therefore subsist with less nutrition. Marsupials save on energy, too, by having small brains—particularly the koala, whose brain occupies less than half of its cranial cavity. Wombats lay low and keep cool in their burrows, and the kangaroo's springy hop is actually a highly energy-efficient way to get around. Rats and mice have smaller litters than their counterparts elsewhere and birds lay fewer eggs. As for plants, many of Australia's trees and bushes have hard, dry leaves rich in compounds that make them unpalatable to browsing animals.

With resources tight, the strategies devised to maximize nutrients often involve biological alliances and interdependencies. In other words, survival is contingent on the success of a long chain of other species, which leaves existence even more tenuous than it already is in nature. Whether it's flowers vying for the few pollinators the environment can support, or gum trees that, when on infertile soil, produce toxins to deter possums, this entails a delicate balance. The equilibrium is easily thrown off when another species comes along and shakes up the system. This is why, writes Flannery, it didn't take much for humans to undermine the biodiversity of Australia, and therefore their own future.

It is not clear whether our species is to blame for the wholesale extinction of Australia's large megafauna, including the diprotodon, about one-third the size of an elephant and the largest marsupial known to have lived. *The Future Eaters* contentiously suggested that Aborigines could have hunted them out with their spears.[10] But we do know that a whole menagerie of fanciful creatures vanished around the time humans arrived on Australia's shores. Among these beasts were 400-pound horned turtles, with elephant-like feet and an armored club-like tail; the giant goanna, a carnivorous lizard capable of eating a large animal; and a veritable flock of flightless birds, the largest among them thought to exceed 1,000 pounds. There were some egg-laying mammals, ancestors of today's platypus and echidna (spiny anteater), and a wide array of marsupials.

Though gone tens of thousands of years, this primeval zoo retains a hold on the national imagination. Debates over what killed this or that species still play out in the media.[11]

We may never learn exactly why all these great mammals died out, nor how long they overlapped with humans. New research indicates that the disappearance of large inland lakes around 50,000 years ago was a factor.[12] But we can talk about the *consequences* of their departure, and why their absence has been pivotal to the making of today's Australia.

As we've seen, plant-eating animals have a significant impact on the landscape. Megafauna like the diprotodon lived in forests, savanna woodlands and grassy areas, and so likely both browsed and grazed. In so doing, they would keep down fuel for fires and their waste would return moisture and nutrients to the soil. Upon the species' demise, this dynamic would have changed, with important environmental repercussions. The absence of large herbivores meant that nutrients weren't being recycled, plants were left to die and oxidize, and little new topsoil was created. Instead, the ground would dry out and plants, other than in established rainforests, would struggle for moisture.

Gregory Retallack, a geologist and paleontologist at the University of Oregon and an Australian himself, reveals how critical this was to the continent's environmental fortunes. Without megafauna the soil didn't have the same opportunities to improve itself as it did in other parts of the world. Nor were these bygone mammals ungulates—hoofed animals like cattle, deer or horses. This is significant, says Retallack, because ungulates evolved in tandem with grasslands and helped create the deep, carbon-rich soils—called Mollisols—that characterize grassland ecosystems. In the climatic belt of grasslands on other continents, Australia had mallee, a semi-arid ecosystem with grasses, shrubs and small trees. Retallack's research demonstrates that African grassland soils contain significantly more carbon than do Australian mallee soils, even when mean annual precipitation is the same. Retallack attributes the difference to the wealth of hoofed mammals in Africa's savanna. "Australia presents us with a view of what the world was like before the evolution of grasslands," says Retallack.[13]

The presence of pack-hunting animals was also vital to the development of grasslands, Retallack said in a phone interview. "What we see about 19 million years ago is the advent of a particular set of brain indentations around the same time we see the first Mollisols and the first dung cakes." Retallack refers to Allan Savory's insight about grasslands—the choreography of predator and prey that kept grazing animals on the move—when he added, "The whole grassland ecosystem is a dream of a dog."

Australia never had pack hunters, he said. "Australia was always out of the way."

In any event, the dearth of animal life in Australia served to perpetuate the nutritional impoverishment that had constrained animals' success from the start.

The conditions created by the limited animal populations may help explain why Aboriginal people were so reliant on fire. Without large browsers and grazers to manage brush and grasses, they resorted to clearing land with the fire-stick. Because a chief source of protein was the kangaroo, they used fire to create the kind of environment in which kangaroos thrive, which tends to be open savanna with short, green grass. Bill Gammage, author of *The Biggest Estate on Earth: How Aborigines Made Australia,* says this is why parts of Australia looked to European newcomers like a "park," and why kangaroos are often found on golf courses.[14]

Another reason Aboriginals needed to be adept with fire was that with megafauna missing, the wildfires were burning hotter, Walter Jehne has written.[15] As Australia emerged from the last ice age, plants with hard, dry leaves (a type of vegetation called sclerophyllous plants, which includes eucalypts) became more prominent. Analysis of pollen and charcoal in sediment cores confirms that fuel levels and wildfires intensified. "The Aboriginal custodians had to rapidly adopt regular cool fuel reduction burns to limit these intense wildfires for their own survival," he explained to me in an email.

More fiery burns further tilted forests in the direction of eucalypts, which have an affinity with the fire cycle, and away from fire-sensitive trees like cypress, beech and mountain ash. The shift in fire regime has particularly affected rainforest trees, which support plant and animal communities not found elsewhere. Since rainforests sustain and recycle moisture, the shrinking of Australia's rainforests also pushed the climate toward aridity.

There are several hundred species of eucalypt, far beyond the common tall gum trees that are now all over California. Most of these species sprout and regenerate quickly in response to fire stress; they even "store" food in swellings low on the trunk in anticipation of fire. For many of these plants, seeds are released from their woody pods only upon burning. When the ground cools, the bed of mineral-rich ash is ideally suited to germination. Meanwhile the fire has cleared out competing plants and hungry herbivores, leaving the eucalypts plenty of room to grow.[16] Since fires give eucalypts a competitive edge, the trees have cannily devised tricks to promote burning. They produce volatile, highly flammable oils that intensify fires once they catch. Plus, their flinty leaves are slow to break down so they lie on the ground and accumulate, dry and ready to ignite.

The upshot of this environmental walkabout through time is that numerous trends conspired to render Australia fire-prone. A situation the Aboriginal people learned to manage, in part by generating controlled, often cool, burns of their own. And so Captain James Cook, whose exploration of Australia's eastern coastline set the stage for European colonization, noted the ubiquitous cultivated fires and called the land "This continent of smoke."[17]

On September 17, 2014, Chris Henggeler woke up at 2 a.m. and saw flames in the cliffs to the south of camp. Coming out of winter, things were quiet; he and Jacqueline were the only ones at home. Against the night sky the blaze was small, bright and intense—an incandescent gem. He wasn't anticipating a fire. "The nights were still unusually cool, and we were still enjoying days with blue skies," he recalls.

Henggeler sprang into action. That hard, white flare, that glowing jewel, would not stay neat and contained for long. And so, as he's done more times than he would care to count, he gathered fire-fighting equipment—the sprayers and protective gear that are a mainstay of life in the Kimberley—and set off in his truck to tame the blaze. With the combination of danger, the early hour, and the awareness that the fire could devastate his property, he felt the adrenalin boost such situations call for—and a deep weariness.

"Fire means an instant recognition of the fact that over the next few hours everything that we have worked for in the last twenty-five years is on the line," he says. "Until the fire is out, our fate depends on wind direction and strength, daily temperature fluctuations, fuel loads, where the fire is burning at a particularly time of day, and how soon until the sun loses its sting, which is generally around 3:30 p.m. Then there's our luck, our wits and what help we can get. And then the cleanup is the salt in the wounds." For only afterward can you know the full extent of the damage.

By 3:55 a.m. the fire had surged. A photo Henggeler took just west of a spot called Goanna Vlei shows flames leaping and enveloping brush, the white heat still at the core and growing. But wind, luck and topography were with him, and within an hour the fire was out. Just before 5 a.m. the sky slowly brightened over a quiet horizon, the red-orange band of sunrise an echo of the fire that just a short while ago had threatened to ravage the land. By 6 a.m. Henggeler felt there'd been sufficient time for the ground to cool and that it was safe for him to return home. And start his day's work.

When he checked the spot later, he was relieved to see that the impact was restricted to one hectare (about two and a half acres). The fire, he believes, was caused by rock fall—rock hitting rock to create sparks that then ignite a fire. If Henggeler had not happened to wake up, the fire would likely have continued to build through the night.

As he does after every fire emergency, Henggeler asked himself: What could we do better next time?

I can only imagine how disheartening it must be to continually be hit with fires. A single episode of burning can cost tens of thousands of dollars to fight as well as devastate the land, sometimes undoing years of prior efforts to restore it. Sometimes, as Henggeler puts it, "nature pulls the trigger." But more frequently bushfires are the handiwork of firebugs. "On average we get an arson-related fire coming over the hills to our east every three years. Over the last three years we had fires every year," he says.

Still, Henggeler remains philosophical about the setbacks. He, his family and business partners were clear from the start that they were in this for the long haul. Underlying their vision was the understanding that wealth derives from ecological function and that building this foundation can take years, even a generation.

Thinking as a capitalist, Henggeler's guiding principle is to build carbon in the landscape. He regards Kachana's prime asset as carbon, and his mantra vis-à-vis carbon is "use it or lose it." The goal is to keep carbon cycling in the system rather than going up in smoke.

This is where the cows come in.

Holistically managed cattle make use of the carbon in plant matter; they eat the forage before the plants die, dry out, oxidize and become irresistibly burnable. In this way they keep the fuel load under control. At the same time the animals help generate carbon in the soil. A grass plant's response to being nibbled is to release sugars in the root zone. Also, by dunging, urinating and stomping down mulch, the cattle return organic material to the earth. Worms and dung beetles create paths for air and water. Plus, they act upon carbon-rich biomass so that it remains in the soil and it can be processed by microorganisms—the "little beasties" above and below the ground that, in Henggeler's lexicon, are "the workers," the labor force that upper management strives to keep productive.

Building carbon in the landscape is essential for the water cycle in several ways. Enhanced carbon maintains moisture, and this supports the growth of green plants. This sets up a beneficial feedback loop since the growth of green plants, in turn, maintains moisture in the environment, thereby deterring fire. Furthermore, accumulating carbon helps prepare the land for rain. Enhancing ground cover or "armor," says Henggeler, "changes raindrops from bombshells into mist-irrigators that help to grow grass. Reinvest your carbon and you can become productive."

As someone living in the bush, Henggeler is mindful of how fire has shaped the continent, and its usefulness.

From an ecological standpoint, however, he's acutely aware of the violence fire does to the land. The environmental degradation wrought by excessive fire is a story he reads across much of Australia's rural north. "Fire often lays bare the surface of the earth, exposing soil to solar radiation, dehydration, and wind and water erosion," he says. "This short-circuits nature's complex recycling process." Soil that is charred and stripped bare is not able to make use of rain, he says: "In the absence of ground cover— plants, mulch and litter—less water is retained, and much of it is then soon lost to soil-surface evaporation. And when it rains, more water runs off quicker in the form of flash-flooding."

With rainfall rendered ineffective, the land desertifies—this in an area with predictable annual monsoons and an average of 29.5 inches of rain. Trouble is, a fire-seared landscape makes it harder for all kinds of life forms to thrive. The aftermath of fire, says Henggeler, is "not much fun if you are a small animal, bird, insect or soil organism. Many die. Many of the larger animals and livestock can pull through but over time the country supports less of them."

Under the auspices of the organization Healthy Soils Australia, Walter Jehne has written a document called "Regenerate Australia," a comprehensive program to restore ecological resilience to the continent and which offers critical insights for the rest of the world. He presented a version of the paper at Global Soils Week in Berlin in 2015. In the paper Jehne invites us to consider the fate of a molecule of carbon.

Every carbon molecule that has ever been fixed by photosynthesis, he says, has either been:

1. oxidized by fire or by respiration; or
2. biologically sequestered into stable soil carbon.

Jehne writes: "It is the balance between these two processes that governs if . . . systems build natural capital, resilience and productivity or degrade as their soils are oxidized to re-form inert mineral detritus. It is the balance between these processes that governed the evolution of the Australian landscape."[18]

The first British colonists disembarked at Sydney Cove in 1788, marking the advent of European immigration to Australia. On the southeast coast, the first area colonized, the newcomers encountered an exotic, unfamiliar landscape. Some forests were dense, nearly impenetrable; others were sparsely treed, with grasses of varying height filling the spaces between. There were wide-mouthed rivers and swampy areas lined with reeds, waterways for ferrying goods and materials between small coastal communities and the wild, unexplored interior. (A novel that beautifully evokes this period is Kate Grenville's *The Secret River*.)

The arrivals wasted no time in chopping down trees for timber and clearing fields for planting and husbandry. Cattle and sheep, transported to the new land on the First Fleet (along with pigs, horses, rabbits, turkeys and ducks), flourished on grassland pasture.[19] The nineteenth century brought plows that churned the earth and riverboats that tore through the reeds. Swamps were drained and dams put in to stop flooding—though as it turns out, wetlands and floodplains were crucial to maintaining water and fertility on the landscape.

As Tim Flannery wrote, people endeavored "to create a second Britain in Australia." Boom-times continued into the twentieth century, a long crescendo during which Australia's economy "rode on the sheep's back." Meanwhile, a parallel narrative went unnoticed by an increasingly urban population in part because there was so much untouched country to exploit. Troubles like erosion, drought and loss of soil fertility began showing up as early as the mid-1800s. Introduced animals, infamously rabbits and foxes—the latter so the far-off subjects of the Crown could enjoy the venerable pastime of fox hunting—have wreaked havoc on the continent's vaunted diversity of animal species.[20]

Back to Flannery: "People found that a second Britain could not be established, but that old Australia could be too easily destroyed."

The basic problem was twofold: first, the colonists regarded the continent's resources, notably timber and fertile soil, as endless. And second, they approached agriculture as if they were dealing with the same conditions as home. As Peter Andrews emphasizes in his books *Back From the Brink: How Australian Landscape Can Be Saved* and *Beyond the Brink: Peter Andrews' Radical Vision for a Sustainable Australian Landscape*, the two locales represent completely different conditions. For starters, England is cool and wet while Australia is hot and dry, and Australia was never host to the grazing animal/grassland interaction that resulted in soil rich in organic matter. Rather, the typical profile consists of a thin horizon of organic matter on top of dry clay subsoil.

Andrews says he became a student of the terrain the day in 1943 that a dust storm ripped through his family's farm near Broken Hill, New South Wales. He was three years old. When he emerged from the underground room where he and his siblings hid until the squall passed, the land was a desert. Meadows of grass were now bare soil. The foliage from trees and bushes had blown away, leaving ghostly twigs. Haunted by having witnessed how rapidly land can succumb to the elements, he devoted himself to this question: Ecologically speaking, what makes Australia tick?

A farmer and racehorse breeder, Andrews came to recognize the delicate water-land relationships that have sustained Australia's environment over time. He observed that water moved through chains of ponds that slowly released nutrient-rich sediments; the pools filled and seeped in rhythm with the rains. The chief actors, he concluded, were plants: vegetation held back erosion when it rained and maintained ground moisture when it was dry. Plants, including those considered weeds, brought up water from the layer of clay—the in-ground sponge—suppressing the salts beneath. He noted that the water sources of Australia's vast interior were not lakes and rivers as was the case in the mother country. Rather, water flowed between the soil horizons. Given the warm, arid climate, this meant protection from evaporation.

Australia's native fauna are soft-footed, Andrew notes. Managed as they were, the hard-hoofed livestock imported from abroad damaged vegetation. This altered the floodplains' ebb and flow. Cultivating crops according to European methods swiftly depleted the soil. Andrews explains: "Whenever rain falls on the soil it will start to move and transport soluble nutrients in the soil unless there are plants there to control it. If there are no plants there, whether because they were sprayed out or plowed out, the nutrients will be washed out of the soil by the moving water—that is, leached."[21]

The removal of plants by fire, clearing and inappropriate grazing led to several developments: a loss of moisture and fertility, and increased salinity, as salts accumulated downstream. Farmers became dependent on pesticides, fertilizers and expensive machinery. Despite this, Andrews says, many farmers are scrambling financially. Soil carbon levels are a fraction of what they were before white settlers arrived, and the extent of land covered by plants has drastically diminished.

This is exactly the kind of scenario Chris Henggeler hopes to reverse.

"So often Australian history begins 200 years ago when Captain Cook landed here," he says. "Humans today and humans thousands of years ago were basically opportunistic—they were using the environment for their own needs. We haven't changed much in our thinking, but we need to understand that our actions leave footprints. The first humans in Australia unleashed a chain reaction that left an impression, and the net result was the deterioration of our landscapes. Arguably, two to three hundred years ago the Australian continent could sustain its population. But with 20 million-odd new Australians, we are simply not harvesting enough sunshine to sustain that. The only thing to do is to go back to a situation where we harness sufficient energy. In the absence of native megafauna, we need to harness new megafauna—livestock—to perform on our landscapes and harness more solar energy. All of this is beyond politics, beyond race. We need to rewind and ask how Australia can and must function ecologically. We need to work with nature and not fight against it."

A major motivation for writing this book has been my conviction that water needs to be brought into discussions of climate change. Not merely from the perspective that a changing climate will put stress on available water sources worldwide—a link that is generally known—but also *the influence of water on climate*. For the water cycle is a powerful ally. I've learned about this from several people, including the group in eastern Europe whose publication *The New Water Paradigm: Water for the Recovery of the Planet* is available free on the web.[22]

Walter Jehne is another. I was introduced to Jehne through an Internet discussion group called Soil-Age. A dispatch from Jehne always got my attention, in part because he was writing from the other side of the world where it was likely already tomorrow. But also because each post was erudite and dense. Over the years I've watched the "Regenerate Australia" project evolve, and I see it as the most promising approach to addressing climate change that's out there. That's because it addresses the significance of the water cycle to climate in addition to CO_2.

As we've seen throughout this book, there is much we can do to influence how water moves through our landscapes and the atmosphere. We definitely need to curtail CO_2 emissions. However, we cannot *un*burn the fossil fuels we've already used. The power of Jehne's work is that it speaks to the multidimensional nature of climate, incorporating the biology as well as the physics. From a pragmatic standpoint the program demonstrates how we can work with water processes in order to buy time for CO_2 reduction strategies, in accordance with the agreement signed at COP21 in Paris, to take effect.

First, the inescapable question: If water has an impact on climate, why isn't water discussed in these terms? Jehne would say we've tended to emphasize CO_2 over H_2O largely because it's easier to measure in the atmosphere.

Earth enjoys a climate conducive to a diversity of life thanks to the temperature-moderating effects of water, he writes. This is "due to the unique capacity of water to absorb and transfer vast quantities of heat via its phase changes and the role of the immense quantities of water, in its oceans, ice, atmosphere and on land, in governing 90 percent of the Earth's natural heat dynamics . . . and global climate."

He continues:

> While this has been accepted scientifically for centuries it was because water was such a dominant driver of the Earth's climate, including of some 60 percent of the natural greenhouse effect, that it was assumed that humans could not possibly have altered its dynamics and thus the global climate. These hydrological processes are also highly variable in time and space and thus difficult to model mathematically or demonstrate how they could be contributing to the observed climate reality and changes . . . By contrast the clear abnormal rise in CO_2 levels and the fact that it is a greenhouse gas, made it easy to assume and promote that this was the dominant and primary cause of the recent global warming, climate changes and its increasing dangerous hydrological feedbacks and extremes.[23]

Walter Jehne is part of a third wave of immigration to Australia, the few hundred thousand who came from Europe during and after the Second World War. Like Peter Andrews, and unlike previous cycles of immigrants, Jehne came of age in an ecologically diminished Australia; the continent had been subjected to the Aboriginal fire regime for millennia and industrial agriculture for nearly two centuries. Also like Andrews, he came to appreciate that the problems plaguing the land—bushfires, droughts, floods, heat waves, lack of soil fertility—were connected.

Earlier we explored Jehne's analysis of aerosols, and how the balance of tiny particles—condensation nuclei and haze micronuclei—have a profound if largely unheeded impact on climate. For a scientist working in Australia, the consequence of haze micronuclei is more than abstract; the country suffers plenty of humid droughts, unpleasant hazy humidity that sits heavily in the air. Toward the end of the millennium drought, Jehne told an Australian Broadcast Corporation interviewer, "We can restore the rainfall that is currently not falling." Every day, he said, there's a massive amount of water floating over Australia; the problem is that it's not being nucleated so as to descend as rain. However, by restoring forest biosystems we can reinstitute "natural dense cloud formation, with high albedo so that heat is reflected back to the sky. Clouds have a massive cooling effect. At any time, half the earth is covered by dense clouds. This is how the Earth regulates its temperature."[24]

Jehne maintains humans have altered the effects of clouds, and that this has happened independently of the precipitous rise in CO_2 levels. "Deforestation was occurring well before the sharp increase in fossil fuel use that started around World War II," he says. In Australia and throughout the world, "deforestation and land degradation have massively altered the hydrology."[25]

The "Regenerate Australia" brief begins with the acknowledgement that Australia, "the driest inhabited continent, is already in the front line of climatic extremes that threaten the stability of natural and regional communities." Therefore it is incumbent upon Australia to take leadership in forging and demonstrating ways to reverse these trends. Jehne writes: "Fortunately Australia still has the natural and economic means to make these changes. To do so we must urgently regenerate the health and resilience of our soils and landscapes so as to restore their natural capacity to buffer extremes and sustain these bio-systems."

The program particularly targets Australia's vulnerable inland and northern regions, places like the Kimberley where vast expanses of land are deteriorating. Key components include:

- limiting the extent of wildfires and their oxidation and degradation of landscapes;
- building resilience so restored ecosystems are able to buffer and cool climate extremes;
- enhancing the natural ability of Australia's soils to infiltrate, retain and sustain water supplies;
- drawing down carbon from the air and back into soils to support both processes;
- limiting soil carbon loss through the bio-conversion of biomass into stable soil carbon rather than burning it.

These strategies, Jehne writes, can be applied to the billions of hectares of similar marginal rangeland areas and "man-made deserts" around the globe.[26]

Chris Henggeler emphasizes that to restrict the impact of fire, you've got to manage the amount of fuel that's standing around waiting to burn. Keeping fire-ready fuel under control involves utilizing the power of his "middle management" and "workers"—livestock and soil organisms, respectively. Basically, the goal is to get animals to consume plant matter that would otherwise dry out and catch fire. As Jehne writes: "Australia's 300 million hectares of inland and northern rangelands produce some 3 billion tons of grass that if not eaten dries to become fire fuel that threaten the collapse of these bio-systems."

With small marsupials like the bandicoot and large grazers like cattle eating and cycling the vegetation, the soil accumulates carbon and moisture. This extends the period of green growth, minimizing the risk of fire.

"Some 60 percent of the Australian landscape may be dry and dormant at any time," writes Jehne. "By regenerating the extent and longevity of green vegetation across the land surface we can not only restore their natural transpiration and thus fluxes of latent heat to cool these soils and habitats but also directly protect the surface soils from exposure, heating, wind scour and erosion."

Enhancing green growth will allow for fire-sensitive trees—trees that have been eclipsed by fire-tolerant eucalyptus—to naturally regenerate in the landscape. The trees would provide windbreaks, which mean fewer dust storms, as in the kind that swept through Broken Hill. Plus, it lowers the chance of fire ripping across parched, dormant landscapes. And we know trees maintain moisture in the environment. Writes Jehne: "Currently over 50 raindrops out of every 100 that fall on Australia are lost by runoff or evaporation. By contrast the former grassy shelterwoods that covered most of Australia protected the soils from surface wind shear and thus evaporation."[27]

In Henggeler's organizational chart, plants are "lower level management": "They not only feed us and other animals, but control what happens under the ground by the way in which they release energy. They also do a whole lot more."

Peter Andrews, who as a child saw the vegetation around his home go *whoosh!* with the gritty wind, seconds the "whole lot more" part. In *Beyond the Brink,* he draws attention to the vegetation loss as an important yet unacknowledged factor in global warming. He writes: "Every plant is a solar-powered factory producing the organic material on which all life depends. Every plant is also a pump, which is constantly raising water from the ground to keep the factory operating."[28]

Plants' capacity to regulate temperature—cooling during the day and warming at night—has been incidental to climate discussions and policies. And yet, Andrews points out, "each day the planet takes in a certain number of units of heat, which it somehow has to manage. In the past, billions of plants helped to manage the heat in situ. . . . Around a quarter of the planet has now been stripped almost entirely of vegetation. In other words, one quarter of the planet has been stripped of its ability to moderate temperature."[29]

In the 200 years since European settlement, he says, Australia's green cover has been reduced by 70 percent. "The fact that all the major problems of our landscape have a common cause, a lack of vegetation, means that they also have a common solution," he writes. And that, he says, is to grow more plants—trees, grass and weeds alike—and stop killing plants that are already growing.

Central to Aboriginal culture is the notion of "the Dreaming" or "Dreamtime." This reflects the era of creation, in which ancestral spirits came to earth and formed animals, plants and other natural phenomena. Creation is an ongoing process, the tales of which are continually shared through story or song. The ancestors are embodied in the forms that they created; the stories represent a spiritual and narrative thread that connects people to their past, their surroundings and each other.

In the north, often slapped by tumultuous storms in the wet season, Water Dreaming stories are common. Aboriginal artists have painted beautiful, evocative Water Dreaming pieces that depict the reverberating dynamism of storm centers and the way water settles in pools. "In northern Australia, Dreamtime is a time of electrical storms and water that the ancestor spirits conjured up to create the world that we know," writes Greg Retallack. Finely attuned to the nuances of the land and weather, Aboriginals experience a reality in which water is continually creating the land and the land continually creating the water.

A typical day for Chris Henggeler begins around 3:30 a.m. "I get up and it's dark. That means office time," he says. "With daylight animals have to be shifted. Overnight, the small animals have to be protected from snakes." By snakes he means pythons, which, he says, may exceed three meters in length and "could easily eat a few chickens for breakfast." Afterward come little chores, like checking on gardens and sprinklers, and then he turns his attention to middle management, especially the horses and cattle. Once middle management has their jobs, it is time for breakfast.

One ongoing focus is to reintroduce herd behavior to the cattle. Under previous management the stock had tended to go feral, wandering off on their own. In part for this reason, Henggeler, unlike many Australian farmers, does not shoot or bait dingoes. Instead, he considers the wild dogs tools for stimulating herd activity in the livestock. While he has lost calves, Henggeler says he's also observed changes that suggest the cattle are coming together as a herd. For example, the animals have been clustering together. There's also improvement in mothering ability, and breeding cows have been running "nurseries." This is the bovine equivalent of day care: calves stay with a matriarchal cow and a heifer or two as the herd disperses to graze. When a calf is in distress, the herd now mobs together for protection. One time, this action flushed out three dingoes caught hunting. The wild dogs emerged from the huddle and fled, tails between their legs.

Henggeler calls animal impact a "power tool." Specifically, he describes it as "the effect of energy transmitted by animals into their surroundings." He says livestock wield their impact "primarily via hoofs, mouths, dung and urine. As does an air-compressor with air, so does bunching animals into a herd enable us to harness and put to use this energy."

He adds the caveat that as with any power tool, mistakes will cost you.

"My assessment is that as humans we have been very successful environmental opportunists," Henggeler says. "We need to become environmental *capitalists*." In regard to what any of us is striving for, "my theory is that natural forces, the subtle ones as well as the more violent ones, will begin to work for us if we manage to get our landscape goals in tune with what nature was and is working towards."

EIGHT

GOOD RIDDANCE TO THE INFERNAL ANTS

Helping the Water Poor and

Avoiding Water Wars

It is no coincidence that more than 75 percent of the world's conflicts occur in dryland areas—home to only 35 percent of the world's population.

—Bianca Jagger, speaking at the 2013
Caux Dialogue on Land and Security

We only have to look at our own bodies to recognize the sacred purpose of water on Mother Earth. We must recover our sacred relationship with the spirit of water.

—Candace Ducheneaux, grandmother,
activist and founder of Mni, a grassroots
movement for justice in the U.S. tribal lands

THE PEOPLE OF SIANYANGA VILLAGE, A COMMU-
nity of 150 households in the Hwange Communal Lands in Zimbabwe,
have suffered their share of privations. But what made me take notice was

the story of the ants. For it offered a glimpse into the vexations that mark everyday life for people in impoverished, rural areas: a cascade of indignities that flow from one to the other and often have an origin in ecological disruption. In this case, the trouble began with the loss of water.

Balbina Nyoni, a single mother of four adult children, told me over the phone about the ant troubles. It all started in the late 1980s, she said, when the Nalomwe River, which provided water to the community and where she enjoyed swimming as a child, went dry. Soon the area, once productive and dappled with shade trees, could no longer support the livestock that had flourished there. When the rains came, the water carved deep ditches in the earth, and each year meant longer forays for water and forage for cattle.

There was one creature that thrived on bare ground: the crawling ants, or *izinyebe*, and the 1990s brought an infestation of them. These ants had a bite. Now, we're not talking the nip or brief smarting of a typical annoying bug. Being rushed on by izinyebe, she said, is like having boiling water poured on your skin. At least one man bitten by ants had to go to the hospital. The ants are known to gouge out the eyes of baby goats, killing them within minutes, so the kids were kept inside and covered with ash. People who lacked shoes, like Nyoni at the time, wrapped their feet in plastic to avoid getting stung. Being bitten could mean losing toenails, so open shoes were of no use. Plus, the ants ravaged low-growing plants, such as groundnuts and cowpeas, both local staples. With food scarce, hunger became a serious problem. Parents were reluctant to send children to school, concerned that without food, they'd lack the strength to walk there and back.

Fast-forward several months and I'm in Sianyanga, touring with a group of twenty or so community leaders, including members of the village garden. Spirits are high. My companions, mostly women, are excited about showing what they've accomplished in the seven years since working with the Africa Centre for Holistic Management (ACHM). An older man has us pause in a grassy field, a *vlei*. He says, "This used to be so bare, you could pick up a needle from the land." A few minutes later we're walking on a narrow, single-file-only path when Nyoni grabs my shoulders and shouts, "Look! *An ant!*"

I had to crouch down and squint to see it scuttling in the reddish dirt. It was such a tiny thing. I'd have never noticed the ant, had Nyoni not pointed it out. I couldn't imagine this creature causing the kind of epic, near-biblical devastation she'd described. Cheerfully, Nyoni says she's glad to be able to show me an ant, since they don't often see them anymore.

I notice the women are all wearing sandals.

One of the cornerstones of ACHM is its work with agropastoral communities within the Hwange Communal Lands in Matabeleland North, the poorest province in an extremely poor country. In the Hwange District, about 132,000 people subsist on marginal land with limited access to electricity or any prospect of employment. These factors plus erratic rains leave many dependent on international food aid. The district is in the general area between Victoria Falls, one of sub-Saharan Africa's top tourist attractions, and the Hwange National Park, Zimbabwe's largest game reserve. ACHM's staff has been working with twenty communities in the district, providing training in Holistic Management and ongoing education and support. Sianyanga, a fair distance from the Victoria Falls–Bulawayo road, is among the most remote. And conditions had so deteriorated that it was hard to imagine things turning around.

A slender woman with bright, engaging eyes and an energetic, can-do manner, Nyoni is chair of the Grazing Committee, a data collector and an animal health worker. She also works with the village garden and grows food—maize, sorghum, cowpeas, squash and millet—for her family. On our walk, she has brought along a sheaf of photos and charts, the sheets enclosed in plastic. At one point she strides over to a large tree, a species of baobab, and calls for everyone's attention. The photos are from before the village began holistic planned grazing, she says. On the page, the tree stands alone, surrounded by bare ground. "We started bringing goats here in 2008," she says. Nyoni herself owns no cattle, but everybody listens to her. "Now it's the dry season and we have grass. I am committed to the cause of the land."

Precious Phiri, a community trainer with the Africa Centre whom I've gotten to know from her visits to the United States, bubbles over with pride as Nyoni flips through her pages, highlighting the improvements over time. "Look, they're doing the monitoring themselves," Phiri says. She tells me that in recent years mushrooms have started to grow beneath this type of tree during the rainy season. "The ants left and now we have mushrooms," she says. "They get to be the size of a hat—and they're delicious."

Phiri confides that when she came to Sianyanga back in 2007, she initially balked at taking on the task. "I wasn't sure I wanted to work here because it was extremely bad," she says. "People had given up hope. I was shaking inside at the thought of starting on this project. They started to see changes in 2009. And now," she pauses, gesturing at the cluster of people around Nyoni, "to see ordinary people doing this!"

During the time we stayed at the Africa Centre, Tony and I took side trips into rural communities. On Wednesday after an early breakfast we set off with Phiri and Elias Ncube, the training manager, who drives the van. We head south on the Bulawayo road, past indistinguishable stretches of unsettled bush and dried river beds, though many of the absent rivers are named. Ncube periodically nods toward the window and says, "We used to swim in that river," or, "This hill had grass."

Here and there we see people at the roadside selling hand-carved wooden curios, and occasional groups of huts: some round and some square; some tidy and others off-kilter. Ncube translates the village names: "Path of the Rock Rabbit," "Pool of the Turtles," "Klipspringer." This last one refers to a lithe, dainty-looking antelope that ambles over rocks—hence its name, Afrikaans for "rock jumper." I'm amused by the road signs warning drivers to be alert for animals. While in the United States we generally see the standard deer crossing sign, with its silhouette of an antler-topped stag midleap, here there are signs for elephants, big-eared wild dogs, and kudu with their unmistakable spiral horns.

After about an hour we approach Hwange town, a bit of industrial sprawl where coal is mined and sold to other African nations, notably South Africa, which depends heavily on coal for electricity. We see women walking along the road with thatch or large bags bulging with grain balanced on their heads. Tony says this is what always strikes him about southern Africa: wherever you go there are people walking.

Beyond the town, Ncube points out his grandmother's hut, barely visible from the road, where he spent his childhood with his family. The village is called Lupote, which he says means "the thicket." "It used to be very dense," he says. "People have cut down the trees." Like the Sianyanga villagers, Ncube is ethnic Tonga. The Tonga people have traditionally lived in the fertile valleys of the Zambezi River in Zambia and northern Zimbabwe and speak their own language. (Zimbabwe has sixteen official languages, though English and Shona dominate.) In the 1950s, tens of thousands of Tonga people were removed to allow for the construction of the Kariba Dam and relocated elsewhere, including here in the Hwange corridor. The hydroelectric dam, among the largest in the world, was once considered a marvel of modern engineering, and touted—by the Queen Mother, no less—as "one of the wonders of the world."[1] Tony recalls seeing films about the Kariba Dam as a schoolboy, with the unmistakable message, "Look how we're taming the African wild." The Kariba Dam is now deemed on the verge of collapse.[2] In late 2015, Zimbabwe and its neighbor Zambia faced widespread power outages as a poor rainy season left the dam "running out of water."[3]

Further along Phiri shows us the area to the west where she grew up. She was in her early teens when her grandmother died, at which point she became head of the household. I've seen Phiri give presentations in the United States and Paris, and there's a slide in which her younger self stands in a doorway on the packed-dirt ground, hands clasped demurely, in a white cap and white T-shirt. A photo taken the same day shows her with four younger children, two to each side, in front of a round mud-daub hut with one small, square window. She alone is smiling. The caption she's given the picture reads: "No one else should live like this."

Phiri still has that lovely, expansive smile and an easy laugh. I admire her warmth and spirit, the patience and clarity of mind of someone who knows what it means to struggle and doesn't take anything for granted. She will never forget the stress and deprivation of her childhood; she draws on it for motivation in her community work, and to bear witness. "I know poverty," she says to audiences in the United States, for whom this level of hardship is an abstraction. "I know it by name, surname and nickname."

Soon we're turning left onto a dirt road with strips of pavement hardly wider than a tire width. We brush past green shrubs, which Ncube says are used for hedging and building. "We'll go up a hill and when we come down we'll be in Sianyanga," he says.

"It's no-man's-land here," says Phiri.

Our visit to Sianyanga begins and ends with a gathering under the shade of a tall winterthorn tree. The villagers put out a large canvas mat, where they sit, and carved wooden stools for Tony and me. As we offer our greetings Tony dips into his repertoire of African languages and, in a resonant voice, says, *"Ngiyabonga."* This prompts hoots of laughter. "You are now in the Tongas," a woman named Busie Nyachari says good-naturedly. "You are supposed to say '*malo.*'" Tony's faux pas is to say "thank you" in Ndebele. But the friendly intent comes through nonetheless.

In a village like Sianyanga, few families are wealthy enough to own more than a few animals, so the community's cattle are pooled and moved as a single herd onto common areas and from one small garden plot to another. This way everyone receives the benefit of animal impact. For example, the animal hooves chip at hard soil so that water can begin to soak into the ground. The increase in water infiltration can mean the difference between feeding your family for two months versus the better part of a year, says Jody Butterfield, Allan Savory's wife and cofounder of ACHM. Research in the Chikomba District, another area of Zimbabwe where ACHM has worked, found that animal-treated fields had crop yields between two to four times greater than controls.

Many adults in the Hwange region cannot read or write, so Butterfield and her team have developed pictorial training materials that illustrate ecological processes. An example is the "Problem Tree," a cause-and-effect tool. The trunk represents the chief problem (bare soil), beneath are the "root causes" (brush fires, ineffective grazing, lack of plant litter, etc.), and the crown shows the effects—the "fruits" of the situation (poverty, hunger, lack of water). There's a corresponding "Solution Tree" in which the trunk is the goal: healthy land.

Rather than using a top-down teaching approach, the program is set up so that local people train each other while ACHM staff members step back and serve as facilitators. Butterfield says this has greatly helped the communities move forward. "We need to listen to the people, and the goals and motivation have to come from them, not from us," says Phiri. "They know their land better than anyone else."

The people I met clearly had a sense of ownership of their success. As we strolled, several offered comments and observations: about how grass is growing on the riverbank, which means fewer floods; how they can now harvest thatch for their dwellings, which means they no longer have to walk thirty kilometers in order to buy it elsewhere.

We regroup under the tree to continue the conversation. Nyoni stresses how big a hardship the lack of water had been. "We would pump for twenty minutes before we could fill a twenty-liter bucket," she says. "We used to get water from other villages, but we would sometimes get chased away. It meant walking ten kilometers to get water, with a bag on your back." The community went to extreme lengths to conserve water, she says. "Children going to secondary school would go without water. After age eighteen, young people didn't wash their hands. When the Africa Centre came in, they assisted the community with water for handling large livestock numbers. The village was in deep water crisis but willing to implement the process."

Thomas Mudimba speaks up. He says he is seventy-eight years old, and that when he was growing up there was plenty of water—not shortages as has recently been the case. "To get water, if I left at midday, I came back from the other village at six in the evening," he says. "If I took five animals for water, maybe I come back with two." For losing livestock to predators, mostly lions, is a continual concern. This is another example of how problems ripple from one to the next: when there was no water, people had to travel distances with their cattle; traveling with cattle left the animals highly vulnerable to predators, and also compromised their productivity and body condition. Goats, sheep and cattle are such an important source of wealth that, come nighttime, people would camp with their animals. Since they've installed boma sheeting corrals, there have been no predator attacks.

The substantial leap in quality of life in Sianyanga results from an enhanced water cycle, an upward trajectory that continues. The animals acted upon the land in a way that kick-started processes that maintain moisture: adding organic matter, breaking capped soil surfaces with their hooves, and trampling dried plants to create mulch. The people of Sianyanga employed animal behavior to transform the water infrastructure of the village—not the metal pipes and concrete conduits we associate with a working water system, but the land itself.

Water stress is rife in the developing world. Here are some quick facts: 663 million, or one in ten people in the world, lack access to clean water. Every ninety seconds a child dies of a water-related disease, usually diarrhea from inadequate drinking water, sanitation or hygiene—death and suffering that is preventable. Women and children collectively devote an astounding 125 million hours a day to water gathering, which can mean carrying across long distances heavy vessels of water of dubious quality on their heads or backs. This is time that could be spent on schooling, caring for children or other relatives, and income-yielding work. And another surprising water statistic: more people have a mobile phone than a toilet.[4]

Water insufficiency is also implicated in many regional conflicts. The Pacific Institute maintains a continually updated list and timeline of water-related clashes throughout the world. These include disputes over water sources and instances where control of water is used as a political or military tool.[5] But even in the case of conflicts presented as driven strictly by politics, water concerns often figure in the backstory. For example, the Islamic extremist group Boko Haram has been responsible for deplorable acts of violence—most infamously the kidnapping of 276 Nigerian schoolgirls in 2014 and the displacement of more than 2 million people.[6] Many familiar with the area link the growth of the militant group in northeast Nigeria to the political vacuum that resulted when water shortages drove people to leave. Lake Chad, once among the world's largest inland lakes and a center for fishing and agriculture, has shrunk to one-twentieth of its size since the 1960s.[7]

The dwindling of Lake Chad, land degradation and shifting monsoon patterns have combined to create water and food stress; as the Nigerian newspaper *Vanguard* puts it, "The sun eats our land."[8] This makes for prime recruiting conditions for a radical group, particularly among young people who see no viable future. According to *Africa News*, many Boko Haram "footsoldiers" are refugees from neighboring Niger and Chad who have been displaced by shortage and drought.[9] As of late 2015, 2,000 migrants per week were fleeing back to Niger, en route to escape "violence, house-burning, kidnapping and arson."[10] The result is a revolving door of poverty, terror and environmental collapse.

As another example, let's look at Syria. The circumstances that led to Syria's civil strife are clearly complex; it's an uneasy brew of political and demographic factors—including the influx of more than a million refugees from Iraq, casualties of the ill-advised U.S.-led war. But lack of water, too, has played a role. From 2006 to 2010, the years immediately preceding the ongoing unrest, much of the country faced severe, persistent drought marked by water shortages and water-related violence. Rampant crop failure and loss of livestock sent rural people into cities already overwhelmed by Iraqi and Palestinian refugees.[11] In 2010 the United Nations reported that 80 percent of Syria was susceptible to desertification, and since then conditions have only deteriorated.[12]

When water stressors like Syria's are brought to light, they tend to be couched in the more general terms like drought and climate change without mentioning land degradation. However, a close look at evolving environmental conditions helps explain how things in Syria grew so dire, seemingly so fast. According to a 2014 publication from the United Nations Convention to Combat Desertification: "In addition to drought, Syria's arable land is severely impacted by unsustainable farming techniques." The report particularly targets "overgrazing, water-intensive cotton and wheat production and ineffective irrigation techniques."[13]

Gianluca Serra, an Italian conservation biologist who spent more than a decade in Syria, points to a factor you're unlikely to hear about in geopolitical debates: unrestricted grazing across the Syrian steppe, dry grasslands that cover more than half of the country. He says that for centuries, Bedouin pastoralists grazed their herds sustainably in a way that allowed for plant regrowth before reintroducing animals. The advent of the modern Syrian state, however, changed that. In 1958 the central government nationalized the steppe. The result was something of a terrestrial free-for-all in which urban investors bought high-value livestock, such as cattle, and put them out on the land. Serra writes: "The customary link between the natural resource and its user was interrupted—abruptly disowning the traditional ecological knowledge of this ancient people."[14]

Like Serra, Francesca de Chatel, a journalist based in the Netherlands who focuses on water concerns in the Mediterranean basin, puts Syria's drought and the uprisings that followed into a larger context. The drought did not cause the humanitarian crisis that preceded the political revolt; rather, the drought aggravated an already troublesome situation of rising poverty, hunger and unemployment in agricultural areas. Attributing the tensions to drought misses the point, she says:

While climate change may have contributed to worsening the effects of the drought, overstating its importance is an unhelpful distraction that diverts attention away from the core problem: the long-term mismanagement of natural resources. Furthermore, an exaggerated focus on climate change shifts the burden of responsibility for the devastation of Syria's natural resources away from the successive Syrian governments since the 1950s and allows the Assad regime to blame external factors for its own failures.[15]

The Syrian government and media regarded water management as a sensitive matter tied to national security, she says; as a result, these institutions made a point of depicting the country as modern and agriculturally self-sufficient—even highly productive. This "culture of secrecy around water" interferes with the Syrian people's ability to grapple with the water challenges inherent in a semi-arid, "brittle" environment that has long experienced wet and dry periods.

Johan Rockström, now executive director of the Stockholm Resilience Centre, has noted that in many cases, crop failures ascribed to drought may result more from poor rainwater management than a lack of rain.[16] We use the word *drought*, but lack of water often signals a poor use of resources—specifically, a failure to ally with the water cycle so that rainfall soaks into the soil and can be put to use.

And so, the backstory of much poverty and conflict is a shortage of water, and the backstory of many water shortages is land degradation. As Precious Phiri says, because of how we've managed—or failed to manage—the land, in lots of places around the globe "there is drought even when it rains."

In an era of climate change it's crucial to make the connection between land practices and water availability. Tiny margins can be consequential. As Jody Butterfield points out, something as simple as chipping hard soil to allow water to soak in can mean the difference between savanna or desert, between food security or chronic hunger and malnutrition.

When it comes to weighing a region's water situation—whether farmers can make their quota, whether reservoirs are sufficiently full, whether levees will hold—we all tend to emphasize what's coming down (or not) from the sky. As the stories in this book have shown, this is far from the whole picture. A shift in our attention toward land function and water processes will highlight the many ways that we can work with the water cycle.

Heeding the ways of water makes sense everywhere, whether in sleek, first-world suburbs or near-forgotten villages along the Zambezi River. As California's plight shows, wealth and technological prowess offer scant immunity to water stress. For places that are geographically and economically isolated (like Sianyanga), or have erratic rainfall and a rapidly growing population (like Syria), paying attention to the logic of water is imperative, and can keep things on the side of peace.

Not that water stress makes warfare inevitable. Research has not shown water shortages cause conflict; just as often, water stress drives people to work things out and find ways to cooperate.[17] It's also worth noting that traditional cultures have generally had systems in place for the equitable distribution of water. As Brendan Bromwich, who for several years served as program director for the United Nations Environment Programme in Sudan, puts it, we need to be mindful of "the social aspects of water."

Sandra Postel has observed and written about international water dynamics for three decades and is the executive director of the Global Water Policy Institute. She says, "Twenty years ago I raised the issue of possible wars over water. I've come to be less worried about water wars per se than of a constellation of threats that stem from droughts and water shortages."

She says that the relationship between water scarcity, food insecurity and political instability is growing in many parts of the world—and that a changing climate will intensify this. "Water may not be the cause of a given set of events, but a significant factor. As for food, it's not only shortages, but rising prices. If you look at FAO [Food and Agriculture Organization of the United Nations] food price statistics, you'll see two spikes, in 2008 and 2010–2011. In 2010 there was a heat wave in Russia that knocked out

40 percent of its wheat crop. This was extreme weather combined with the overall trend of water stress."

She says when food prices surge, "you get unrest and humanitarian crises that you wouldn't otherwise have had." Many political analysts attribute the Arab Spring to the rise of food prices. "The relationships between water, food and political volatility have the potential to be more destabilizing than in the past," says Postel. "Many countries are suffering from land degradation, so if you have an unstable or ineffective government any additional water or climate stresses will likely have a much bigger impact."

She notes that another issue relevant to conflict and destabilization is the prevalence of "land grabs"—large land purchases in developing countries by foreign governments and corporations. Many large-scale land acquisitions are ultimately "water grabs" driven by water shortages in wealthier nations: the value of the land is in the water. The World Bank estimated that the extent of land acquired from 2010 to 2018 will exceed the size of California.[18] Most land transfers involve large tracts, in the tens of thousands of acres. The local people are often not consulted, and some may be moved off the land. According to a 2013 report from the Proceedings of the National Academy of Sciences (PNAS), upon procuring the land, investors may clear forests and make other changes that have an impact on regional water resources. For example, in the Sudan, the land most attractive to international buyers is along the Blue Nile, an important water source in an arid area. Once this land is put into commercial production, there is less water for farmers downstream and what they do get is lower quality. As a result, previously self-sufficient communities become dependent on international food aid and subsidies.[19]

The international nonprofit GRAIN stresses that the quest to control water has driven the "global land rush." As an example of "hydrocapitalism," GRAIN's article "Squeezing Africa Dry" points to Saudi Arabia's land investment in Ethiopia. "Saudi Arabian companies have been acquiring millions of acres of lands overseas to produce food to ship back home. Saudi Arabia does not lack land for food production. What's missing in the Kingdom is water, and its companies are seeking it in countries like Ethiopia."[20]

The PNAS report concluded that global land grabs account for 454 billion cubic meters a year: that's 5 percent of the water used annually throughout the world.[21] Given this reality, says Postel, "I think the 'water war' fear has distracted us. Not that the potential for conflicts over water is unimportant, but this has distracted from a more complex set of issues that are happening every day."

Maude Barlow, national chair of the Council of Canadians and author of three books about water, has long championed water justice and has been critical of water privatization schemes and other means of water appropriation. She says that water conflict isn't necessarily a matter of geopolitics, pitting nation against nation. Rather, it's important to understand that as water stress increases, "most of the conflict is between the rich and the poor."

It's demeaning to be dependent on international food aid. As Precious Phiri makes plain to audiences, "there is no pride in being given food." She refers sardonically to "the African salute, the outstretched hand." Nor is the acquisition of donated food without stress. In Sianyanga, Busie Nyachari describes how it was always a rush to secure an auspicious spot in the distribution line so as to be picked to receive aid.

So when the people in Sianyanga were again able to grow their own food, this meant not only could they fill their stomachs—they could also reclaim their dignity, along with a measure of autonomy and independence. Today, says Nyachari, "neighboring communities now come to us for food." Trace Gezha, a former ACHM program manager, adds that overall health has improved, and the number of children attending school is up.

Introducing restorative grazing to rural villages does present challenges. For example, some communities are wary of combining animals into a single herd in the belief that it allows bad *muti,* or witchcraft, to take hold. Also, says Gezha, livestock have traditionally belonged to men. "We mostly have women in the program because men tend to go out to work in town or out of the country," she says. "Initially it was hard for men to accept women working with the livestock. But men finally can appreciate it." As a result of this experience, she says, women in the community have more respect and the power to make decisions: "Men realize that women can take leadership roles."

A few days later we visit Sizinda, a village of 140 households who are Nambyan, a regional tribe related to the Shona, Zimbabwe's most populous group. The community is just a short drive on the route between Dimbangombe and Victoria Falls. After days of rattling along mostly dirt roads, the glistening paved road prior to the turnoff takes me by surprise. On the return trip I realize that the nice road with its neatly painted lines stops just after the airport, as this short stretch is all that most diplomats, businesspeople or tourists visiting the area would typically see.

Joining Tony, Phiri and me are Savory, Butterfield, some visitors from Switzerland, and three Zimbabwe-based staff members of an international NGO. No one is sure what to expect since the project here has had a different trajectory from that of Sianyanga. Some community members chose not to participate—including one fellow making a business of selling manure for fertilizer—and people brought their animals back to their huts at night rather than leaving them together as a group. As a result, the land wasn't receiving the full herd benefit.

And so, expectations are low as we gather near a narrow stream, the Mwalanga River. Members of our group find a comfortable place to stand, ideally out of direct sun, catching whatever shade is thrown by nearby trees or each other; our village hosts squat, as does Savory, in his khaki bush hat, wooden walking stick angled at his side. With the sense of a great moment, two men, representatives of the core committee, unfold a poster on brown utility paper and hold between them a hand-drawn chart. This is their holistic village plan.

The man on the right deciphers the lines on the diagram. "What do we want exactly from our lives?" he says. "Healthy livestock. Enough food for people, livestock and wildlife. Life of peace and harmony. Knowledge. Water. Enough wealth. What will bring this? Knowledge for how to impact land and cover our land. A diversity of life."

After a brief discussion, all who are squatting stand up: it's time for a walking tour. I see Savory glance between the riverbed and the nearby ground. I hear him say, "It's a lot better than last year." Phiri comes over and points to the land near the water. She says, "Before, every year there was more cutting into the land and more gullies. Now that has stopped, and the water is flowing. Starting in 2012, the river lasts into November. Ten kilometers up, it will join with the Zambezi. Now people are drawing their own maps and planning their own grazing. The river doesn't flash flood and it doesn't dry up. People bring picnics down to the river to talk about our dreams and aspirations. Elephants and buffalo are now coming to drink here."

Along the river, we are shown the village garden, and where the cattle have recently been. Savory confides that he'd been wary when he heard about land improvements here. "But this is about making mistakes, coming back in and adjusting the practices. You have to have a very long outlook."

The stories of restorative grazing in Zimbabwe and the Chihuahuan Desert highlight how the impairment of the water cycle is the crux of desertification—and how enhancing water function reverses the process, bringing landscapes back to health. This is important, because two-thirds of the world's lands are vulnerable to desertification. Among Allan Savory's insights is the distinction between "brittle" and "nonbrittle" environments. A nonbrittle environment is a place like Vermont, where I am now, and much of the eastern United States and northern Europe, where humidity is spread fairly evenly throughout the year. In areas like this, you can do a lousy job of managing the land and plants will still grow. A brittle environment has wet and dry seasons; absent moisture in the soil, the loss of life during dry periods can lead to desertification: the soil dries out, carbon oxidizes and microorganisms die. Savory points out that only one-third of the world is nonbrittle. However, it's these places—New York, London, Paris, et al.—where many global decisions are made.

Climate change, biodiversity loss and desertification are all facets of the same problem: that the world's carbon, water and energy cycles are out of whack. While many intuit a connection between a hotter climate and desertifying terrain, the two are more entwined than is commonly understood.

Throughout this book we've explored this dynamic in various ways. In a presentation for Biodiversity for a Livable Climate's "Restoring Water Cycles to Reverse Global Warming" conference at Tufts University in 2015, Walter Jehne said we can look at global warming from the perspective of what happens to the sunlight that reaches the earth, which amounts to 342 watts per square meter. When the climate is in balance, this same wattage comes in and goes out. Changes to the climate, he says, have meant that we're retaining an additional three watts per square meter.

Jehne said, "The challenge is how do we retransmit an additional three watts per square meter back out to space. That is a 1 percent rebalancing of heat dynamics. Can we by managing the hydrology of the planet do that safely and naturally? What are the processes that govern the natural heat dynamics of the planet? How have we changed those natural processes? And what can we do to restore those processes?"[22] The answers run through this book: restoring soil function, reestablishing plant cover, rebuilding biodiversity, and minimizing haze-producing aerosols (microdirt) in favor of rain-producing nuclei. In short, by looking at how nature manages water and, by extension, regulates heat.

Another concept helpful for understanding the interrelation of land and water is the small water cycle. This is hydrologist Michal Kravčík's term for the closed loop of water or moisture evaporating to form vapor and returning as precipitation, replenishing the area from which it derived. This is the "keep it local" ethic applied to water function: the rainfall nourishes the soil, sustains plants and supports wildlife before it leaves the environment. A functioning small water cycle ensures an economical use of water: within the system, the moisture is used and reused before it flows away into streams, rivers and ultimately back to the ocean.

In a literal sense, retaining water on the landscape preserves local wealth because the nutrients, the minerals and organic matter that lend soil its fertility, remain in the area rather than being wind-blown as dust or sluiced off to sea.

Precious Phiri has recently launched Earth Wisdom Consulting Company to support entrepreneurs in Zimbabwe's Hwange region who are working with nature to build food and water security. When describing Sianyanga's new attitude toward water, she—perhaps inadvertently—evokes economic security as well: "We do not miss a drop. We have it in our pockets," she said at the Conference on Restoring Water Cycles to Reverse Global Warming.[23] It's interesting to note that the word *currency* is connected to "current," one word for running water.

Kravčík, the lead author of *The New Water Paradigm*, says the way we've treated the land—intensive agriculture, improper grazing, field and forest burning, and urbanization—disrupts the small water cycle, thereby depleting soil moisture and limiting what's available to plants. Without hydration, the soil loses its sponge function and becomes lifeless, bare and inert—just the kind of environment that unwanted pests like the izinyebe are waiting for.

The impairment of the small water cycle over large areas results in the drying of the continents, says Kravčík. Water courses away from where it's needed—tearing down deforested hillsides, carving out gullies through degraded southern Africa savanna—to be spent at the coast. Kravčík links this to the phenomenon of sea level rise. It may seem absurd to connect desertification in a land-locked place like Zimbabwe with tides sneaking up on low-lying islands and coastal cities like Miami. But he lays out the math: research in his home country of Slovakia reveals that each year 250 million cubic meters of rainwater leaves the land through runoff. If we accept this as an average rate, across the globe this amounts to 760 cubic kilometers (a cubic kilometer is 1 billion cubic meters) of water draining away and ultimately making its way to the sea.[24] According to Kravčík, this corresponds to 2.1 millimeters of sea level rise a year (since 1992, oceans have risen at an annual rate of 3.048 millimeters).[25]

The more water that's drained from the land, the more water needs to be pumped to serve agricultural and other needs. The resulting depletion of groundwater sources is also associated with rising sea levels, adding about .6 millimeters to the annual toll.[26] The sediment carried by streaming water into larger bodies of water is yet another factor in sea level rise, though little research has been done on this.[27]

Beyond what I've shared in this book, there are plenty of instances of people restoring local water conditions using simple structures, community labor or animal impact. Such programs not only address environmental concerns, but also poverty and related social problems.

In the 1990s, the Slovakian government was set to construct a dam to supply water to cities at a cost of US$350 million. This alarmed Michal Kravčík, who was concerned about the dam's impact on the environment— and the survival of several 700-year-old villages sure to be destroyed by the project. He proposed a "Blue Alternative": to manage the flow of water along the Upper Torysa River with swales, slopes and small dams or steps made of wood or stone to slow and retain water. With water moving into aquifers and held in the landscape, springs appeared and the valley has dependable streams. This effort, implemented primarily by volunteers with the Slovakian organization People and Water, cost almost nothing and earned Kravčík the 1999 Goldman Environmental Prize.

Based on this success, the Slovak Republic government instituted a rainwater retention program on a large scale under Kravčík's management.

Over eighteen months, 488 communities built some 100,000 water-holding structures across degraded land areas.[28] These towns avoided the floods that afflicted much of the country in 2011, saving the government an estimated 500,000 euros. Kravčík adds that the project offered meaningful work for 7,700 people, most of whom had been chronically unemployed.

Sandra Postel of the Global Water Policy Institute notes the irony that throughout the world, so many hungry people live on farms. "In many rural areas this is in part because people can't access the water needed to make crop production more viable," she says. "In Bangladesh and all over South Asia, during the long dry period there is water right there beneath the ground—beneath the farmers' feet—but fallow fields." The problem, she says, is that the irrigation age largely bypassed the poor farmer.

One development to address this has been the advent of low-cost water pumps for rural farmers—often manually operated, without the technological bells and whistles that add to the cost. When she was in Bangladesh, says Postel, a simple treadle pump cost about $35. "For a dollar-a-day farmer that's a lot, but it could be paid back in a season or two," she says. "This can enhance people's ability to grow crops, increase their nutritional value and bring them to market." She notes affordable drip irrigation methods available in India and Nepal.

Postel stresses the promise of community-based water systems over large-scale projects for lifting rural farmers out of poverty and hunger. "If you're distributing water on a large scale with big dams, reservoirs, et cetera, this can contribute to land degradation and water can be lost along the way. Large irrigation delivery systems can cause salinization of the soil. Smaller systems tend to be more cost-effective and present less in the way of environmental costs."

In India, Rajendra Singh's work shows that moribund rivers can flow again. Singh, popularly known as the "waterman of India," initially came to the hot, dry Rajasthan area as a young doctor. He quickly saw that here, in what's commonly referred to as the Great Indian Desert, people's greatest need was not the medical services he had planned to provide, but access to clean water. His approach was building *johads,* small crescent-shaped stone or earthen dams that were traditionally used to collect rainwater. This simple technique began to replenish wells, while brown, parched land turned green. Upon this initial success, villagers joined in to make these structures as well. Over close to thirty years, tens of thousands of johads have been built, returning water and land fertility to more than 1,200 villages. Singh is the recipient of the 2015 Stockholm Water Prize.[29]

I had the chance to hear Singh speak at the Restoring Water Cycles conference at Tufts University. He reported that seven previously dry rivers in his region are now flowing with water—quite an accomplishment in a place that receives nine centimeters (3.5 inches) of rain a year and has a population density twice that of the United States. "We've been converting 'red heat' to 'green heat' by constructing small-scale water-harvesting structures on the ground and making a disciplined and efficient use of water sources," he said. "Now the clouds come and bring the rain." He emphasized that this transformation was brought about "by the community, not government or business," and believes that people—not technology—are central to ensuring access to clean water for all.

These examples offer tremendous hope—and suggest that there are multiple ways to fill the water bucket.

The stories from Zimbabwe and Chihuahua highlight the use of restorative grazing to revitalize the water cycle. I devote space to this in part because exploring the concepts underlying Holistic Management was my route to understanding how water connects to other living processes. In addition, Holistic Management goes beyond ameliorating the symptoms of disturbed water cycles; it directly addresses the sources of water loss in the landscape: the lack of organic matter in the soil and the absence of the kind of soil disturbances that provide places for water to tarry. It is hard to imagine another approach that would set all cycles of life—the energy, nutrient, carbon, and water cycles—moving in the right direction with one strategic spin.

I also appreciate in this model the centrality of biology—the elegance of the way animals maintain the landscape. This understanding of how animals like the ordinary cow spark and sustain biological activity has prompted my own personal Copernican shift. As a child of the suburbs in postwar America, who assumed that food was born in plastic wrap and water lived in pipes, I came to see the relevance of animals as aesthetic (pandas are cute) or sentimental (I adored my calico cat). If a species like the whooping crane or grizzly bear were threatened with extinction, this was sad because we liked them. There was always a sense that humans were at the center and the role of other living creatures was to serve or amuse us.

I've since come to see how all life forms depend upon and nourish each other. For us humans to try to stand above or apart from the ongoing processes that cycle and replenish water, energy and nutrients is to court disaster. And yet, this is what we've been doing.

The Africa Centre for Holistic Management is now launching a project with pigs and chickens. Pigs graze as well as forage, and can get 80 percent of their nutritional needs from grazing; table scraps can provide the balance. The animals' rooting behavior adds another dimension: they loosen and aerate the soil and break up roots and rocky spots. Chickens control insects and produce nitrogen-rich manure for gardens. Their scratching quickly disperses the dung, so there's no pigsty smell, and mixes plant mulch and seeds into the soil. Apparently, the pigs and chickens form an affectionate bond. Come morning, the piglets look out for the birds so they can play.

Then there's the social benefit: the introduction of small livestock will allow more people to launch small food enterprises. This is especially relevant for women, who are less likely to be in a position—either culturally or financially—to own larger animals. This provides the most marginalized people in the community with an income opportunity, a new means of bettering their lives while bettering the land. Notably, the land's way with water.

Water, intrinsic to all life forms, is the ultimate shape-shifter. It expands in volume or retrenches; it retains or releases energy. It changes state, moving from gas to liquid to solid and back again, in an ongoing dialogue with the earth and sun. However, water is sometimes discussed as if it were a static resource, a commodity to be owned, controlled and divvied up. My goal in this book has been to draw attention to the way water functions in the environment, to bring concepts like infiltration, transpiration and condensation into our discussions of water problems and solutions. Doing so, I believe, broadens our repertoire of strategies with which to provide clean water to everyone on the planet. And to show that regenerating landscapes can revive water sources: this is where we'll find our water—in plain sight.

Water bridges geographical distance. Poor land management on one ranch can lead to flooding on a neighbor's land. Atmospheric moisture from one continent wafts toward another, and the resulting balance of aerosols can determine whether you get rain or a persistent haze. In this way, deforestation in one location diminishes water resources elsewhere.

And water links topics that we tend to look at in isolation. We can't talk about water without talking about land. We can't achieve food security unless water access is secured. Water is key to ensuring biodiversity just as biodiversity plays a role in water quality and availability. Finally, we can't truly take on climate change without incorporating the heat-modifying effects of water and water-based processes.

What approach to water best serves us? When we're focused on what does or doesn't come down from the sky—whether there's enough rain or too much all at once—there's the impression that we're at the mercy of the elements. However, once we attend to land function, we regain a sense of agency: specifically, this steers our thinking toward the many ways to enhance the land's ability to retain water, organic matter and microbial life, thereby offering resilience in the face of flooding and dry skies.

This is not to dismiss the problems of access to water, pollution of water sources, the specter of water privatization, or water as a weapon of war.[30] The power politics of water is a real concern—and a threat to human rights. In 2010, the United Nations General Assembly officially recognized the human right to water. But as Rajendra Singh said before accepting the World

Water Prize: "On paper, you have declared water is a human right. But water as a human right is only possible after river rights and nature rights. Without the clean flow of the river you can't ensure the human right."[31]

In essence, every piece of land offers a choice: restoration or deterioration. Even in harsh, dry climates it is possible, as Phiri says, to have water "in our pockets."

Water is rich in symbolism. Its cultural meanings include transformation and motion, life and rebirth, intuition and reflection. All of which are relevant to this particular moment in time, a moment in which certainty of the fundamentals of life seems to be slipping beyond our grasp. This may be too scary to face head-on, so the tendency is to look at aspects in pieces: a polar bear and cub stranded on an ice floe; temperature trends with arrows pointing up; the impact of the California drought on the price of broccoli. Yet approaching the situation as a whole allows us to see how our challenges connect in ways that present possibilities for restoration, new ways to respin that wheel so that we stop the vicious cycle and start a virtuous one. We can pause and look at those water words again: transformation and motion, life and rebirth, intuition and reflection.

It has become a truism that future wars will be fought over water rather than oil. But we don't need to let that happen. We can acknowledge that the freshwater we want and need derives from natural processes in healthy ecosystems. Whenever there's environmental degradation, those processes are distorted or interrupted. However, we've seen that many forms of environmental restoration can help revive the water cycle. Such strategies can ameliorate the sorts of water-related problems that mark this era of emerging climate instability. And in bringing balance back to the water cycle, these efforts can have a moderating effect on climate.

It's all possible. It's now up to us to think outside the rain gauge and the reservoir.

ACKNOWLEDGMENTS

THIS WORK IS ONLY POSSIBLE THANKS TO THE IN-
terest and generosity of the many who shared with me their knowledge and
ideas. Through all the travel and correspondence conducted for the book,
I benefited from the insights and hard-won wisdom of people who have
devoted their lives to understanding the water dynamics of their regions. In
particular, I want to note the warmth and hospitality of those in Zimbabwe,
Mexico, Texas and California. I also owe appreciation to colleagues in the
growing movement centered on soil and ecosystem restoration, who keep
me motivated and inspired.

The Pulitzer Center on Crisis Reporting and the Food and Environment Reporting Network supported reporting for articles on Zimbabwe; the
Studios at Key West provided time and space for me to move forward on
new work. I want to say a special thank-you to Elisabeth Dyssegaard, my
editor at St. Martin's Press, and to Laura Gross, my literary agent: your ongoing encouragement ensured I never felt I was in this alone. Finally, love
and appreciation to Tony Eprile, my traveling companion on assignment
and in life, whose gifts as a photographer make up for my lack of them,
and to our son, Brendan Thabo Eprile, who keeps me humble and looking
toward the future.

NOTES

CHAPTER ONE: THE ELEPHANT POOLS

1. Roxana Isabel Duerr, "Singapore's 'Toilet to Tap' Concept," DW.com, June 25, 2013, http://www.dw.com/en/singapores-toilet-to-tap-concept/a-16904636.
2. "Reducing Cases of Chronic Malnutrition," UNICEF, April 2013, http://www.unicef.org/zimbabwe/overview_12923.html.
3. Brian Latham and Franz Wild, "Hunger Stalks Zimbabwe as Drought with Floods Hit Food Crops," *Bloomberg Business*, December 6, 2013, http://www.bloomberg.com/news/articles/2013-12-05/hunger-stalks-zimbabwe-as-drought-combined-with-floods-hit-crops.
4. "Brace for More Floods," *NewsDay*, January 7, 2015, https://www.newsday.co.zw/2015/01/07/brace-floods/.
5. Secretariat of the United Nations Convention to Combat Desertification, "A Stronger UNCCD for a Land-Degradation Neutral World," United Nations Convention to Combat Desertification, September 2013, http://www.unccd.int/Lists/SiteDocumentLibrary/Rio+20/issue%20brief%2004_09_13%20web.pdf.
6. "Frequently Asked Questions," United Nations Convention to Combat Desertification, n.d., http://www.unccd.int/en/resources/Library/Pages/FAQ.aspx, accessed January 11, 2016.
7. "Floods Kill Scores in Malawi And Mozambique," Al-Jazeera, January 13, 2015, http://www.aljazeera.com/news/africa/2015/01/floods-kill-scores-malawi-mozambique-201511322271825906.html.
8. Larry Kopald, "Nature Wants Her Carbon Back," *Huffington Post*, November 17, 2014, http://www.huffingtonpost.com/larry-kopald/nature-wants-her-carbon-b_b_6173358.html.
9. If you have cattle appropriately managed on healthy grassland, the methane cycle will be in balance. For a more in-depth discussion of the environmental impact of cattle, see Nicolette Hahn Niman, *Defending Beef: The Case for Sustainable Meat Production* (White River Junction: Chelsea Green Publishing, 2014).

CHAPTER TWO: PIPES, PUMPS AND BEAVER PONDS

1. David Carle, *Introduction to Water in California* (Berkeley and Los Angeles: University of California Press, 2004).

2. Ian James, "USGS Estimates Vast Amounts of Water Used in California," *The Desert Sun*, August 21, 2014, http://www.desertsun.com/story/news/environment /2014/08/21/usgs-estimates-vast-amounts-water-used-california/14400333/; "Water Use in the United States," United States Geological Survey, June 18, 2015, http://water.usgs.gov/watuse/wuto.html.

3. "In Drought-Stricken California, How Much Water Does Agriculture Use?" *Forum with Michael Krasny*, KQED, April 15, 2015, http://www.kqed.org/a/forum /R201504151000.

4. Matt Weiser, "Feds Say Many Central Valley Farmers Will Get No Water Deliveries," *Sacramento Bee*, February 27, 2015, http://www.sacbee.com/news/local /environment/article11355200.html.

5. Jeff Daniels, "2014 California Drought Was Bad. 2015 Will Be Worse," CNBC. com, March 3, 2015, http://www.cnbc.com/2015/03/03/california-drought -seen-having-worsening-3-billion-economic-impact-in-2015.html.

6. Ted Robbins, "In Time of Drought, U.S. West's Alfalfa Exports Are Criticized," NPR.com, August 12, 2014, http://www.npr.org/2014/08/12/339753108/in-time -of-drought-arizona-s-alpha-exports-criticized.

7. Sarah Miller, "Almonds Are Sucking California Dry," *Good*, January 20, 2015, http://magazine.good.is/articles/almonds-california-drought.

8. Garance Burke, "California Drought: Plan Would Reverse Aqueduct Flow to Send Water Back to Farms," *San Jose Mercury News*, May 6, 2014, http://www .mercurynews.com/science/ci_25709331/california-drought-plan-would-reverse -aqueduct-flow-send.

9. Ian James, "California Board Approves Emergency Water Rules," *USA Today*, May 6, 2015, http://www.usatoday.com/story/news/nation/2015/05/05/ca lifornia-water-restrictions-missed-targets/26928275/.

10. "South-North Water Transfer Project," International Rivers, n.d., http://www .internationalrivers.org/campaigns/south-north-water-transfer-project, accessed January 12, 2016.

11. Savory Institute, "Effective Rainfall Demo," YouTube, published November 5, 2013, https://www.youtube.com/watch?v=Vk3KHrqb7Uc.

12. Alice Outwater, *Water: A Natural History* (New York: Basic Books, 1996), 65.

13. David F. Salisbury, "Using a High-speed Camera to Study the Interaction between Individual Raindrops and Soil Particles Provides new Insights into the Physics of Water Erosion," Exploration (website), Vanderbilt University, January 18, 2007, http://www.vanderbilt.edu/exploration/stories/rainsplash.html.

14. Northern Rivers Catchment Management Authority, "Soil Erosion Solutions," fact sheet, New South Wales, Australia, n.d., http://www.ruralresidentialliving .com.au/soil/resource_downloads/Soil%20Erosion%20Solutions/1.%20Types %20of%20erosion.pdf.

15. United States Department of Agriculture National Resources Conservation Service, "Soil Health Lessons in a Minute: Soil Stability Test," YouTube, published December 27, 2012, https://www.youtube.com/watch?v=9_ItEhCrLoQ.

16. Holistic Management International, "Holistic Management: The Soil Surface," YouTube, published December 8, 2009, https://www.youtube.com/watch?v=fH UPKPqbcLI.

17. Christine Jones, "Recognize Relate Innovate," Department of Land and Water Conservation, New South Wales Government, Armindale, NWA, 2003, 4, http:// www.amazingcarbon.com/PDF/JONES-RecogniseRelateInnovate.pdf.

18. Christopher W. Lanman et al, "The Historical Range of Beaver in Coastal California: an Updated Review of the Evidence," *California Fish and Game* 99, no. 4 (Fall 2013): 193-221, http://oaec.org/publications/historical-range-of-beaver -update/.

19. Outwater, *Water,* 32.

20. Don Comis, "Glomalin, the Unsung Hero of Carbon Storage," United States Department of Agriculture, Agricultural Research Service, September 6, 2002, http://www.ars.usda.gov/is/pr/2002/020906.htm.

21. "Soil Health: Key Points," United States Department of Agriculture, Natural Resources Conservation Service, February 2013, http://www.nrcs.usda.gov/In ternet/FSE_DOCUMENTS/stelprdb1082147.pdf.

22. Judith D. Schwartz, "Soil as Carbon Storehouse: New Weapon in Climate Fight?," *Yale Environment 360,* March 4, 2014, http://e360.yale.edu/feature/soil_as_carbon _storehouse_new_weapon_in_climate_fight/2744/.

23. R. Lal, "Soil Carbon Sequestration to Mitigate Climate Change," *Geoderma* 123 (2004): 1, https://sustainability.water.ca.gov/documents/18/3407623/Soil+carb on+sequestration+to+mitigate+climate+change.pdf.

24. Selman A. Waksman, *Humus: Origin, Chemical Composition, and Importance in Nature* (Baltimore: Williams & Wilkins, 1936), 342, accessed online at http:// www.soilcarboncoalition.org/files/Waksman-Humus.pdf.

25. "Selman Waksman's HUMUS: Origin, Chemical Composition, and Importance in Nature (1936)," *Soil Carbon Coalition,* February 28, 2011, http://soil carboncoalition.org/selman-waksmans-humus-origin-chemical-composition- and-importance-nature-1936.

26. Peter Donovan, "Measuring Soil Carbon Change: A Flexible, Practical, Local Method," online pamphlet, October 2013, 2, http://soilcarboncoalition.org/files /MeasuringSoilCarbonChange.pdf.

27. David A. Salazar, "The LA River: A Brief History," United States Army Corps of Engineers, Los Angeles District, October 3, 2013, http://foresternetwork.com /daily/water/streamwater/the-real-dirt-on-the-jersey-shore/.

28. Hillary Rosner, "Los Angeles River: From Concrete Ditch to Urban Oasis," *National Geographic,* July 18, 2014, http://news.nationalgeographic.com/news /2014/07/140719-los-angeles-river-restoration-kayaking-greenway/.

29. "Southern California Storm Updates: Snow Where It's Needed; 2 Inches of Rain in Parts," *Los Angeles Times,* December 12, 2014, http://www.latimes.com/local /lanow/la-me-storm-live-updates-20141211-htmlstory.html.

30. Andrea Thompson, "Storm Pounds Calif., but to the Drought, Just a Spritz," *Climate Central,* December 11, 2014, http://www.climatecentral.org/news/storm -pounds-calif-for-drought-just-a-drop-18433.

31. Justin Doom, "California Drought Needs 17 Million Olympic-sized Pools," *BloombergBusiness,* December 16, 2014, http://www.bloomberg.com/news/arti cles/2014-12-16/california-drought-needs-17-million-olympic-sized-pools.

32. Council for Watershed Health, "Elmer Avenue Water Augmentation Study: Neighborhood Retrofit Demonstration Project," Watershed Health, n.d., http:// watershedhealth.org/Files/document/702_Elmer%20brochure_lores.pdf, accessed January 13, 2016.

33. David C. Richardson, "The Real Dirt on the Jersey Shore," Barnegat Bay Partnership, October 2011, http://bbp.ocean.edu/pages/109.asp?item=687.

34. Rebecca Lindsey, "Looking for Lawns," NASA Earth Observatory, November 8, 2005, http://earthobservatory.nasa.gov/Features/Lawn/.

35. Brad Lancaster, "How to Harvest Water," Planet Experts, September 8, 2014, http://www.planetexperts.com/harvest-water-interview-brad-lancaster/.

36. Anne Schwartz, "Trying to Create a More Permeable New York," *Gotham Gazette*, May 19, 2011, http://www.gothamgazette.com/index.php/city/754-trying-to-cre ate-a-more-permeable-new-york.

37. "Water Resources Protection Program," City of Charlottesville, Virginia, n.d., http://www.charlottesville.org/departments-and-services/departments-h-z /public-works/environmental-sustainability/water-resources-protection-program, accessed January 13, 2016.

CHAPTER THREE: THE BIRDS OF CHIHUAHUA

1. Simeon Tegel, "Chihuahua: Where the Rain Doesn't Fall Any More," *The Independent* (UK), July 10, 2012, http://www.independent.co.uk/environment /climate-change/chihuahua-where-the-rain-doesnt-fall-any-more-7932695 .html.

2. Tom Barry, "The Coming Water Wars," *Desert Exposure*, April 2013, http://www .desertexposure.com/201304/prt_201304_water_wars.php.

3. Diana Washington Valdez, "Fracking May Be Coming to the Chihuahua Border, Mexican Officials Say," *El Paso Times*, August 18, 2014.

4. Duane B. Pool et al., "Rapid Expansion of Croplands in Chihuahua, Mexico Threatens Declining North American Grassland Bird Species," *Biological Conservation* 170 (February 2014): 274–281, doi:10.1016/j.biocon.2013.12.019.

5. "Corona Del Mar Today: Restored Buck Gully Is Now Thriving," *Los Angeles Times*, January 19, 2015, http://www.latimes.com/tn-dpt-me-0118-cdmtoday-20 150116-story.html.

6. Alice Outwater, *Water: A Natural History* (New York, Basic Books, 1996), 73.

7. Ibid., 175.

8. Ibid., 181.

9. Julia Whitty, "Big Changes in Ocean Salinity Intensifying Water Cycle," *Mother Jones*, April 26, 2012, http://www.motherjones.com/blue-marble/2012/04 /warming-climate-driving-huge-salinity-and-water-cycle-changes-ocean.

10. Jennifer Francis, "Linking Weird Weather to Rapid Warming of the Arctic," *Yale Environment 360*, March 5, 2012, http://e360.yale.edu/feature/linking _weird_weather_to_rapid_warming_of_the_arctic/2501/.

11. Gretel Ehrlich, "Rotten Ice: Traveling by Dogsled in the Melting Arctic," *Harper's Magazine*, April 2015, http://harpers.org/archive/2015/04/rotten-ice/.

12. "Your Shot: Prairie Dog," *National Geographic*, n.d., accessed January 14, 2016, http://animals.nationalgeographic.com/animals/mammals/prairie-dog/.

13. Gerardo Ceballos Gonzalez, "Return of the Black-footed Ferret," *Discover Wildlife*, July 27, 2010, http://www.discoverwildlife.com/animals/return-black -footed-ferret.

14. Colette Derworiz, "Look to the Beaver for Flood Prevention, Scientists Say," *Calgary Herald*, March 27, 2014, http://www.calgaryherald.com/news/alberta/Look %2Bbeaver%2Bflood%2Bprevention%2Bscientists/9674728/story.html.

15. Brock Dolman, "Sorax, the Ghost of Coho Salmon Past, Addresses the Sonoma County Board of Supervisors," Occidental Arts and Ecology Center, n.d., http://

oaec.org/wp-content/themes/oaec/docs/Sorax_speech_Sonoma_County_Board _of_Supervisors.pdf, accessed January 14, 2016.

16. Outwater, *Water,* 176.

17. "Ancient Fertile Crescent Almost Gone, Satellite Images Show," *National Geographic,* May 18, 2001, http://news.nationalgeographic.com/news/2001/05/0518 _crescent.html.

CHAPTER FOUR: MISSING THE WATER FOR THE TREES

1. "History of the Propagation of the Coffee Plant," Coffee Tea Etc., n.d., http:// www.coffee-tea-etc.com/coffee/history, accessed January 14, 2016.

2. "Daily Chart: Drought in São Paulo," *Economist,* April 9, 2015, http://www.eco nomist.com/blogs/graphicdetail/2015/03/sao-paulo-drought.

3. Claire Rigby, "São Paulo—Anatomy of a Failing Megacity: Residents Struggle as Water Taps Run Dry," *Guardian* (UK), February 25, 2015, http://www .theguardian.com/cities/2015/feb/25/sao-paulo-brazil-failing-megacity-water -crisis-rationing.

4. Antonio Donato Nobre, "The Future Climate of Amazonia: Scientific Assessment Report," CCST, 2014, http://www.ccst.inpe.br/wp-content/uploads/2014/11/The _Future_Climate_of_Amazonia_Report.pdf.

5. "LBA-ECO Project Summary," LBA-ECO, n.d., accessed January 18, 2016, http://lbaeco-archive.ornl.gov/summary.htm.

6. "Science Quotes by Baron Alexander von Humboldt," Today in Science History, n.d., http://todayinsci.com/H/Humboldt_Alexander/HumboldtAlexander -Quotations.htm, accessed January 18, 2016.

7. George Perkins Marsh, *Man and Nature* (Cambridge, MA: Belknap Press of Harvard University Press, 1965), 42.

8. Gary Sabourin, "The Connection between Healthy Forests and Clean Water," *Ripples: The E-Newsletter of the Vermont Agency of Natural Resources* (Montpelier, VT, 2014), https://files.ctctcdn.com/a2bee447101/9b341a2d-fc73-40d 8-aad3-88d70b8fb128.pdf?utm_source=Ripples+January+2015&utm _campaign=RipplesHoliday2014&utm_medium=email.

9. He later specified that this came from U.S. Forest Research Lab at UC Davis. Calculations on root-zone "sponge" of a large (100 feet in diameter canopy) California native oak tree situated in a natural, undisturbed setting. He elaborates: "According to the lab, the sponge area is the highly permeable zone created over many decades or hundreds of years of leaf [litter] building into soil—from mulch to compost to humus to soils—and hosting a community of decomposers and diggers and drillers (fungi, bugs, reptiles and mammals). The area can fully capture the 58,000 gallons that would fall on the tree canopy during a massive 12-inch storm event, plus it has additional capacity to capture water flowing by and/or to the tree. The water is held, treated and recharged to the aquifer below."

10. Home page, Shinrin-yoku.org, n.d., http://www.shinrin-yoku.org/, accessed January 18, 2016.

11. Bill Mollison, "Trees 1," video, Networks Productions, Permaculture Lecture Series Online, Vimeo, 57:08, n.d., https://vimeo.com/140885116.

12. Alice Outwater, *Water: A Natural History* (New York: Basic Books, 1996), 64.

13. Neil McMahon, "Can Melbourne Lower Its Temperature 4 Degrees?," Citiscope, January 30, 2015, http://citiscope.org/story/2015/can-melbourne-lower -its-temperature-4-degrees.

14. Colin Tudge, *The Tree: A Natural History of What Trees Are, How They Live, and Why They Matter* (New York: Crown, 2006), 254.

15. Mollison, "Trees 1," video.

16. Antonio Donato Nobre, "The Future Climate of Amazonia: Scientific Assessment Report," São José dos Campos, Edition ARA, CCST-INPE e INPA, 2014, 13.

17. Scott Jasechko et al., "Terrestrial Water Fluxes Dominated by Transpiration," *Nature* 496 (April 18, 2013): 347–350, doi:10.1038/nature11983, http://www.nature.com/nature/journal/v496/n7445/full/nature11983.html.

18. Nobre, "The Future Climate of Amazonia," 18.

19. T. J. Goreau and W. Z. de Mello, "Effects of Deforestation on Sources and Sinks of Atmospheric Carbon Dioxide, Nitrous Oxide, and Methane from Central Amazonian Soils and Biota during the Dry Season: A Preliminary Study," in *Proceedings of the Workshop on Biogeochemistry of Tropical Rain Forests: Problems for Research*, D. Athie, T. E. Lovejoy, and P. de M. Oyens, eds. (São Paulo, Brazil: Centro de Energia Nuclear na Agricultura & World Wildlife Fund, Piricicaba, 1985), 51–66.

20. Nobre, "The Future Climate of Amazonia," 15.

21. Douglas Sheil, "How Plants Water Our Planet: Advances and Imperatives," *Trends in Plant Science* 19, no. 4 (April 2014); Scott Jasechko et al., "Terrestrial Water Fluxes Dominated by Transpiration."

22. D. V. Spracklen et al., "Observations of Increased Tropical Rainfall Preceded by Air Passage Over Forests," *Nature* 489 (September 13, 2012): 282–285, doi:10.1038/nature11390.

23. "Pollen and Clouds: April Flowers Bring May Showers?," press release, American Geophysical Union, May 4, 2015, http://news.agu.org/press-release/pollen-and-clouds-april-flowers-bring-may-showers/.

24. V. G. Gorshkov and A. M. Makarieva, "Biotic Pump of Atmospheric Moisture as Driver of the Hydrological Cycle on Land," *Hydrology and Earth System Sciences Discussions* 3 (2006): 2621–2673, doi:10.5194/hess-11-1013-2007.

25. David M. Schultz, "Accepted at *Atmospheric Chemistry and Physics* after Nearly Two and a Half Years," *Eloquent Science* (blog), February 22, 2013, http://eloquentscience.com/2013/02/accepted-at-atmospheric-chemistry-and-physics-after-nearly-two-and-half-years/.

26. Gorshkov, "Biotic Pump."

27. "The Biotic Pump: Main Findings," Biotic Regulation, http://www.bioticregulation.ru/pump/pump.php.

28. Douglas Sheil and Daniel Murdiyarso, "How Forests Attract Rain: An Examination of a New Hypothesis," *BioScience* 59, no. 4 (2009): 341–347, doi:10.1525/bio.2009.59.4.12, http://bioscience.oxfordjournals.org/content/59/4/341.abstract.

29. R. J. van der Ent, *A New View of the Hydrological Cycle Over Continents*, dissertation, Technical University of Delft, 2014.

30. Deborah Lawrence and Karen Vandecar, "Effects of Tropical Deforestation on Climate and Agriculture," *Nature Climate Change* 5 (2015): 27–36, doi:10.1038/nclimate2430.

31. "Dom Phillips, "Report Suggests Forest-cutting Can Immediately Harm Climatic Patterns," *Washington Post*, December 19, 2014, https://www.washingtonpost.com/world/report-suggests-forest-cutting-can-have-an-immediate-effect-on-climate/2014/12/18/ba392600-86f6-11e4-abcf-5a3d7b3b20b8_story.html.

32. "'We Are Heading for the Abattoir,' Says Brazilian Scientist Antonio Nobre," Latin American Bureau, November 29, 2014, http://lab.org.uk/"we-are-heading -for-the-abattoir"-says-brazilian-scientist-antonio-nobre.

33. Judith D. Schwartz, "Clearing Forest May Tranform Local—and Global— Climate," *Scientific American,* March 4, 2013, http://www.scientificamerican .com/article/clearing-forests-may-transform-local-and-global-climate/.

34. "Farmer-Managed Natural Regeneration (FMNR): A Good News Story," World Vision Australia, 2010, https://www.youtube.com/watch?v=E9DpptI4QGY, accessed February 8, 2016.

35. Willie Smits, "How to Restore the Rainforest," March 2009, https://www.you tube.com/watch?v=E9DpptI4QGY.

CHAPTER FIVE: FARMING FOR WATER

1. Nicholas Kristof, "Our Water-Guzzling Food Factory," *New York Times,* May 31, 2015, http://www.nytimes.com/2015/05/31/opinion/sunday/nicholas-kristof-our -water-guzzling-food-factory.html?_r=0.

2. "Product Gallery: Tomato," Water Footprint, n.d., http://waterfootprint.org/en /resources/interactive-tools/product-gallery/, accessed January 25, 2016.

3. Kyle Kim, Jon Schleuss, and Priya Krishnakumar, "624 Gallons of Water Were Used to Make This Plate," *Los Angeles Times,* April 7, 2015, http://graphics .latimes.com/food-water-footprint/.

4. David C. Johnson, private correspondence.

5. "The Farming Systems Trial: Celebrating 30 Years" (Kutztown, PA: Rodale Institute, 2012), 7, http://rodaleinstitute.org/our-work/farming-systems-trial/far ming-systems-trial-30-year-report/.

6. Emily C. Kelley, "NMSU Researcher's Carbon Sequestration Work Highlighted in 'The Soil Will Save Us,'" New Mexico State News Center, July 2014, https://newscenter.nmsu.edu/Articles/view/10461/nmsu-researcher-s-carbon -sequestration-work-highlighted-in-the-soil-will-save-us.

7. John Kempf, "Insights: Cutting-Edge Agriculture Science," http://www.john -kempf.com/insights/, accessed February 8, 2016.

8. Sandra Postel, *Pillar of Sand: Can The Irrigation Miracle Last?* (New York: W. W. Norton, 1999), 4.

9. "Irrigation Timeline," Irrigation Museum, n.d., http://www.irrigationmuseum .org/exhibit2.aspx, accessed January 25, 2016.

10. "World Losing 2,000 Hectares of Farm Soil Daily to Salt-Induced Degradation," United Nations University, McMaster University, Hamilton, Ontario, Canada, n.d., http://inweh.unu.edu/world-losing-farm-soil-daily-salt-induced-degradation/, accessed January 25, 2016.

11. Sandra Postel, "Water: Adapting to a New Normal," *The Post Carbon Reader Series: Water* (Santa Rosa, CA: Post Carbon Institute, 2010), 4, http://www.post carbon.org/publications/water-adapting-to-a-new-normal/.

12. Tom Philpott, "California Farmers: Drill, Baby, Drill (for Water, That Is)," *Mother Jones,* April 2, 2014 http://www.motherjones.com/tom-philpott/2014/04 /california-drought-groundwater-drilling.

13. Nathan Halverson, "California Is Literally Sinking Into the Ground," *Mother Jones,* June 10, 2015, http://www.motherjones.com/environment/2015/06/califo rnia-sinking-drought-ground-water.

14. Christine Jones, "Nitrogen: The Double-Edged Sword," *Amazing Carbon*, July 21, 2014, http://amazingcarbon.com/PDF/JONES%20%27Nitrogen%27%20 (21July14).pdf.
15. Robert Sanders, "Fertilizer Use Responsible for Increase in Nitrous Oxide in Atmosphere," *Berkeley News*, April 2, 2012, http://news.berkeley.edu/2012/04 /02/fertilizer-use-responsible-for-increase-in-nitrous-oxide-in-atmosphere/.
16. Marc Ribaudo et al., *Nitrogen in Agricultural Systems: Implications for Conservation Policy*, a report from the Economic Research Service, United States Department of Agriculture, 127 (September 2011): 4, http://www.ers.usda.gov /media/117596/err127.pdf.
17. "Fertilizer Use to Surpass 200 Million Tonnes in 2018," U.N. Food and Agriculture Organization, n.d., http://www.fao.org/news/story/en/item/277488/icode/, accessed January 25, 2016.
18. "Soil Health Study: Grazing Management and Infiltration," USDA NRCS South Dakota, published April 22, 2013, https://www.youtube.com/watch?v=Iq B4z7lGzsg.
19. Paul and Elizabeth Kaiser, "Soil Is Life, Tillage is Death: A Future With No-Till Agriculture," *Bodega Land Trust Journal* (Bodega, CA) (Winter–Spring 2015): 7.
20. "Cover Crops and Water Infiltration of Soil," USDA NRCS California, published June 11, 2014, https://www.youtube.com/watch?v=wGimp3tx7xc.
21. Kristin Ohlson, *The Soil Will Save Us: How Scientists, Farmers, and Foodies Are Healing the Soil to Save the Planet* (New York: Rodale, 2014), 231.
22. Ibid., 233.

CHAPTER SIX: DEW AND THE DESERT

1. "Africa: Namibia," World Wildlife Fund, n.d., https://www.worldwildlife.org /ecoregions/at1315, accessed January 25, 2016.
2. BBC News, "Namib Desert Beetle Inspires Self-Filling Water Bottle," BBC.com, November 23, 2012, http://www.bbc.com/news/technology-20465982. Industrial applications have since proved a more promising market so the company, NBD Nano, is no longer making "self-filling water bottles."
3. Liz Stinson, "A Bamboo Tower That Produces Water from Air," *Wired*, January 9, 2015, http://www.wired.com/2015/01/architecture-and-vision-warkawater/.
4. Thomas Nørgaard and Marie Dacke, "Fog-Basking Behaviour and Water Collection Efficiency in Namib Desert Darkling Beetles," *Frontiers in Zoology* 7, no. 23 (2010): 7–23, doi: 10.1186/1742-9994-7-23, http://www.frontiersinzoology .com/content/7/1/23.
5. "Camels in Texas," Lone Star Junction, n.d., http://www.lsjunction.com/facts /camels.htm, accessed January 25, 2016.
6. Permaculture Research Institute, "Greening the Desert," Permaculture News, March 1, 2007, http://permaculturenews.org/2007/03/01/greening-the-desert -now-on-youtube/.
7. Masanobu Fukuoka, *The One-Straw Revolution: an Introduction to Natural Farming* (New York: New York Review Books Classics, 2009).
8. Renee Cho, "The Fog Collectors: Harvesting Water From Thin Air," *State of the Planet* (blog), Earth Institute, Columbia University, March 7, 2011, http://blogs .ei.columbia.edu/2011/03/07/the-fog-collectors-harvesting-water-from-thin-air/.

9. Alexandra Ossola, "Chilean Fog Nets Pull Beer From Desert Air," *Popular Science*, May 18, 2015, http://www.popsci.com/chilean-brewery-only-uses-water -harvested-fog.

10. Warka Water website, http://www.warkawater.org/design.

11. P. K. Read, "Innovation for Sustainability: the Groasis Waterboxx Fights Desertification, One Tree at a Time," Foodtank, March 26, 2014, http://foodtank .com/news/2014/03/the-groasis-waterboxx-fights-desertification-one-tree-at-a -time.

12. Karin Kloosterman, "Tal-Ya Water Makes the Most of Dew," Israel21c.org, June 4, 2009, http://www.israel21c.org/tal-ya-water-makes-the-most-of-dew/.

13. Ellen Shehadeh, "Mist Opportunity," Bohemian.com, July 22, 2015, http://www .bohemian.com/northbay/mist-opportunity/Content?oid=2731567.

14. "Peter Andrews, A Hero of the New Agricultural Revolution," *Late Night Live*, presented by Phillip Adams, ABC-RN, http://www.globalartscollective.org/nsf .htm#.VvQRrGQrK2w, retrieved February 8, 2016.

15. Ibid.

16. Michael Tennesen, "Clearing and Present Danger? Fog That Nourishes California Redwoods is Declining," *Scientific American*, December 9, 2010, http://www .scientificamerican.com/article/fog-that-nourishes-california-redwoods -declining/.

17. Brendan Francis Newnam, "Cynthia Barnett Drops a Little Rain Knowledge," *Chattering Class* (blog), Dinner Party Download, April 24, 2015, http://www .dinnerpartydownload.org/cynthia-barnett/.

18. Adam Voiland, "Aerosols: Tiny Particles, Big Impact," Earth Observatory, November 2, 2010, http://earthobservatory.nasa.gov/Features/Aerosols/.

19. Ibid.

20. Mary Beth Griggs, "The Middle East Is in the Middle of a Horrific Heat Wave," *Popular Science*, July 31, 2015, http://www.popsci.com/iran-middle-horrific -heat-wave.

21. Alan Dupont and Graeme Pearman, *Heating Up the Planet: Climate Change and Security*, No. 12 (New South Wales, AU: Lowy Institute for International Policy, 2006), 65, http://www.lowyinstitute.org/files/pubfiles/LIP12_Dupont _WEB.pdf.

22. Fred Pearce, "The Long Strange Journey of Earth's Traveling Microbes," *Yale Environment 360*, August 22, 2011, http://e360.yale.edu/feature/the_long_stra nge_journey_of_earths_traveling_microbes/2436/.

CHAPTER SEVEN: STORM WATERS DREAMING

1. "Australia's Deadliest Creatures," Telegraph.co.uk, November 4, 2013, http:// www.telegraph.co.uk/travel/destinations/oceania/australia/galleries/Australias -deadliest-creatures/.

2. Barry Traill and John Woinarski, "The Modern Outback," Pew Charitable Trusts, October 14, 2014, http://www.pewtrusts.org/en/research-and-analysis/reports /2014/10/the-modern-outback.

3. Janet Stanley and Paul Read, "Bushfire Arson: Prevention Is the Cure," The Conversation.com, January 9, 2013, http://theconversation.com/bushfire-arson -prevention-is-the-cure-11506.

4. Nick Bryant, "Firebugs: Australia's Dangerous Summer Arsonists," *BBC News*, January 18, 2013, http://www.bbc.com/news/world-asia-21072349.

5. Rachel Monroe, "Fire Bugs," *The Awl*, December 4, 2013, http://www.theawl .com/2013/12/fire-bugs; Sue Russell, "Catching Arsonists Red-Handed," *Pacific Standard*, February 15, 2010, http://www.psmag.com/politics-and-law /catching-arsonists-red-handed-9062.

6. Walter Jehne, "The Role of Wildfires in the Ecology of the Australian Landscape and Its Regeneration," Future Directions International, April 9, 2014, http:// www.futuredirections.org.au/files/Associate%20Papers/The_Role_of_Wildfires _in_the_Ecology_of_the_Australian_Landscape_and_its_Regeneration_by _Walter_Jehne.pdf.

7. Linda Marsa, "The Continent Where Climate Went Haywire," *Discover Magazine*, March 26, 2012, http://discovermagazine.com/2011/dec/17-continent-whe re-climate-went-haywire.

8. "Tim Flannery," About section, ABC.net.au, n.d., http://www.abc.net.au/sci ence/future/abouttim.htm, accessed January 25, 2016.

9. Tim Flannery, *The Future Eaters: An Ecological History of the Australiasian Lands and People* (New York: Grove Press, 2002), 77.

10. Ibid., 181.

11. Yasmin Kaye, "Australia: Tasmanian Tiger 'Sighting' Proves It Is Not Extinct," *International Business Times*, July 12, 2015, http://www.ibtimes.co.uk /australia-tasmanian-tiger-sighting-proves-it-not-extinct-1510479.

12. Oliver Milman, "Drying Out of Vast Inland Lakes May Have Caused Australia's Megafauna Extinction," *Guardian* (UK), February 25, 2015, http://www .theguardian.com/australia-news/2015/feb/26/drying-out-of-vast-inland-lakes -may-have-caused-australias-megafauna-extinction.

13. Gregory J. Retallack, "Global Cooling by Grassland Soils of the Geological Past and Near Future," *Annual Review of Earth and Planetary Sciences* 41 (2013): 69–86, http://blogs.uoregon.edu/gregr/files/2013/07/Retallack -2013-grassland-cooling-q8ay9r.pdf.

14. Bill Gammage, "Aboriginal Land Management in 1788," Proceedings of the 12th Conference of the Australasian Urban History / Planning History Group, Morten Gjerde and Emina Petrović, ed. (Wellington: Australasian Urban History / Planning History Group and Victoria University of Wellington, 2014).

15. Walter Jehne, "Regenerate Australia," *Healthy Soils Australia*, http://www .healthysoilsaustralia.org/wildfire-impacts.html.

16. "Eucalypts and Fire," Forest Education Foundation, n.d., accessed January 25, 2016, http://www.forest-education.com/sites/forest-education/files/explore_cat egory/files/eucalypt_adaptations.pdf.

17. Flannery, *Future Eaters*, 217.

18. Walter Jehne, "Regenerate Australia," delivered at Global Soils Week, Berlin, 2015, http://www.healthysoilsaustralia.org/regenerate-australia.html.

19. "Australian Farming and Agriculture: Grazing and Cropping," Australia.gov. au, n.d., accessed January 25, 2016, http://www.australia.gov.au/about-australia /australian-story/austn-farming-and-agriculture.

20. Christopher Johnson, "Is It Too Late to Bring the Red Fox Under Control?" The Conversation.com, February 12, 2013, https://theconversation.com/is-it-too-late -to-bring-the-red-fox-under-control-11299.

21. Peter Andrews, *Beyond the Brink: Peter Andrews' Radical Vision for a Sustainable Australian Landscape* (Sydney: ABC Books, 2006), Kindle Edition.

22. "Welcome to Our Webpages," WaterParadigm.org, n.d., accessed January 25, 2016, http://www.waterparadigm.org/.

23. Walter Jehne, "The Processes Governing the Earth's Climate: The Scientific Reality and Our Assumptions from Models," Healthy Soil Australia, http://www.healthysoilsaustralia.org/processes_scientific_reality_assumptions.html.

24. http://blogs.abc.net.au/files/walter-jehne.mp3.

25. Walter Jehne, private correspondence with author.

26. Walter Jehne, "Regenerate Australia," Executive Summary, http://www.healthysoilsaustralia.org/regeneration-to-secure-water.html.

27. Walter Jehne, "Regenerate Australia," Shelterwoods section, http://www.healthysoilsaustralia.org/regeneration-of-shelterwoods.html.

28. Peter Andrews, *Back from the Brink: How Australia's Landscape Can Be Saved* (Sydney: ABC Books, 2014), Kindle Edition.

29. Ibid.

CHAPTER EIGHT: GOOD RIDDANCE TO THE INFERNAL ANTS

1. Greg Mills, "Kariba Dam and Power Crisis," *The Independent* (Zimbabwe), October 2, 2015, http://www.theindependent.co.zw/2015/10/02/kariba-dam-and-power-crisis-the-cost-of-poor-management/.

2. Greg Mills, "Zambia's Power Woes: All Roads Lead to Kariba Dam," Daily Maverick, September 2, 2015, http://www.dailymaverick.co.za/article/2015-09-02-zambias-power-woes-all-roads-lead-to-kariba-dam/#.VgbSsmRVhBc.

3. Matthew Hill, "Minister Says World's Biggest Dam Kariba Is 'Empty,' As Zambia's Power Deficit Widens to 42%," *Mail & Guardian Africa*, November 12, 2015, http://mgafrica.com/article/2015-11-12-minister-says-worlds-biggest-dam-kariba-is-empty-as-zambias-power-deficit-widens-to-42.

4. "Sanitation Facts," Water.org, http://water.org/water-crisis/water-sanitation-facts/.

5. "Water Conflict Chronology List," Worldwater.org, n.d., http://www2.worldwater.org/conflict/list/, accessed January 25, 2016.

6. Michelle Nichols, "U.N. Appeals for Help for Boko Haram Displaced; Nigeria a No-Show," Reuters, September 25, 2015, http://www.reuters.com/article/2015/09/25/us-un-assembly-boko-haram-aid-idUSKCN0RP2IF20150925.

7. "Lake Chad: Almost Gone," Vital Water Graphics, UNEP.org, n.d., http://www.unep.org/dewa/vitalwater/article116.html, accessed January 25, 2016.

8. Hugo Odiogor, "Special Report on Desertification in Nigeria: The Sun Eats Our Land," *Vanguard*, May 3, 2010, http://www.vanguardngr.com/2010/05/special-report-on-desertification-in-nigeria-the-sun-eats-our-land/.

9. Nafeez Ahmed, "Behind the Rise of Boko Haram: Ecological Disaster, Oil Crisis, Spy Games," *The Guardian*, May 9, 2014, http://www.theguardian.com/environment/earth-insight/2014/may/09/behind-rise-nigeria-boko-haram-climate-disaster-peak-oil-depletion.

10. Manipadma Jena, "Safe Haven Elusive for Africans Fleeing Conflict, Climate Stress," Thomson Reuters Foundation News, November 11, 2015, http://www.trust.org/item/20151111103702-lwas6/.

11. Brad Plumer, "Drought Helped Cause Syria's War. Will Climate Change Bring More Like It?," *Washington Post*, September 10, 2013, http://www.washington post.com/news/wonkblog/wp/2013/09/10/drought-helped-caused-syrias-war -will-climate-change-bring-more-like-it/.

12. "Act Now to Stop Desertification, Says FAO," *IRIN: Humanitarian News and Analysis*, June 15, 2010, http://www.irinnews.org/report/89492/syria-act-now-to -stop-desertification-says-fao.

13. *UNCCD News: A Quarterly Newsletter About Achieving a Land-Degradation Neutral World*, 6, no. 1 (2014): 6, http://newsbox.unccd.int/imgissue/UNCCD News6_1.pdf.

14. Gianluca Serra, "Over-Grazing and Desertification in the Syrian Steppe Are the Root Causes of War," *Ecologist*, June 5, 2015, http://www.theecologist.org /News/news_analysis/2871076/overgrazing_and_desertification_in_the_syr ian_steppe_are_the_root_causes_of_war.html.

15. Francesca De Châtel, "The Role of Drought and Climate Change in the Syrian Uprising: Untangling the Triggers of the Revolution," *Middle Eastern Studies* 50, no. 4 (2014): 521–535, doi: 10.1080/00263206.2013.850076.

16. Sandra L. Postel, "Getting More Crop Per Drop," Washington, DC: Worldwatch Institute, State of the World 2011: Innovations that Nourish the Planet, chapter 4, 6.

17. "Commentary Versus Evidence in the Climate/Conflict Debate," UK Climate Change and Migration Coalition, n.d., http://climatemigration.org.uk/commen tary-versus-evidence-in-the-climate-conflict-debate/, accessed January 25, 2016; Joel Jaeger, "Will Climate Change Lead to Conflict or Cooperation?" Inter Press Service, August 4, 2014, http://www.ipsnews.net/2014/08/will-climate-change -lead-to-conflict-or-cooperation/.

18. Maria Cristina Rulli, Antonio Saviori, and Paolo D'Odorico, "Global Land and Water Grabbing," *Proceedings of the National Academy of the Sciences* 110, no. 3 (January 15, 2013): 892–97, http://www.pnas.org/content/110/3/892.full.pdf.

19. Ibid.

20. "Squeezing Africa Dry: Behind Every Land Grab Is a Water Grab," GRAIN. org, June 11, 2012, https://www.grain.org/article/entries/4516-squeezing-africa -dry-behind-every-land-grab-is-a-water-grab.

21. Brian Bienkowski, "Corporations, Investors 'Grabbing' Land and Water Over- seas," Environmental Health News, February 12, 2013, http://www.environmen talhealthnews.org/ehs/news/2013/land-grabbing.

22. Walter Jehne, "The Natural History of Water on Earth," Biodiversity for a Liv- able Climate's Restoring Water Cycles to Reverse Global Warming Confer- ence, Tufts University, October 17, 2015, https://www.youtube.com/watch?v=ei PDUDT9HjA.

23. Precious Phiri, "Community Grazing for Community Abundance," Biodiver- sity for a Livable Climate's Restoring Water Cycles to Reverse Global Warm- ing Conference, Tufts University, October 17, 2015, https://www.youtube.com /watch?v=lr9HwkLxPww.

24. Jan Lambert, ed. *Water, Land and Climate—The Critical Connection: How We Can Rehydrate Landscapes Locally to Renew Climates Globally* (Lone Leaf Graphics, n.d.), 27; Michal Kravcik and Jan Lambert, "A Global Action Plan for the Restoration of Natural Water Cycles and Climate," *Terra Nova Voice* (blog),

October 19, 2015, http://terranovavoice.tamera.org/2015/10/a-global-action-plan -of-climate-restoration/4074.

25. "Is Sea Level Rising?" National Oceanic and Atmospheric Administration, n.d., http://oceanservice.noaa.gov/facts/sealevel.html, accessed January 25, 2016.

26. Richard Lovett, "Groundwater Depletion Accelerates Sea-Level Rise," *National Geographic*, June 1, 2012, http://news.nationalgeographic.com/news/2012/05/1 20531-groundwater-depletion-may-accelerate-sea-level-rise/.

27. Rubin Zhang et al., "Another Important Factor of Rising Sea Level: Soil Erosion," *Soil Air Water* 41, no. 2 (February 2013), doi: 10.1002/clen.201200127, http://www.researchgate.net/publication/264326755_Another_Important_Fac tor_of_Rising_Sea_Level_Soil_Erosion.

28. Lambert, *Water, Land and Climate*, 35.

29. Karl Mathiesen, "Rajendra Singh: Clean Flowing Rivers Must Be a Human Right," *The Guardian*, August 25, 2015, http://www.theguardian.com/global-dev elopment-professionals-network/2015/aug/25/waterman-of-india-rajendra -singh-stockholm-water-prize.

30. "Red Cross: Water Being Used as Weapon of War in Syria," *Al Jazeera*, September 2, 2015, http://www.aljazeera.com/news/2015/09/red-cross-water-weapon -war-syria-150902114347090.html.

31. Mathiesen, "Rajendra Singh: Clean Flowing Rivers Must be a Human Right."

INDEX